Locke and Blake

Locke and Blake

*A Conversation across
the Eighteenth Century*

Wayne Glausser

University Press of Florida
*Gainesville Tallahassee Tampa Boca Raton
Pensacola Orlando Miami Jacksonville*

Copyright 1998 by the Board of Regents of the State of Florida
Printed in the United States of America on acid-free paper
All rights reserved

03 02 01 00 99 98   6 5 4 3 2 1

Library of Congress Cataloging-in-Publication Data

Glausser, Wayne.
Locke and Blake: a conversation across the eighteenth century
/Wayne Glausser.
p. cm.
Includes bibliographical references and index.
ISBN 0-8130-1570-7 (acid-free paper)
1. Blake, William, 1757–1827—Knowledge and learning. 2. Great Britain—Intellectual life—18th century. 3. Great Britain—Intellectual life—17th century. 4. Influence (Literary, artistic, etc.) 5. Locke, John, 1632–1704—Influence. I. Title.
PR4147.G54 1998
821'.7—dc21   97-40248

The University Press of Florida is the scholarly publishing agency for the State University System of Florida, comprised of Florida A & M University, Florida Atlantic University, Florida International University, Florida State University, University of Central Florida, University of Florida, University of North Florida, University of South Florida, and University of West Florida.

University Press of Florida
15 Northwest 15th Street
Gainesville, FL 32611
http://nersp.nerdc.ufl.edu/~upf

In memory of Audrey O'Brien Glausser

CONTENTS

Preface   ix

Chapter 1: From Caricature to Conversation   1

Chapter 2: Mothers, the Matrix, and Marriage   13

Chapter 3: Two English Physicians   43

Chapter 4: Slavery   62

Chapter 5: Seditious Plots   92

Chapter 6: Possessions   121

Chapter 7: Printing   141

Chapter 8: Epitaphs   163

Notes   166

Bibliography   183

Index   191

Preface

To my knowledge, this book has no obvious model. It might best be described as a composite critical biography, organized by topics of cultural significance for the long eighteenth century. Although the sequence of chapters loosely suggests a progress from cradle to grave, the biographical narratives are neither continuous nor complete, and I am primarily concerned with useful critical topics rather than thorough coverage of either life. My intention is to find a middle ground between biography, with its emphasis on identifying the unique subject, and social history, where details of individual lives are neutralized and absorbed by cultural paradigms.

The project grew from a conference paper about Blake's printing imagery in which Locke was to play a minor (and conventionally oppositional) role. An unexpected lingering over Locke upset the original purposes of that paper. Over time I found it productive to think about a number of topics from the double perspective of Locke and Blake, who have traditionally been positioned as adversaries at the edges of the eighteenth century. In revisiting their lives and works I am trying to discover more complicated patterns of comparison. Each chapter begins with a biographical connection between Locke and Blake. Some of these connections are quite specific—for example, the fact that both had to defend themselves against sedition charges, or (on a smaller scale) their respective angry fits about a picture stolen by a friend. Other connections are more general, as in the chapter about medicine and the body. Each biographical parallel suggests a broader topic of textual as well as contextual importance for Locke and Blake. The topics offered here are by no means the only ones that might come to mind: prominent topics that I tried out but finally dropped include language, education, and fathers. I abandoned these topics not for lack of material but because the symbiotic benefits of the composite analysis seemed less significant.

Blake scholars have produced several comparative books in which Blake is clearly the foreground figure. Within this genre of "Blake and _____" books,

Blake typically either anticipates a later writer whose imagination does not quite measure up (like Freud or Marx) or improves upon the imagination of a precursor (Newton, for example, or Milton). I propose to study Locke and Blake with equal attention and critical distance. Perhaps this sounds like a naive interpretive strategy—an effort to annul the contingencies of reception by a mere declaration of neutrality. Absolute neutrality in interpretation as in adjudication is no more than an enabling illusion. But by weaving topical chapters from the warp of Blake and the woof of Locke I hope to avoid the most obvious simplifying effects of an alliance with one or the other and to expose some familiar texts to new interpretive conditions.

I am obviously indebted to a number of Locke and Blake scholars for their work with primary biographical materials. I have particularly relied on Cranston, DeBeer, and Ashcraft for Locke and Erdman and Bentley for Blake. The Bodleian Library courteously provided access to the Lovelace collection of Locke's papers. DePauw University supported my work at the Bodleian and elsewhere with generous research grants.

Tom Vogler at the University of California, Santa Cruz, and Leslie Brisman at Yale guided my early interest in Blake, and Frances Ferguson (Johns Hopkins) has been very helpful in later work with Locke and the current project. I am grateful to DePauw students and colleagues over several years for intelligent discussion. For fruitful ideas and subtler kinds of encouragement, I would especially like to thank Keith Nightenhelser, Andrea Sununu, David Field, Martha Rainbolt, Istvan Csicsery-Ronay, Tom Chiarella, and (above all) Marnie McInnes.

A version of chapter 3 appeared in *Reading the Social Body,* edited by Catherine B. Burroughs and Jeffrey David Ehrenreich (University of Iowa Press, 1993); the first half of chapter 4 was published in *Journal of the History of Ideas* (April–June 1990); and chapter 7 adapts a few passages from my essay on "Atomistic Simulacra" in *The Eighteenth Century: Theory and Interpretation* (Spring 1991). I thank the University of Iowa Press, Johns Hopkins University Press, and Texas Tech University Press for permission to reprint these pieces.

Quotations from Locke's work (cited parenthetically by section number) are taken from the following editions: *An Essay Concerning Human Understanding,* ed. Peter H. Nidditch (Oxford: Clarendon Press, 1975); *Two Treatises of Government,* ed. Peter Laslett (Cambridge: Cambridge University Press, 2nd ed., 1967); and *Some Thoughts Concerning Education,* ed. John W. Yolton and Jean S. Yolton (Oxford: Clarendon Press, 1989). All other quotations from

Locke's published works (cited parenthetically by volume and page numbers) are taken from *The Works of John Locke,* 3 vols. (London, 1751).

Quotations from letters and unpublished writings are cited in the endnotes.

Quotations from Blake (cited parenthetically by plate and line numbers where appropriate and by page numbers otherwise) are taken from *The Complete Poetry and Prose of William Blake,* ed. David V. Erdman, commentary by Harold Bloom (New York: Doubleday, 1988).

Chapter 1

From Caricature to Conversation

The first chapter of Northrop Frye's *Fearful Symmetry* is called "The Case against Locke." For appreciative interpreters of Blake, Locke has always made a plausible, convenient foil. The two are commonly situated at opposite borders of the Age of Reason. Blake carefully instructed his audience in this strategy. Over and over he named Locke as a principal architect of the fallen world. Locke and a handful of colleagues had degraded consciousness so effectively that people became vulnerable to spiritual failure on many levels. Symptoms included atheism, political and economic exploitation, sexual frustration, bad art, cosmic alienation, and (most generally) a sort of mental dullness: Lockean common sense made humanity less interesting.

Locke lived a century before Blake, of course, and could not literally make "the case against Blake." But the case is plain enough if one reads Locke proleptically. One of the last sections he added to his *Essay Concerning Human Understanding*, "Of Enthusiasm," delivers a strong warning against excited pseudoprophets. Enthusiasts rely on "the ungrounded Fancies of a Man's own Brain" as a "Foundation both of Opinion and Conduct" (4.19.3). Whether their pretensions are caused by weak judgment or simply a "warmed" or "melancholic" brain, they "feel the Hand of GOD moving within, and the impulses of the Spirit, and cannot be mistaken in what they feel" (4.19.8). But their claims are pathetically circular. "They are sure, because they are sure"; "It is a revelation, because they firmly believe it, and they believe it, because it is a Revelation" (4.19.10). Such people are dangerous to modern, rationally stable societies. Inner light "is a very unsafe ground to proceed on, either in our Tenets, or our Actions . . . The strength of our Perswasions are no Evidence at all of their own rectitude: Crooked things may be as stiff and unflexible as streight" (4.19.11).

Blake would point to this last metaphor as a sure sign of imaginative weakness. Locke sees a world full of crooks and kinks to be straightened out by empowered reasoners. He becomes a model for Urizen in Blake's favorite narrative of the Fall: a perceptive but self-absorbed, insecure character who tries to organize the universe against threats to his stability. A century earlier Locke observed and predicted self-absorbed, insecure enthusiasts like Blake. Feeling inhibited or otherwise victimized by the institutions of modern thinking, they claim divine privilege to challenge sane, rational ideas.

This book is an attempt to move beyond adversarial caricatures of temperament, faculty, ideology, and intention and to open up the lives and works of Locke and Blake for richer conversation. The adversarial caricatures have stayed fairly securely in place, however, and it is not difficult to understand why. Scholars who specialize in Blake tend either to adopt his distaste for Locke or to grant Locke a distantly respectful cameo role. Frye, for example, closes "The Case against Locke" with the following deflection: "Though Blake is an interesting eighteenth-century phenomenon even in philosophy, Locke's reputation can perhaps be left to take care of itself." The disciplinary separation of philosophy from literature may not be fully justified, Frye suggests, but it allows him to send Locke back to the Lockeans and get on with the study of his literary antagonist. Locke and Blake have come to be separated by period as well as by academic discipline. *The Norton Anthology of English Literature,* for example—certainly a useful index of mainstream literary history—positions Locke as a "terminus" at the threshold of the eighteenth century and opens the Romantic period with Blake. If confidence in periods has recently ebbed as a result of Foucauldian and associated poststructuralist strategies,[1] Locke and Blake remain influential transitional figures in a history of English letters that many still take for granted.

It would be easy enough to construct a period sufficiently extensive and heterogeneous to include both of them. Indeed, many scholars now like to refer to "the long eighteenth century," roughly 1660–1830. Inviting Locke and Blake into a putative common period is no less artificial than separating them as founders of distinct periods, but it does suspend certain assumptions that might obscure cultural and textual continuities. The problem of disciplinary separation has diminished in recent years as literary scholars have increasingly appropriated texts outside the canon of imaginative literature. Certainly marriages of literary and philosophical texts are common enough to require no special justification. Blake, it should be noted, wanted to keep philosophers duly subordinate to poets: "There are always two classes of learned sages, the poetical and the philosophical ... Let the Philosopher always be the servant and scholar of inspiration and all will be happy" (*A Descriptive Catalogue*, 537).

The essays that follow belong more or less to the genre of critical biography, but with a double focus and a primary concern for productive critical topics rather than thorough coverage of either life. Thorough biographers of both Locke and Blake have had to work around gaps in the evidence.[2] Locke was good at keeping secrets, and records are scarce from his years in political exile. Blake's extant correspondence is much slighter than Locke's, some of his works have apparently been lost, and he slipped into greater obscurity as his engraving career foundered. If biographical records are somewhat defective, the body of critical analysis is dauntingly voluminous. Despite these contrary problems of shortage and surplus, a critical biographical approach remains attractive. Fredric Jameson has complained that the traditional history of ideas simply "wishes away the gap between philosophy and daily life or lived experience."[3] Some such gap may be inevitable, but here the ideas of Locke and Blake will be mingled with records of at least their own daily lives.

I use "conversation" in the title for its contemporary as well as its eighteenth-century implications. Richard Rorty uses "conversation" to label an antifoundational paradigm for intellectual history, well suited to this project. In conversation, "Our focus shifts from the relation between human beings and the objects of their inquiry to the relation between alternative standards of justification, and from there to the actual changes in those standards which make up intellectual history." Knowledge becomes "a matter of conversation between persons, rather than a matter of interaction with nonhuman reality."[4] Both Locke and Blake also subverted commonsense assumptions about the relationship of knowledge to nonhuman reality—as in Locke's treatment of nominal essence and Blake's deconstruction of nature—although neither man would have been quite comfortable with Rorty's antifoundational premises.

Locke and Blake themselves used "conversation" with the broader sense of "company" still implicit within the narrower modern usage. It was a word they both reserved to name a particularly rewarding experience. Locke wrote about the pleasure of conversation with friends, and for him the pleasure was enhanced rather than diminished by differences: "Difference of Opinions in conversation" brings about "the greatest Advantage of Society . . . where the light is to be got from the opposite Arguings of Men of Parts, shewing the different Sides of things" (*Education*, 145). Blake describes "Eternity" as a state of delightful conversation:

> When in Eternity Man converses with Man they enter
> Into each others Bosom (which are Universes of delight)
> In mutual interchange. (*Jerusalem* 88:3–5)

At the end of *Jerusalem*, he generously grants Locke (along with Bacon, Newton, Chaucer, Shakespeare, and Milton) a place among the conversants of eternity.

This generous reference to Locke was very much the exception, however. Blake scorned, even demonized Locke throughout his life. As a young man he read the *Essay Concerning Human Understanding* and wrote notes expressing his "contempt and abhorrence" ("Annotations to *The Works of Sir Joshua Reynolds*," 660). His copy of the *Essay* has never turned up, unfortunately, but several references to Locke elsewhere give us a good idea of what he must have written in the margins. In the early satire *An Island in the Moon*, the character Scopprell refers to "An Easy of Huming Understanding by John Lookye Gent." Someone else corrects him—he must mean "John Locke"—and Scopprell agrees: "O ay Lock" (456). Blake subverts Locke with a flurry of puns. The *Essay* presents the easiest or laziest of epistemologies (convenient for a comfortable gentleman); it leads to Hume's more radical skepticism; it locks up the intellect in a prison of sensory impressions. "Lookye" reinforces the comment on sensory information and also suggests the compelling influence of the *Essay* ("look ye" or "look'ee" meaning "mind this").

In a little song from *An Island in the Moon*, he acknowledges the popular opinion of Locke as an exemplary English genius: "To be or not to be / Of great capacity, / Like Sir Isaac Newton / Or Locke." Blake often paired Newton and Locke. Whether or not he knew that they were friends (and to some extent collaborators, although Locke never understood Newton's physics very well and Newton was uneasy with some implications of Locke's *Essay*),[5] he considered their work a coordinated effort to debase humanity. They are blamed for propagating a "Philosophy of Five Senses" ("Till a Philosophy of Five Senses was complete / Urizen wept & gave it into the hands of Newton & Locke" [*The Song of Los* 4:16–17]). Locke and Newton had elevated reason and memory to such prominence that better, more inspired faculties atrophied. Blake explains one of his paintings as "The Horse of Intellect . . . leaping from the cliffs of Memory and Reasoning; it is a barren Rock: it is also called the Barren Waste of Locke and Newton" (*A Descriptive Catalogue*, 546). He likes to describe the Lockean world with rock images. When the "Reasoning Power in every Man" dominates mental life, Albion becomes "a Rocky fragment from Eternity," "Constricting into Druid Rocks" (*Jerusalem* 54:6, 26). (Blake would have been amused to learn that Locke's favorite boyhood playground was the Druid stone circle near Stanton Drew.)[6]

His other favorite images for Locke come from weaving. He refers to Satan "weaving the Woof of Locke" (*Milton* 4:11). The narrator of *Jerusalem* uses similar imagery as part of a prophetic overview of fallen Europe. Locke's influence is so pervasive that academic Europe produces truth strictly from the fabric of his reasoning. For Blake this produces not enlightenment but a funeral pall:

> I turn my eyes to the Schools & Universities of Europe
> And there behold the Loom of Locke whose Woof rages dire
> Washd by the Water-wheels of Newton. black the cloth
> In heavy wreathes folds over every Nation . . . (15:14–17)

Weaving imagery also calls attention to contemporary industrial conditions that Locke helped prepare. As Nelson Hilton remarks, "The Industrial Revolution, practically coterminous with Blake's life, was nowhere so evident as in the textile industry."[7] Blake, whose father worked as a hosier, knew well the machines and institutions that drove the industry. "The Looms & Mills & Prisons & Work-houses" (*Jerusalem* 13:57) converged in his mind as tangible evidence of the Woof of Locke. Perhaps he knew that Locke supported compulsory spinning schools and workhouses for children of the poor. In notes toward poor-law reform, Locke wrote, "All children at five years old or sooner of parents that receive alms or pay noe taxes to be sent to the spinning schools there to learn to spin"; cities must build workhouses for the employment of these children as well as "all Strangers and foreigners that shall beg . . . and vagrants that shall be found there."[8] Blake was understandably bitter over this sort of thing from Locke and other gentlemen who could be idle if they wished. Probably he did not know that Locke worried frequently about living conditions of the poor. "If any City Corporation or Burrough suffer any of their poor to perish for want of due reliefe," he wrote, they are "to be punished according to the heinousness of the fact."[9] Just before his death he left careful instructions for the simplest of funerals, as the cost of elegance "will be better laid out in covering the poor."[10] Had he known of Locke's sympathy, Blake might have considered him a better candidate for redemption, but he would not have tempered his criticism of the Loom of Locke. Charity soothes a properly guilty conscience and keeps the Loom running. "Pity would be no more / If we did not make somebody Poor" ("The Human Abstract," 27).

For Blake, Locke's way of thinking impoverished humanity on many levels. He denounced its epistemological and spiritual poverty even more frequently than literal economic effects. If humans come to believe that their minds start out empty and are gradually furnished by empirical reasonings, they will feel shrunken and humble. "Bacon & Newton & Locke . . . teach Humility to Man!" (*Jerusalem* 54:17); "The feminine Tabernacle of Bacon, Newton & Locke" tricks humans into giving up their eternal imaginative powers. (Blake used "female space" to mean an illusory infinity that makes someone feel small and impotent.) Blake told Henry Crabb Robinson that Locke was an atheist. Robinson, a conventional thinker who was intrigued and a little alarmed by Blake, soberly objected: "[When] I remarked that Locke wrote on the evidence of Christianity and lived a virtuous life, Blake had nothing to say in reply. Nor did he make the charge of willful deception. I admitted that Locke's doctrine leads to Atheism, and with this view Blake seemed to be satisfied."[11] More likely Blake just tired of Robinson's conventional defense. For Blake the distinction between what Locke "was" and what his "doctrine leads to" would not be worth an argument: the man who wrote the *Essay* steeped himself and all of Europe in atheism, whether he knew it or not. Blake suspected that Locke did know but kept it secret. In the margins of Bishop Watson's *An Apology for the Bible,* near a reference to Locke's theory of conscience, he wrote, "I believe that the Bishop laught at the Bible in his slieve & so did Locke" (613).

Blake could not have known just how seriously Locke took the Bible. He certainly knew it at least as well as Blake did. He owned twenty-eight copies (in many languages) and another twenty-four copies of the New Testament by itself, along with a number of interpretive works.[12] His journals are full of biblical citations, often mingled with notes sketching preliminary ideas toward the *Essay*. He once spent several pages working out an exact chronology from the creation to the end of the world.[13] Even if Blake knew all this, he would probably persist in calling Locke an atheist. Reading the Bible is no guarantee of anything: "Both read the Bible day & night / But thou readst black where I read white" ("The Everlasting Gospel," 525.)

A Coincidence of Bishops

Blake liked to draw this sort of sharp distinction between himself and his adversaries. In mental war as in design he loved the clean line and detested blurring. He also loved minute particulars, however, and the reopening of tightly englobed conclusions. Thus it does not simply violate Blakean principles to look for moments of confluence in the lives of Locke and Blake that lead to interpretive complications.

A small example of such a moment has just surfaced. When Blake accused Locke of laughing at the Bible, he was responding to Richard Watson, bishop of Landaff, whose defense of the Bible against Tom Paine had irritated him. As it happens, Locke ran into trouble with a similarly irritating bishop. Edward Stillingfleet, bishop of Worcester, published a series of objections to the *Essay*. He worried that it threatened fundamental church doctrines, including the Trinity and the Resurrection of the Body. Locke answered each time—first with a polite letter, then a sharper second and third that showed his increasing irritation. The two bishops were similar enough to make the coincidence interesting: both were scholarly, Whiggish moderates who gained a reputation for defending revealed religion against untoward incursions by nonconformity or new philosophy. What can be discovered from Locke's and Blake's testy answers to moderate bishops?

For one thing, both of them express distinct anticlerical sentiments. Blake's remarks along these lines are much more vivid than Locke's, as might be expected; but he did not write them for publication, and Locke's hostility is no less significant for being more decorous. Blake's attacks focus primarily on priestly administration of state religion. Where Watson announces his purpose of "stopping that torrent of infidelity which endangers alike the future happiness of individuals, and the present safety of all christian states," Blake underlines the last two words and calls Watson a defender of "Antichrist." He calls him a "State trickster," full of "sly insinuations." "I should Expect that the man who wrote this sneaking sentence would be as good an inquisitor as any other Priest." He supports his accusations with a gospel reference: "Read the XXIII chap. of Matthew & then condemn Paines hatred of Priests if you dare." He attributes "the English Crusade against France" to "State Religion." One of Watson's published sermons was called "The Wisdom and Goodness of God, in having made both Rich and Poor"; Blake noticed this title and wrote, "God made Man happy & Rich but the Subtil made the innocent Poor. This must be a most wicked & blasphemous book" ("Annotations to *An Apology for the Bible* by R. Watson," 611–20).

Although Blake associated Locke with Bishop Watson as kindred conspirators, Locke attacked his own bishop with an indignation that Blake would have appreciated. Noting that Bishop Stillingfleet withheld his name from his response to the *Essay*, Locke explains that "anyone . . . may be well ashamed of his name, when he raises such a doubt as this, viz. whether an infinitely wise and powerful being, be veracious or no; unless falshood be in such reputation with this gentleman, that he concludes lying to be no mark of weakness and folly" (*Works*, 1:438). Frequently he mocks Stillingfleet with ironic praise. The bishop complained that Locke had discussed substance "childishly"; Locke replies, "I did not publish my Essay for such great masters of knowledge as your lordship" (1:490). At the end of his last reply he recognizes "the obligation I have to you, for the pains you have been at, about my Essay, which, I conclude, could not have been any way so effectually recommended to the world, as by your manner of writing against it" (1:587). In *The Reasonableness of Christianity* Locke writes more straightforwardly about priestly arrogance. He emphasizes that "the Scribes and Pharisees and chief priests" could not believe in Christ because of their narrow allegiance to institutions and rules: "Had God intended that none but the learned scribe, the disputer or wise of this world, should be Christians, or be saved; thus religion should have been prepared for them, filled with speculations and niceties, obscure terms, and abstract notions . . . [But such men] are rather shut out from the simplicity of the gospel, to make way for those poor, ignorant, illiterate, who heard and believed the promises of a deliverer, and believed Jesus to be him; who could conceive a man dead and made alive again" (*Works*, 2:588). At least in this context, Locke sides with the innocent poor against priestly overseers. He and Blake both resented the substitution of clerical establishment for the simpler vigor of original Christianity. Both also suggested that their bishops had strayed from fidelity to the Holy Spirit. Locke, correcting Stillingfleet on a scriptural point, admonishes him "to keep close to the words of Scripture" unless he pretends to be "wiser than the Holy Spirit himself" (1:507). Blake likewise corrects Watson and dares him to "prove that he has not spoken against the Holy Ghost who in Paine strives with Christendom as in Christ he strove with the Jews" (614).

As this last note indicates, Blake wants to stand with Paine against Watson. But he is not entirely comfortable doing so. He can embrace Paine's politics more easily than his religion. In defending *The Age of Reason* against the Bishop of Landaff, Blake finds himself aligned with a person who admired Locke and to some extent resembled him. A few of Blake's notes betray the awkwardness of this situation. Alongside Watson's smug toleration of Paine—"If you have made the best examination you can, and yet reject revealed religion, I think that you are in error; but whether that error be to you a vincible or an invincible error, I presume not to determine"—Blake writes: "Paine is either a Devil or an Inspired man. Men who give themselves to their Energetic Genius in the manner that Paine does are no Examiners. If they are not determinately wrong they must be Right or the Bible is false. as to Examiners in these points they will be spewed out. The Man who pretends to be a modest enquirer into the truth of a self evident thing is a Knave" (613–14). What stands out here is Blake's unwillingness to declare Paine right or wrong. Although the note sounds characteristically forthright, its argument is fractured. He denounces modest examiners like Watson in favor of inspired geniuses like Paine who refuse to equivocate about the "self evident" truths of "Inspiration." At the same time he equivocates about Paine's status as "either a Devil or an Inspired Man." (Note the slightly skewed parallel, which may indicate Blake's uneasiness with starkly binary questions of this sort.) He admires Paine's decisiveness but can't quite decide about Paine.[14]

Blake's best answer to Watson, and the one that distinguishes him most clearly from Locke, has to do with miracles. Watson argues that "the evidence for the miracles recorded in the Bible is . . . so greatly superior to that for the prodigies mentioned by Livy, or the miracles related by Tacitus, as to justify us in giving credit to the one as the work of God, and in withholding it from the other as the effect of superstition and imposture" (616). Locke had offered a similar argument one hundred years earlier in a short "Discourse of Miracles." Blake answers by subverting the assumption that reason precedes and enables belief in miracles:

> Jesus could not do miracles where unbelief hinderd hence we must conclude that the man who holds miracles to be ceased puts it out of his own power to ever witness one The manner of a miracle being performd is in modern times considerd as an arbitrary command of the agent upon the patient but this is an impossibility not a miracle neither did Jesus ever do such a miracle. Is it a greater miracle to feed five thousand men with five loaves than to overthrow all the armies of Europe with a small pamphlet. look over the events of your own life & if you do not find that you have both done such miracles & lived by such you do not see as I do True I cannot do a miracle thro experiment & to domineer over & prove to others my superior power as neither could Christ But I can & do work miracles such as both astonish & comfort me & mine. (616–17)

Blake's perspective differs as much from Paine's as from Watson's. He does not doubt Christ's miracles, but neither does he argue that they can be proved or disproved by reason. Blake's position on miracles anticipates Wittgenstein's remark in his "Lecture on Ethics" in which he dismisses as absurd the sentence, "Science has proved that there are no miracles." Imagine the most miraculous event you can, says Wittgenstein, such as a lion's head suddenly appearing on a human body; as soon as a team of scientists arrives to study the cause, the miracle will always become just another natural phenomenon, the causes of which have not yet been perfectly understood.[15] Blake similarly subverts the continuity of reason and miracle. He redefines miracle as an event in which a person's power of belief makes possible some experience of wonder or transformation.

Locke's position on miracles turns out to be more complicated than Watson's and less strictly adversarial with Blake's than it first appears. One important complication emerges during his exchange with Stillingfleet. The bishop dislikes Locke's definition of knowledge ("the perception of the agreement or disagreement of our ideas"), as it may undermine certainties of faith. Locke replies that "the certainty of faith . . . has nothing to do with the certainty of knowledge":

> And to talk of the certainty of faith, seems all one to me as to talk of the knowledge of believing, a way of speaking not easy to me to understand. Place knowledge in what you will; 'start what new methods of certainty you please, that are apt to leave men's minds more doubtful than before' [Locke is quoting Stillingfleet]; place certainty on such grounds as will

leave little or no knowledge in the world; . . . this shakes not at all, nor in the least concerns the assurance of faith; that is quite distinct from it, neither stands nor falls with knowledge. Faith stands by itself, and upon grounds of its own; nor can be removed from them, and placed on those of knowledge. (*Works,* 1:416)

The point sounds rather closer to Blake than to natural religion. Indeed Locke's answer to Stillingfleet goes against the grain of his own writings elsewhere about miracles. In *The Reasonableness of Christianity,* for example, he concludes that Christ's miracles "produced faith" in those who saw them. Christ gave "such a manifestation of himself, as every one at present could not understand; but yet carried such an evidence with it . . . to convince them he was the Messiah" (*Works* 2:530). A similar argument dominates his "Discourse of Miracles." Rational inquiry proves biblical miracles to be genuine. "Such care has God taken that no pretended revelation should stand in competition with what is truly divine, that we need but open our eyes to see and be sure which came from him" (*Works* 3:434). The theory sounds better in the abstract than in practice. Locke dismisses supposed miracles of Indian and Persian religion as "wild stories" too "manifestly fabulous" to be taken seriously; at the same time he accepts Judeo-Christian miracles as presenting "no manner of difficulty." Perhaps he worried about the distinction a little more than he admitted. Once he asked a friend traveling to India to find out about magical effects he had heard of—"which must needs be beyond leger de main and seeme not within the power of art or nature. I would very gladly know whether they are really done as strange as they are reported."[16] In any case, Locke liked to think that apparent miracles could be evaluated successfully by reason. He had not discovered any modern miracles. They were no longer necessary, he thought; after Moses and Christ, a rational person needed no more special evidence. If miracles were briefly useful as "credentials of a messenger delivering a divine religion," now they would merely disrupt "the established, steady laws of causes and effects" (*Works* 3:432).

Blake thrived on the continuing astonishment and comfort of miracles; Locke was more comfortable with the orderly patterns of a postmiraculous age. And yet Locke told Bishop Stillingfleet that religious belief must not be confused with rational knowledge. Belief must be allowed to exceed knowledge, however well aligned they might appear to a professional believer like the bishop. Even in the "Discourse of Miracles," where he called on reason to verify miracles, Locke admitted that "a miracle to one . . . will not be so to another," and "I doubt whether any man, learned or unlearned, can in most cases be able to say of any particular operation . . . that it is certainly a miracle" (*Works*

3:436). Although he never says so with Blake's zeal, Locke sometimes implies that belief must precede reason rather than the other way around. In the *Essay* he tries to have it both ways. No revelation that contradicts reason can be trusted as such. On the other hand,

> There being many Things, wherein we have very imperfect Notions, or none at all; and other Things, of whose past, present, or future Existence, by the natural Use of our Faculties, we can have no Knowledge at all; these, as being beyond the Discovery of our natural Faculties, and above *Reason*, are, when revealed, *the proper Matter of Faith*. Thus that part of the Angels rebelled against GOD, and thereby lost their first happy state: And that the dead shall rise, and live again: These, and the like, being beyond the Discovery of *Reason*, are purely Matters of *Faith;* with which *Reason* has, directly, nothing to do. (4.18.7)

His two examples of suprarational truth sketch a sort of Blakean redemptive plot: Satan's fall into rational self-sufficiency must be overcome by faith in miraculous resurrection. For Blake this resurrection comes as a consequence of inspired belief, as in the Lazarus story: "If ye will believe your Brother shall rise again" (*The Four Zoas,* Night 7b, 87:6). Locke was determined not to let inspired belief supplant reason, but he recognized that some versions of rational faith were shallow and mundane. Stillingfleet, for example, argued mightily that Locke had subverted the doctrine of the Resurrection of the Body. The bishop insisted on the resurrection of each person's actual body as it existed on earth. Locke scoffed at this notion. Stillingfleet was unable or unwilling to imagine something beyond his ordinary body. Locke relied on Paul to envision a miraculous transformation: "It is very remarkable what St. Paul says . . . [that] we shall not all sleep, but we shall all be changed in the twinkling of an eye . . . because this corruptible thing must put on incorruption, and this mortal thing put on immortality. How? By putting off flesh and blood in an instantaneous change."[17] Blake also liked Paul's account of Resurrection, as in 1 Corinthians: "It is sown a natural body; it is raised a spiritual body." He engraved the second clause on the plate of "To Tirzah." Locke was skeptical of latter-day St. Pauls who announced disruptive miracles. But he was no more patient than Blake with a bishop's plodding, official desiccation of spiritual truth.

This coincidence of bishops has provided a minor opportunity for the sort of conversation I propose. The resulting analysis will not simply erase differences between Locke and Blake, but it should alter interpretive coordinates sufficiently to replot their relationship within the long eighteenth century. Chapters that follow all begin with biographical connections and move into analysis of relevant texts and contexts. In each case, the focal topic emerges from an event or situation in Locke's life that corresponds suggestively with something in Blake's life. These correspondences include several elements of their public careers along with a few more private matters of family, health, and happiness. Although topical organization does not allow a strictly chronological sequence, the order of chapters loosely follows the course of their lives: beginning with mother's milk, and ending with epitaphs.

Chapter 2

Mothers, the Matrix, and Marriage

Biographical records of Locke's and Blake's mothers are frustratingly minimal. Neither man said much of anything about his mother. Arguing primarily from evidence in his work, some psychoanalytical interpreters of Blake find a "deep animosity towards women, linked with a feeling of maternal deprivation."[1] A few clues from Locke's life and writings seem to point in a similar direction. But Locke's and Blake's attitudes about mothers, women, lovers, and marriage are complicated enough that no straightforward thesis, psychoanalytical or otherwise, can stand as a sufficient account. Both of them participated in conventional representations of gendered desire, yet both of them resisted traditional romantic plots and looked for alternatives to ordinary marriage.

LOCKE THE LOVER

We know far too little about Agnes Locke to claim that she was one or another sort of mother. A few biographical hints might suggest that she and her son were not especially close. He talked about her very rarely and never wrote about her. He once referred to her as "a very pious woman and an affectionate mother," says Cranston, "but it seems that he never talked much about her."[2] He and she did share an interest in home remedies: an early notebook inscribed with both their names contains therapeutic recipes for stomachache, coughing, back pain, and the like.[3] He came home from Oxford when he learned her health was precarious but arrived too late to see her before she died. His mother was ten years older than his father; this means nothing, perhaps, except in its possible connection to one of Locke's "Atlantis" notes sketching social regulation: "Who ever marys a woman more than 5 years older than him self shall forfeit half of all she brings him in marriage."[4]

Other "Atlantis" notes suggest the following law: "The son that is not nursed by the mother inherits not the estate of the father. Unlesse upon testimony of

2 physicians & the mid wife that it could not be donne without evident danger to the mother & the child."[5] Here he is taking a position against the cultural norm of the period: most English families of comparable position used wet nurses.[6] Whatever his other reasons for inserting this provision—including concern over the hygiene and habits of wet nurses—he clearly wanted mothers to participate more fully in the nurture of their children. Elsewhere in his writing various clues can be found about the value he attached to infant nurture. Indeed, recent feminist critics have noted that, despite "some glimmering of feminist sympathies" (mainly in his emphasis on consent and choice in the marriage contract), Locke effectively subjugated women by making maternity their essential function.[7] In the *Second Treatise*, for example, he writes about the ends of "conjugal society": "and tho' it consist chiefly in such a Communion and Right in one anothers Bodies, as is necessary to its chief end, Procreation; yet it draws with it mutual support, and Assistance, and a Communion of Interest too, as necessary to their common Off-spring, who have a Right to be nourished and maintained by them, till they are able to provide for themselves" (78). Nourishment of children is the one natural purpose that dictates the endurance of marriages; when this purpose has been achieved, there is "no necessity in the nature of [marriage], nor to the ends of it, that it should always be for Life" (81). Both parents bear the responsibility of nurturing, but the child "must certainly owe most to the Mother," who "nourish[es] the Child a long time in her own Body out of her own Substance. There it is fashion'd, and from her it receives the Materials and Principles of its Constitution" (*First Treatise*, 55). In *Some Thoughts Concerning Education* he uses the pleasures of nursing to illustrate the associational origins of fear: "Did a Child suck every Day a new Nurse, I make account it would be no more affrighted, with the change of Faces at Six Months old than at Sixty. The reason then, why it will not come to a Stranger, is, because having been accustomed to receive its Food and Kind Usage only from one or two that are about it, the Child apprehends, by coming into the Arms of a Stranger, the being taken from what delights and feeds it, and every moment supplies its Wants, which it often feels, and therefore fears when the Nurse is away" (115). An unannounced question of maternal intimacy plays beneath the main argument. He assumes that the child will be fed by a nurse, not necessarily the mother. (Perhaps he did not want to dictate maternal nursing to the Clarkes, close friends to whom he addressed *Some Thoughts Concerning Education*.) And the main point suggests that an indifferent succession of nurses would toughen a child against timorousness and anxiety. At the same time, however, the passage shows a sensitive appreciation of the "delights" and "kind usage" of maternal attachment. Locke will not quite let this become a sentimental embrace of the loving mother—the care comes "only from one or two," as if

that difference were trivial—but the older, tougher Locke has not entirely erased hints of earlier vulnerability.

In a letter written from Holland (where he had heard gossip connecting him with three English women), Locke summons an old proverb: "I am . . . confirmed in the opinion that I was wrapt abundantly in my mothers smock but it was still the upper end of it."[8] The proverbial mother's smock points to good luck generally; a man wrapped in the tail of his mother's smock would have good luck with women.[9] Locke lightly welcomes the gossip but keeps himself safely within the upper smock. This double gesture is typical of him. As the *Education* passage quoted above suggests, he felt both a sensitive attraction to the pleasures of maternal nurture and a defensive instinct to preserve himself from any such dependency. His amorous relationships (and his opinions about women and love) show signs of a comparable tension between romance and independence. One intriguing love story deserves particular attention: a close relationship developed between Locke and Damaris Cudworth, daughter of the Cambridge Platonist. This epistemologically unlikely match became his most intimate friendship with a woman.

To some degree Locke followed a fairly ordinary script for amorous roles within his culture. He was capable of treating women quite conventionally as objects of desire. This is most obvious in records of his younger years, although it also shows up here and there in his mature writings. In a letter supplementary to *Some Thoughts Concerning Education,* for example, "having more admired than considered your sex," he disclaims expertise on the rearing of daughters.[10] (After this banal courtliness, he goes on to say that they should be brought up pretty much the same as sons.) In another passage from *Education* he casually compares women to sweets as objects of male longing: "For if the child must have Grapes or Sugar-plumbs, when he has a Mind to them, rather than make the poor Baby cry, or be out of Humour; why, when he is grown up, must he not be satisfied too, if his Desires carry him to Wine or Women? They are Objects as suitable to the longing of one of more Years, as what he cried for, when little, was to the inclinations of a child" (36).

Most signs of conventional romantic behavior appear in earlier records. Earliest of all would be a 1649 entry in his account book from Westminster School. He notes an expense of five shillings for "a pair of gloves for my ___Mary Lower." Locke at some point crossed out the whole entry, but it remains legible except for the word characterizing his relationship to Mary Lower.[11] This sort of embarrassment and disguise in amorous correspondence continues well past adolescence. He wrote letters to women using codes. He liked to use pseudonyms for himself ("Atticus," "Philander") and either a pseudonym for the woman or inverted initials ("PE" for Elinor Parry). He sometimes altered an address from "Madam" to "Sir" and removed names.

Friends complained about his riddling letters. In a 1654 letter to a woman he refers to a message in invisible ink: the postscript tells her to "take out a leaf of clean paper inserted at the beginning of this book, and when you are alone warm it very hot by the fire. Beyond this I dare not trouble you."[12] Cranston presents this postscript and concludes that "however inappropriately for a man who was to be remembered as the founder of the Age of Reason, Locke was romantic in his ways."[13]

His romantic ways were no doubt influenced by college reading. He told Pierre Coste that he "spent a good part of his first years at the university in reading romances, from his aversion to the disputative way then in fashion there."[14] One romance he must have liked was *Cleopatre* by La Calprenède: he sent the English translation to Elinor Parry in 1659. Among the tropes pervading this romance are conventional images of fire and heat to represent erotic passion. It begins with Prince Tyridates in "amorous thoughts," comparing his inner flames to the literal flames of a burning ship: "But my fire finds in my soul an eternal punishment, no hope of relief from a contrary element, nor end of such a substance as may ever burn without consuming." Soon Cleopatra's eyes "shot new flames into great Caesar's soul . . . as he had much ado to hinder his amorous fever from breaking out into the hottest proofs," and so on.[15] Locke wrote to Elinor Parry using similar imagery. As he jauntily delivers his vision of an afterlife, he notes that "the shades have their old passions sticking to 'em and the same flames torment 'em here that scorch them above and the fire that ladies eyes kindle is of such a nature that death hath not coldnesse enough to extinguish it."[16] In another letter to Parry he complains of her insufficient warmth—"Pray tell me whether yours be true love or No, for our old philosophers say that love is a fire and a flame full of heat and warmth."[17] Later, as we shall see, it will be Elinor Parry complaining of Locke's deficient flame; but for a while at least he played a typical romantic lover, chiding her for "robbing me of the use of my reason." His most titillating letter to Parry comes with Platonic trappings. Locke "must be content to carry about a luggage of clay, whilst I (that is my soul) snail like beare about my house with me . . . 'Tis well for you that it is soe for could my body remove with my thoughts I beleeve you would have reason to complaine of my too frequent visits, and possible some times at midnight you would find other company at BH [Black Hall, St. Giles, Oxford] besides sleep and pleasant dreams."[18] Less Platonic was an invitation from Frank Atkins, "perhaps the proverbial 'bad companion' of Locke's youth" (Cranston). Atkins had planned some sort of amorous adventure for Locke and himself.

> It may be Cupid may be one of the actors in a comical journey, and to that purpose I have sent already a footboy to my mistress to meet me on Tuesday or Wednesday night at Chard. She is one of thine own sect, and

if she errs she does it out of pure zeal and simplicity of soul. I cannot promise you she's handsome, but this, though I think she has the more scarlet in her cheeks of the two, yet you shall be the judge . . . I shall desire to meet you at the place near the coalpits, where we last parted when I came from Pensford, about four o'clock in the afternoon. Then we'll have a little love-duel.[19]

We don't know whether he accepted or declined the outing. In any case, young Locke was well enough versed in romantic conventions to make Atkins consider him a plausible companion.

Some enemies of the older Locke regarded him quite otherwise. John Edwards, a testy Calvinist, called him "a Hater of Women."[20] Edwards was hardly an impartial judge of this or any other aspect of Locke's life. However, there are a few hints of mild misogyny in his writings to complement the conventional treatment of women as love objects. The passage to which Edwards refers comes from *Education*. Locke expresses his disapproval of interruptions and "loud wrangling" in conversation: "Was it not, think you, an entertaining Spectacle, to see two Ladies of Quality accidentally seated on the opposite Sides of a Room, set round with Company, fall into a Dispute, and grow so eager in it, that in the Heat of their Controversie, edging by Degrees their Chairs forwards, they were in a little time got up close to one another in the middle of the Room; where they for a good while managed the Dispute as fiercely as two Game-Cocks in the Pit" (145). Locke once recorded (in Latin and English) an undistinguished satirical poem called "Love and Cats," which ends, "You know by experience the hot fit is soon o'er / Puss puss lass not long but turns to cat whore."[21] The sentiment might seem an odd one for Locke to cherish, but his writing does contain a fair number of cynical references to women's appetite and inconstancy.

Despite these hints of conventional misogyny and romance, neither label quite fits him. He was finally neither the lover nor the misogynist. For Elinor Parry, who assumed he was courting her seriously, he was a puzzle she never solved. After all his flirtatious letters and romantic behavior, she must have expected either a marriage proposal or a definitive rejection. She received neither. She noticed only a mysterious change. In late 1666, she began to write of "that change in you" that "London hath wrought."[22] Over the next two or three years she continued to write him in an effort to draw out some decisive confession of desire. "I must tell you from S [Scribelia, her pseudonym] that if you are the yet passionate Att [Atticus, Locke's pseudonym] and the real one you ever was, you will hide nothing from her."[23] Nothing was revealed, and she tried to fit him into another "real" identity: "Are you changed and do you now think indifferently of the affection you have framed in my soul?"[24] In a final letter, she wants to believe that she has finally understood the story of their relationship. He really loves her, but somehow her "folly" has spoiled their prospects: "How hard is it for you to disguise your thoughts, soul and heart to one that knows it so well as I do ... You love me still in spite of all my folly ... You have over-acted the indifferent part, but 'twas only to require a seeming and mistaken letter too too unhappy since it has brought us both to a nearer meeting, I believe, in the next world, since we will not in this."[25] Parry finally blames herself as a way of excusing Locke and preserving him in the role of passionate lover she prefers. She persuades herself that the real lover has retreated behind layers of disguise.

A better diagnosis might be that Locke always held himself a little aloof from traditional scripts of desire that end in "conjugal society." When he was young he may have come close to marrying, but later he tended to see marriage as boring or vaguely distasteful. In a letter to his French friend Toinard he jokes about marriage as a burden ("le fardeau de mariage"), a fate comparable to death ("le mariage et la mort ... sont a peu pres le mesme chose"), and he happily repeats, twice, Toinard's joke about marriage and circumcision. In an earlier letter to Toinard—who obviously brought out this side of Locke—he had joked at rather awkward length about men selling their wives by the pound.[26] Elsewhere he compares men's opinions to "their wives, which when they have espoused them think themselves concerned to maintain, though for no other reason but because they are theirs ... and if 'twere left to their own choice, 'tis not improbable that this would be the more difficult divorce."[27] A passage from the *Essay* implies a similarly jaded view of marriage. As he discusses the utility of "uneasiness," he quotes Paul: "It is better to marry than to burn, says St. Paul; where we may see, what it is, that chiefly drives Men into the enjoyments of a conjugal life" (II.xxi.34). In his later paraphrase and notes to 1 Corinthians, Locke embellishes Paul's treatment of marriage as a necessary evil. Where Paul writes, "If a virgin marry, she hath not sinned; nevertheless, such shall have trouble in the flesh," Locke paraphrases as follows: "But those that are married, shall have worldly troubles; but I spare you, by not representing to you how little enjoyment Christians are like to have from a married life."

Locke's coolness could be explained in a variety of ways. The easiest explanation would be framed as a matter of temperament. Cranston remarks that "Locke was not by temper a voluptuary," and soon enough he "lost the itch for gallantry."[28] Like all such answers this one is hard to refute, but it is opaquely determinate and a little dull. Another dull but reputable answer would lie in his moral firmness: he considered himself one of those strong men whom Paul calls to higher celibacy. More practically, his poor health discouraged him, especially weakness of the lungs. In a letter he told a friend, "I doe not finde that my ague hath much inclined me to the thoughts of [love]. My health, which you are so kinde to in your wishes, is the only mistris I have a long time courted, and is soe coy a one that I thinke it will take up the remainder of my days to obteyn her good graces and keep her in good humour."[29] Perhaps his absorption in public work crowded out romance. He once copied two French poems about a king's call to duty taking precedence over his heart.[30] Or perhaps his lack of enthusiasm could be explained as a sign of other desires, differing sufficiently from heterosexual routine to alter the usual call for conjugal establishment. This sort of analysis could seem strained if it were phrased too simply—that is, if one were to decide that Locke must have been "essentially" gay, however he happened to have figured or deflected his desires. But the explanation could be put more subtly, to position his desires at some remove from his culture's romantic norms along a continuum of sexualities.

These several explanations are not mutually exclusive: all of them could be true. The one thing they all recognize is a discrepancy between Locke's romantic desires and some sort of normalizing expectation: he is physically cooler or weaker, more principled or preoccupied, more receptive to other sexualities. The trouble with all of them is that they do not account very well for his one most intimate, enduring relationship, with Damaris Cudworth. With a mixture of playfulness and anxiety they reshaped their romantic plot and eventually arranged an alternative version of marriage.

Locke met Damaris Cudworth when she was twenty-three and he forty-nine. Her father was Ralph Cudworth, the Cambridge Platonist whose *True Intellectual System of the Universe* had been published a few years earlier. Despite conspicuous differences between Cudworth's ideas and his own, Locke admired the book. In *Education* he recommended it for study of ancient Greek philosophy (193). Still, Locke's epistemology differed so sharply from Platonism that the *Essay* squelched respectable interest in that kind of thinking for a long time. The tension between Platonic Damaris Cudworth and anti-Platonic John Locke helped make their relationship particularly stimulating.

The story survives mainly in some forty letters from "Philoclea" (Cudworth) to "Philander" (Locke). Although very few of his answering letters remain, we can often infer the gist from her reaction. When they first met (1682) they must have spent some time discussing the romances of M. de Scudéry. In her first letter she writes, "You should have let me knowe what new and better forms [of romance] are introduc'd instead of those Antiquated ones of his."[31] Cudworth was probably surprised to find him something of an expert in romances. Locke was well past his *Cleopatra* days, however; soon the focus of their correspondence shifted to philosophy and religion.

In February they exchanged ideas about visionary faith and reason. They discussed *Divine Knowledge* by Platonist John Smith, which Locke purchased and read for this occasion. She writes, "I know not what you may call Vision nor how much you may attribute to the power of Reason, onely as I understood them it seemes to mee that there may be something betweene these two things, there being (I think) such a Degree of Perfection to be attain'd to in this Life to which the Powers of meere Unassisted Reason will never conduct a Man."[32] The term "vision" would carry for Locke a pejorative sense, similar to "enthusiasm." He was defining "enthusiasm" in his journal as "a strong and firme persuasion of any proposition relating to religion," unsupported by reason. Cudworth is willing to entertain his debunking of vision, but only to a point. Her critique of "mere reason" would have pleased Blake, if not her doubts about vision. She posits but does not name a faculty between reason and vision. Locke responds accommodatingly but with firm authority: "Whatever is known, however sublime or spirituall is known only by the naturall faculty of the understanding and reason, however assisted."[33] Cudworth's next letter suggests a rising vexation—she is half attracted to his ideas but a little irritated by his complacency. She discusses Smith's "contemplative man . . . who shooting up above his own Logical or self-rational life, pierceth unto the Highest life . . . which if you will call Enthusiasts in yr next I shall think my self much concern'd, and will resolve to take very Ill."[34]

As Cudworth tentatively defends her father's ideas she begins to link Platonic vision with friendship. "That I have no Ill Opinion of the Platonists I confess, nor ought you to wonder at that seeing I have spent the most of my life amongst Philosophers of that Sect in whom I have always found the most Vertue and Friendship."[35] And a little later, teasing Locke for neglect of correspondence, she refers to "Faith, whose Implicitness is not of less value in Friendship, then it is in Religion. But who can assure me that you are not a Heretick in both?"[36] Her tone is light, but she seems to be reaching for a way to unsettle Locke's rational complacency. Perhaps those who lack vision, she implies, also lack some sort of warmth necessary for the higher fulfillments. In one letter she tries to name the higher faculty to which she aspires: ". . . there being a Natural Cohesion of Truth with impolluted Souls, and also, as Dr. More says, a Principle Antecedaneous to Reason which he calls Divine Sagacitie which is only compatible to Persons of Pure and Unspoted Minds and without which Reason is not successful in the Contemplation of the Highest matters."[37] Years later she will adapt More's "Divine Sagacitie" to question Locke's attack on innate ideas: "I should be glad more Clearly and fully to understand the difference betweene you and some friends of Mine, about that Principle thing, of the Souls haveing no Actual Knowledge; Being not sure the Difference between you, is Really so great as it seemes." Her friends mean "onely an Active Sagacitie in the Soul whereby something being Hinted to Her she runs out into a More Cleare and large Conception ... We have not onely sensible Ideas Passively impress'd from without, but also Intelligible Notions exerted from the Mind It self."[38]

This position conforms fairly closely to her father's. Ralph Cudworth denied the primacy of empirical reason in favor of an antecedent spiritual motive. "The first principle of motion in the soul is not, of course, reason and understanding ... there must be some other spring and motion, or first mover in the soul, that sets the wheels at work and employs the thinking, consulting, and speculative power."[39] This "spring" is hard to name; he calls it "a certain love," or the "instinct" and "desire" that constitutes "the source of life and activity" (terminology that resembles Blake's in *The Marriage of Heaven and Hell*). He derogates those who rely solely on "inferior reason." Such people pursue their "private utility" through a "prudent calculation of consequences." Their utilitarian interests show a "cool" or "passive" soul at work, as opposed to "the active exertion of love itself."[40] A Cudworth might well see Locke as someone who neglects this higher love in the service of prudent utility. Indeed, sometimes Locke calculated his interests so prudently that critics charged him with pagan hedonism or (less dramatically) a cold, practical self-love.

As she worked through her mixed admiration and suspicion of Locke's ideas, Damaris Cudworth was also trying to sort out exactly how cool or warm their friendship would be. Near the end of 1682 she was showing signs of strain from the uncertainty of this relationship and, more generally, from the social pressures accumulating on an unmarried twenty-four-year-old woman. "Instead of thinking (as I used to do) that the Happyness of life consisted Principally in Societie, and Friendship, I now beleeve otherwise, and that to be Happy One must Care for Nothing, nor Nobody, Have no Friends, Love onely ones self, Nor ever take Concerne in the Good, or Ill, of other people."[41] Locke must have been concerned about her sour stoicism. His reply has been lost, but we can infer that he made two guesses about what had caused it: either she has had some disappointment or she has been seized by melancholy (a subject in which he was well versed, having studied the nervous disorders in some depth). She writes again to deny both causes. "It is not any Disappointment that makes me more so now than ever ... nor Melancholy Humour ... so that I would not have you expect if ever you see me againe you should finde me worse company than I use to be."[42] Although she denies any specific disappointment, the letter gently chides Locke for coolness or neglect ("if ever you see me againe").

Shortly after this letter Locke's feelings apparently warmed up dramatically. Perhaps two months later (DeBeer guesses mid-January 1683), she and he wrote pastoral poems with "Damon" and "Clora" posing for John and Damaris.[43] In brief, the story goes as follows: Clora loved Damon and tried to win his love, but Damon offered only friendship; when Damon later discovered that he had been overcome by love for Clora, she returned only friendship. Cudworth's poem begins with Damon as a cool debunker of love:

> Say wherefore is't that Damon flies
> From the weak charms of Clora's eyes?
> Weak charms they surely needs must be
> Which till this hour he could not see.
> Nor is she now more fair than when
> Their first acquaintance they began,
> When the gay shepherd laughed at love,
> Swore it no generous heart could move,
> Disease of fools, fond lunacy . . .

She pretends to attribute Damon's reserve to Clora's "weak charms" but implies that the problem lies more with his defective vision ("he could not see"). When Damon then staggers with love of Clora, he tries to reason himself back to equanimity—"Resolve he would no captive be / But set himself by reason free." He fails and resigns himself to loving her: "Condemned a sacrifice to be / Oppose not then thy destiny." Clora is unimpressed with a lover who feels that destiny has pushed him (St. Paul would say "burning" has "driven" him) to ignore his better judgment.

> The friendship once I gave retain
> But think from me no more to gain
> To whom thy passion comes too late
> That scorn a conquest given by fate.
> With this she left the trembling swain
> Half dead with grief at her disdain.

Cudworth playfully exaggerates the emotions involved, but Damon resembles Locke sufficiently to provoke his sequel. "But this disdain could not yet move / The constancy of Damon's love," he begins, and goes on to answer Clora's complaints about his delayed passion. The tricky part is to explain the transition from friendship to love as something more than fate or appetite:

> I friendship begged and did obtain
> And thought myself a happy swain,
> But 'twas not ignorance nor pride
> Made me ask nothing else beside.
> He that asks friendship asks the heart
> Unless there be some better part;
> And that were only made a toy
> To please some idle wanton boy.
> I thought by this 'twould well be known

I now no longer was my own:
Yours friendship made me; from that hour
Was I not always in your power?
Friendship first warmed me with desire
And lodged in me a secret fire,
Which either time or some kind blast
Was sure to make flame out at last.

He first distinguishes friendship from mere sexual appetite, the latter only a "toy / To please some idle wanton boy." A nobler sexual desire then emanates from friendship. Locke seems to be mixing the rhetoric of his old romances (fires and flames) with a Platonic strain borrowed from Damaris: like the Cudworths' Cambridge friends, Damon has grown warm from the "secret fire" of some virtue higher than reason. He doesn't simply concede her claims of an innate "divine sagacity" but compromises. This secret fire, not innate, was transferred almost Pentecostally by her influence. However this happened, "It matters not now to enquire / Your power prevaild and all's on fire."

The poem ends with one more interesting turn. After all those fiery desires he pictures a gentler, maternal scene: "Then with a sigh closing what he had said / Upon her bosom drop'd his drooping head." This might sound like an insignificant pastoral trope. However, Locke liked to address Damaris as "my Governess" and have her call him "Pupil." This pet name suggests that his ideal female love may be less conjugal than maternal. Governess is as close a substitution for mother as one could find outside the family. The term implies a close but chaste relationship ("governess" safer than "nurse" in this respect), protected from any guilty desires of a "wanton" boy; his sexual inclinations are tamed into manners and transmuted into knowledge. Damaris Cudworth as governess offers intimations of "divine sagacity" to her cool, skeptical pupil.

If the Damon and Clora poems are a reliable key, Cudworth declined Locke's efforts to turn their friendship into something more intimate—perhaps into marriage, but there is no way of knowing. In any case, Locke fled to Holland later in 1683 for political reasons, and in 1685 Cudworth married a widower baronet. Her letters to Locke in the intervening year resume their earlier gloominess. Apparently she is annoyed by the socioeconomic pressures pushing her toward marriage and unhappy with the choices in front of her. In one letter she asks a favor of Locke. She has heard interesting reports of the Labadists, a colony of Pietists in Friesland. Will he please try to find out about them?

Locke did so and sent her a discouraging account. No doubt he was worried by the tone of her letters and her curious infatuation with a sect of zealots. She remained keenly interested despite his report. "Notwithstanding the character which you have giv'n of the Labadies I acknowledge that I like them very well."[44] Her good opinion prevails despite rumors that "under a show and appearance of Religion there are not really greater Libertines in the World." Two months later, "If ever I come to be Perfectly reconcil'd to Matrimonie againe I shall have an extreame Desire to Marry a Labadist, and be one my self for that very Reason."[45] Locke might have been unsure how seriously to take her remarks, but he made an effort to argue against the Labadists. In Cudworth's last letter on the subject, she half-teasingly claims that his arguments have had the opposite of their intended effect. She has now a greater "Zeal for the sect I have embrac'd"; and "should I ever resolve for Matrimonie, You have so far improv'd my Reasons and Arguments for it that I should certainly then go into Freezeland."[46]

If Cudworth wanted to provoke Locke with an enthusiastic attachment, she chose her sect well. The Labadists were more dramatically anti-Lockean than her father's Platonists. Locke found this out directly when he visited the colony at her request. (His letter to her has been lost, but a substantial journal entry records his impressions.)[47] The Labadists had withdrawn from the world of profane modern learning to live like early Christians. Aspirants had to surrender all possessions to the community—a requirement that Locke, theorist of private property, found distasteful and suspicious: "They live all in common and whoever is admitted is to give with himself all that he has to the Lord: i. e. to the church," now run by Pierre Yvon, "who has established to himself a perfect empire over them." Labadists distrusted reason and called for inspired regeneration of faith. The ultimate goal, in the words of Yvon, was to be "overwhelmed by the effects of Jesus's love."[48] Locke found their piety affected (with "a little of Tartouf") and their inspirations dubious: whenever he "enquired after the rationall means and measures of proceeding" they simply "referred all things to the Lord," "as if they did all things by revelation." As to matters of worldly love (and rumors of libertinism), Locke had nothing to report, except that they were "very shie to give an account . . . about their manner of liveing." Other studies give no support to such rumors, but they note that Labadists emphasized marriage as an inspired event. Marriage was valid only between two enthusiasts, whose attachment to each other reflected their passionate Christian faith.

Cudworth's attraction to the Labadists seems easy enough to understand. Irritated by the prospect of an uninspired marriage, she probably used the Labadists as a convenient way of alarming family and friends. But she also had a strong sense of vocation, and the "governess" may have wanted to push Locke toward some vision of higher love. Instead, he felt only annoyance that the Labadists treated him coldly as an unpromising outsider. They made him wait more than two hours for an interview and restricted him to "a little house without the gates."

Whatever her intentions, she did not turn Labadist. She married Sir Francis Masham, a widower with nine children. Cranston pieces together what evidence he can and concludes that Sir Francis "was not a stupid man, but he was a commonplace one"; probably "something of a bore" although "an affable one."[49] Lady Masham worried that the marriage would hurt her friendship with Locke. Three months before the wedding she wrote him about something she had heard from mutual friends—a report "that You Love me Exceedingly."[50] She admits to being "Really Vex'd." She received a letter back from Locke on the day of her wedding, "almost at the very same moment [Mlle Cudworth] was going to quit that name for Another under which you will Always find her as much yr Friend as she ever was."[51] Locke's first letter to Lady Masham distressed her with its formality: "Your last letter seems to me to differ so much from the stile of yr former ones, that I cannot help being Dissatisfy'd with you for it . . . And you make such distinctions between Friendship, and Respect, Your Governess, and my Lady—that if I were at all naturally Suspicious would incline me to beleeve you were growing Wearie of the Former."[52] In the rest of this letter, she tries to reassure Locke that her friendship with him is on a higher spiritual plane than her match with Sir Francis. She uses Platonic terminology of "vehicles" (means by which preexistent souls enter terrestrial life) to convey these feelings: "To my Knowledge I never had so great a Desire as now to talk to you of a Vehicle . . . My ideas are too Sublime to beare the Mixture of any thing that is Material . . . The Objects of all my Thoughts are of an Immortal Nature; and such without doubt is Friendship." The message is clear enough. She has married only in a mundane, corporeal sense; their friendship is sublime.

For both of them, then—because of temperament, virtue, or intimations of something better—ordinary marriage was not the thing. So they invented an alternative. Not long after Locke returned to England, Lady Masham proposed that he come live with her new family at Oates. Locke happily accepted. He occupied three rooms, Cranston notes, "filled his rooms with his own furniture, and it was not long before his belongings had spilled over into other parts of the house . . . [H]is rooms looked out onto a lawn and garden, in which he liked to sit in fine weather to read. He enjoyed gardening too; in some respects he was more the master of the house than the baronet himself."[53] Among his legacies he gave her two rings, of ruby and diamond.[54] John Edwards outraged Locke by referring to his "Seraglio at Oates," but Edwards was better at provoking Locke than understanding him. This was no seraglio. It was a vehicle.

Cominglings in the Matrix

Blake needed no Damaris Cudworth to nudge him toward Platonic intimations of higher love. He was familiar with many writers and religious figures who encouraged him in that direction. A few were strictly Platonic or Neoplatonic. Many others were only loosely so, and a more general label would be safer—perhaps "Protestant visionaries" would be best. The seventeenth and eighteenth centuries saw quite a crowd of such figures, including fairly obscure ones like Jean de Labadie, and a few who became more broadly influential. Three well-known Protestant visionaries who certainly influenced Blake were Boehme, Milton, and Swedenborg. Blake's reception of these writers was not simply positive or negative. He objected to various aspects of their writings, but he was always eager to entertain visionary countermyths to Locke's *Essay*, and he referred to all three of them respectfully in various contexts. In matters of love, sex, and marriage these three sources were ambiguous. To some extent they celebrated a blissful conjugal union achievable by the purest souls. On the other hand they warned repeatedly about the dangers of corporeal entanglements. Often these risks were represented as attraction to a female body or involvement in what Boehme called the "Matrix"—the maternal stuff of fallen, mortal nature, which Blake addressed as Tirzah:

> Thou Mother of my Mortal part
> With cruelty didst mould my Heart.
> And with false self-decieving tears,
> Didst bind my Nostrils Eyes & Ears. ("To Tirzah," 30)

In confluence with his Protestant visionary sources, Blake showed an ambiguous attitude about conjugal love. Like Locke he both participated and withdrew himself critically. Perhaps this ambiguity was conditioned by maternal deprivation, as psychoanalytical readers have suggested. The best biographical support of this thesis, besides the fact that he never talked much about his mother, has to do with his brother John. Tatham tells the story of John as follows:

> The Eldest Son, John, was the favorite of his Father & Mother, & as frequently in life, the object least worthy is most cherished, so he, a dissolute disreputable youth, carried away the principal of his Parents attachment, leaving the four others William, James, Catherine, & Robert, to share the Interest between them. William often remonstrated, & was as often told to be quiet, & that he would bye & bye beg his bread at John's door; but as is sometimes proved to parents Sorrow, their pet will not be petted into honour, nor their darling into any other admiration than their own. John was apprenticed to a Gingerbread Baker with an Enormous premium, served his apprenticeship with reluctance, became

abandoned & miserable & literally, contrary to his parents presage, sought bread at the door of William. He lived a few reckless days, Enlisted as a Soldier & died.[55]

Tatham gets some details wrong, but the core of the story seems plausible, given other evidence. If Blake felt neglected alongside John, he may have been more sensitive to his mother's lesser affection than his father's. But the case for maternal deprivation must depend mainly on analysis of the work rather than biographical information. Tatham briefly fills in a conventional maternal role for Catherine Blake (the mother, not his wife of the same name): she "has been represented as being possessed of all those Endearing Sympathies, so peculiar to maternal tenderness."[56] But this sounds like a hollow formula, and Tatham offers no supporting evidence.

One hint suggests that the adult Blake, like Locke, wanted someone to take on a maternal role. Tatham said that William was at once "lover, husband, and child" to his wife Catherine; he needed her for maternal soothing on nights of "fierce inspiration."[57] The hint is interesting, but in the end we know more about the Matrix and Tirzah than about Blake's literal mother; and more about his wife and marriage than his early childhood. It seems useful, then, to examine Blake's feelings about conjugal love in his life and work, along with relevant material from Protestant visionary sources. How promising is marriage as a vehicle for the soul aspiring to eternity? Often he was inclined to see ordinary love as a torment and marriage as inevitably flawed and fallen. His uneasiness with marriage helps to explain the apparently inconsistent treatment of women in his work: this uneasiness contributes both to the feminist inclinations of *Visions of the Daughters of Albion* and an aggressive misogyny that became increasingly apparent in his later work.[58] Still, he never simply gave up his efforts to reenvision marriage as a suitable vehicle for his wife and himself, and for Enitharmon and Los, their closest counterparts among the Zoas.

Even if the story is apocryphal about the Blakes imitating unfallen Adam and Eve, startling a visitor with their naked leisure, several observers did comment on their happiness. Friends and early biographers tended to see the marriage as nearly ideal. Linnell noted that Blake lived "in perfect harmony with his wife."[59] Tatham needed a high style to describe this harmony: "The morning of their married life was bright as the noon of their devoted love, the noon as clear as the serene Evening of their mutual equanimity."[60] Hayley, who knew the Blakes during particularly trying times, nonetheless told Lady Hesketh how fortunate their marriage was. Blake has an "excellent Wife," "a true Helpmate"; "I wish our beloved Bard [Cowper] had been as happy in *a Wife*, for Heaven has bestowed on this extraordinary mortal perhaps the only female on Earth, who could have suited him *exactly*. They have been married more than 17 years & are as fond of each other, as if their Honey Moon were still shining . . . they seem animated by one Soul, & that a soul of indefatigable Industry & Benevolence."[61] Hayley's speculation about a unified soul received some confirmation after William's death. Catherine said that William's spirit regularly "visited, condoled, and directed her"; on her deathbed, according to Gilchrist, she was "calling continually to her William, as if he were only in the next room, to say she was coming to him, and would not be long now."[62] These accounts of conjugal harmony revolve around William, and they raise a question as to what extent Catherine was molded into his ideal helpmate. Still, for many observers the marriage looked quite happy, including William himself in these lines from a notebook poem: "I've a wife I love & that loves me / I've all But Riches Bodily" (481).

Of course there is evidence of trouble as well, mainly of two types: jealousy (on both sides) and the problem of inequality. Blake's poems are full of the torments of jealousy. A few biographical hints indicate his vulnerability to that emotion. Before he met Catherine, says Tatham, "he fell in love with a young woman who by his own account & according to his own knowledge was no trifler, he wanted to marry her but she refused, & was as obstinate as she was unkind. He became ill & went to Kew near Richmond for a change of air & renovation of health & spirits."[63] Gilchrist adds that Blake suffered severe "attacks of jealousy" in this early relationship: "When he complained that the favour of her company in a stroll had been extended to another admirer, 'Are you a fool?' was the brusque reply—with a scornful glance. 'That cured me of jealousy,' Blake used naively to relate."[64] Few people can cure jealousy so easily, and Blake was not one of them. At Felpham he suspected that Hayley had designs on Catherine: in a notebook poem "On Hayley's Friendship" he writes, "And when he could not act upon my wife / Hired a Villain to bereave my Life."

On the other side, Gilchrist says that Catherine Blake showed "an exaggerated suspiciousness" and a "jealousy of his friends." He continues, "There *had* been stormy times in years long past, when both were young; discord by no means trifling while it lasted. But with the cause (jealousy on her side, not wholly unprovoked), the strife had ceased also."[65] The parenthetical reference suggesting Blake's infidelity has not been confirmed by any useful evidence, and Bentley is right to dismiss all guesses as "speculative gossip."[66] Wilson mentions "the only breath of scandal touching his life" as coming from "a story, based, perhaps, on some wild saying of his own or reference to Mary Wollstonecraft's passion for Fuseli, that he proposed to add a concubine to his household"; one such "wild saying" might be what he told H. C. Robinson, that he advocated "community of women."[67]

The other problem in the marriage had to do with inequality. Catherine may have been illiterate when she married (she signed the certificate with an X),[68] and certainly her husband assumed the dominant, educating position in the relationship. Friends noticed how much she seemed to imitate Blake: "Mrs. Blake's spirit, in truth, was influenced magnetically, if one may so speak, by her husband's. She appears to have had the same *literal* belief in his visions as John Varley . . . Not only was she wont to echo what he said, to talk as he talked, on religion and other matters—this may be accounted for by the fact that he had educated her; but she, too, learned to have visions;—to see processions of figures wending along the river, in broad daylight; and would give a start when they disappeared in the water."[69] Catherine's visions, if we knew them better, might show a distinctive character of their own. But Blake must have thought he had to mold his wife. The discrepancy in power could easily have led to problems of tyranny and resentment. One scene from early in the marriage suggests this sort of trouble.

> One day, a dispute arose between Robert and Mrs. Blake. She in the heat of discussion, used words to him, his brother (though a husband too) thought unwarrantable. A silent witness thus far, he could now bear it no longer, but with characteristic impetuosity—when stirred—rose and said to her: "Kneel down and beg Robert's pardon directly, or you never see my face again!" . . . She, poor thing! "thought it very hard," as she would afterwards tell, to beg her brother-in-law's pardon when she was not in fault! But being a duteous, devoted wife, though by nature nowise tame or dull of spirit, she did kneel down and meekly murmur: "Robert, I beg your pardon, I am in the wrong." "Young woman, you lie!" abruptly retorted he: "I am in the wrong."[70]

Gilchrist's account can't be trusted for details, but the core of the story sounds right. Blake admired his brother in a way that made anyone else recede in importance. Catherine was strong enough to resent this kind of behavior, even if she negotiated her dignity more often by imitation than by rebellion. Because many passages in Blake's works convey struggles for domination between men and women, it is tempting to assume a biographical basis for them. Some of the most strident expressions of male privilege seem to be products of insecurity and pent-up anger: "In Eternity Woman is the Emanation of Man she has no Will of her own There is no such thing in Eternity as a Female Will" (*A Vision of the Last Judgment*, 562).

Females have always been something of a problem for the eternities of male Protestant visionaries. In Blake's mythic narratives a crucial moment comes when the first female appears as a separate entity. This happens first in *The*

Book of Urizen, when Enitharmon emerges from Los's disturbed fibres, and "All Eternity shudderd at sight / Of the first female now separate" (18:9–10— E 78). Enitharmon's separation from Los is retold in *The Four Zoas, Milton,* and *Jerusalem,* with complications arising from the increasing importance of their relationship for redemptive plots. The creation of the first female also occupies Milton, of course, as well as Boehme and Swedenborg. These scenes share certain fears about women and what they represent, but they are far from identical. Blake's scene of the first female has affinities with all of them but does not simply repeat them. His revisions suggest that he was not entirely comfortable with a tradition that still held him in its fibrous matrix.

Jacob Boehme wrote about the creation of Eve in several places, most elaborately in *Mysterium Magnum,* his commentary on Genesis. He gave a full chapter to "The building of the Woman; shewing how Man was ordained to the outward Naturall Life."[71] We do not know which of Boehme's works Blake read (all were available in translation), but *Mysterium Magnum* seems like a good candidate, given his own interest in rewriting Genesis. He might also have seen a briefer account of the Eve separation in *The Way to Christ,* one of Boehme's best-known books, in the section called "Of Regeneration."

Boehme departs from mainstream exegesis in one crucial way that influenced Blake. The creation of Eve from Adam's rib indicates that the Fall had already taken place: it stands as the first obvious manifestation of Adam's deadly error. The serpent and fruit and so on follow inevitably from the separation of Eve. Traditional interpreters reject this as nonsense, because God declared that it was not good for man to be alone. Boehme says that Adam should have been fine on his own. God earlier had pronounced Creation good as it stood; when he announced that now something was *not* good, he was acknowledging Adam's lapse from eternal self-sufficiency. Adam in his original perfection "was a man, and also a woman."[72] As long as he kept the cosmic properties in balance, he had a magical creative potency: "The soules power was so potent before [the Fall] that it could by Magick alter all things whatsoever are in the outward worlds Essence."[73] He nourishes himself, engages in "Love-play," and magically reproduces, all from within his Godlike fullness—"just as God begot the external world without dividing Himself, but by forming in His desires, i. e., in the *Verbo Fiat,* the fashioned properties and qualities . . . and by directing them into a figuration according to the birth of the spiritual world."[74] Eve was never supposed to happen. Boehme like Blake cites a gospel passage that relegates marriage to the fallen world: "In heaven they neither marry nor are given in marriage" (Matthew 22:30). Boehme's paradise earned the praise of Norman O. Brown for its embrace of "an androgynous mode of being and narcissistic mode of self expression," in tune with the unconscious and a liberated "love-play."⁷⁵ To someone like Locke it must have sounded like the outlandish masturbatory fantasy of a man uncomfortable with women.

Boehme's Adam fell into a state of defective desire that resembles Urizen's mistake: both of them turn away from eternity to discover a "self-will" or "egocentric hunger." The fallen Adam conceives of an external other to be desired and consumed. Boehme's God recognizes that Adam has become deformed, puts him to sleep, and implements Adam's new desires by separating Eve from his body. Before the Fall she was "the Matrix" within Adam; after his hungry vanity she stands apart as an object of lust. The creation of Eve marks Adam's loss of magical power. Although Boehme's account, unlike Milton's, appears to deflect blame from Eve, his description of women remains traditionally derogatory. "The woman soone lusted after the vanity; as to this day, meer earthly lust of the flesh is found in most of them: so soone as this sex comes but to any yeares, the selfish will doth predominantly appeare in pride and glistering showes of fleshly desires."⁷⁶ Boehme refers to sexual organs as "bestial," ugly "wormes carkasses" hung upon Adam and Eve. Blake would have detected the workings of conventional morality here (as he did in Swedenborg), but two antifeminist themes suggested here find their way into his work: the disgusting female body (and more generally, an aesthetic antipathy to sexuality) and a female will that makes men lose their original powers.

Milton's Eve starts out quite differently. Her creation is no mistake. *Paradise Lost* actually contains two first females, Sin as well as Eve. Satan's mental creation of Sin, an important source for Blake, resembles Boehme's account of Eve in its general spirit. The female emerges directly from the thoughts of an egocentric male; Sin, like Boehme's Eve, is both attractive and repulsive, and she collaborates in the production of death. Milton's scene of Eve's creation, on the other hand, is nothing like Boehme's version. When Adam suggests that he would like a companion, God teases him a little—"A nice and subtle happiness I see / Thou to thy self proposest" (8:399–400)—but Milton makes it clear that God is "not displeased." Milton raises the Boehme problem of self-centered desire only to expose it as a misreading. Adam needs "conversation" and "solace" to remedy his "single imperfection." Here, as in his divorce tract, Milton specifies that the chief purpose of marriage is good company (above reproduction and associated sexual pleasures). He turns the Boehme threat of egocentric desire into a natural completion of spiritual happiness. Although sexual pleasures are subordinate to the broader purpose of conversation, they are certainly not absent from Eden. Blake told H. C. Robinson that Milton's spirit visited him to warn against *Paradise Lost*'s "doctrine that carnal pleasure arose from the Fall."⁷⁷ Either Blake was misreading Milton perversely or somehow mixing Milton's account with Boehme's.

Boehme's and Milton's versions are obviously different, but it is not far-fetched to imagine Blake blending them into a single scene. The creation of Eve in *Paradise Lost* hints at trouble despite its happiness. Like Boehme's Adam, Milton's Adam begins to narrow his pleasures. Adam fixes his attention on her so keenly that he loses touch with other sources of pleasure.

> She disappeared, and left me dark, I waked
> To find her, or for ever to deplore
> Her loss, and other pleasures all abjure . . . (8:478–80)

Anxiety of weakness accompanies his narrowed pleasure. He feels "weak / Against the charm of Beauty's powerful glance," and wonders whether God "from my side subducting, took perhaps / More than enough." Milton's Adam has not literally lost Edenic powers, but he worries that he has lost some sort of original strength or adequacy. In his divorce tract, Milton described the effects of a disappointing marriage as infinitely worse than the risks of remaining single: "And the solitariness of man, which God had namely and principally ordered to prevent by marriage, hath no remedy, but lies under a worse condition than the loneliest single life: for in single life the absence and remoteness of a helper might inure him to expect his own comforts out of himself, or to seek with hope; but here the continual sight of his deluded thoughts, without cure, must needs be to him . . . a daily trouble of pain and loss."[78] Such a man will be "lost under a secret affliction under an unconscionable size to human strength." In short, the creation of females and marriage retains its Boehmian threats of narrow, deluded desire and sacrifice of male self-sufficiency.

Swedenborg's account of female origin and marriage is the most sanguine of the three. Women are created from men to implement a providential division of labor, both mental and corporeal; women are innately "modest, elegant, pacific, yielding, soft, and tender," and they "love the bonds of marriage."[79] Marriages belong as much in heaven as on earth. If Swedenborg's account resembles Milton's in the abstract, it does not contain the Miltonic undercurrents of distrust, angst, and gloom. Despite or because of Swedenborg's appreciation of conjugal love, Blake was wary. He told Robinson, "Parts of Swedenborg's scheme are dangerous. His sexual system is so."[80]

Blake didn't specify what he found dangerous in Swedenborg's sexual system. Three elements probably contributed. To begin with, Swedenborg insists on strict monogamy. "The angels say that to have a plurality of wives is altogether contrary to divine order";[81] adulterers inhabit hell. Blake was always suspicious when anyone summoned divine or natural order to justify social conventions. Whether or not he had any sexual experience outside his marriage, he wrote repeatedly of the problems afflicting lovers who restrict each other's desires too closely. A second and related problem has to do with Swedenborg's discussion of jealousy. Swedenborg acknowledges the power of jealousy but welcomes it as a sign of genuine love and a providential protection of monogamy. "Jealousy is the zeal of conjugial love . . . the fire of love burning . . . Also it may be called the defender and protector of love."[82] Monogamy and jealousy combine to create a sexual system in which true love is measured by the grip of possessive desire. Boehme's love-play must have sounded much more promising to Blake.

The third troublesome element in Swedenborg is a familiar one—a suggestion that women somehow cause or at least indicate a diminution of male power. In Boehme and Milton the weakening of the male came as a key event in the Fall. Swedenborg, however, treats the manipulation of men by women as a beneficent, providential process. This is one of the few intriguing ideas in *Conjugial Love*. It emerges from his interpretation of the Genesis creation of Eve. "Jehovah God caused a deep sleep to fall upon Adam . . . and took one of his ribs, and built it into a woman; by the man's sleep is signified his plenary ignorance that the wife is formed and created from him, and also the innate prudence and circumspection of wives not to divulge anything concerning their love, nor concerning their assumption of the affections of the man's life." Swedenborg explains that all wives have a special, intimate knowledge of their husbands' emotions, which they gain through a secret sixth sense. This sense, he hears from wives, "we have in the palms, while we touch the breasts, arms, hands, or cheeks of our husbands, especially while we touch their breasts." This sixth sense serves the providential purpose of controlling conjugial love. Wives know their husbands' emotions so that they can "prudently moderate them . . . in the entire ignorance of their husbands." The wives insist on secrecy. Not only do they keep hidden their special knowledge and moderation of men's emotions, they also decline to reveal to their husbands the full extent of their love. Swedenborg, a little puzzled by all this, asks why. "They answered, that if the least thing of the kind should slip from their mouth, cold would invade the husbands and separate them from bed, bedchamber, and presence."[83] In other words, if a man comes to know the extent to which a woman has attached herself to him and gained secret influence over his emotions, he will turn away in alarm. He will feel exposed, dissected, manipulated—victim of secretly powerful women whose work Swedenborg endorses in the name of moral fitness.

Blake expressed many comparable ideas about deceptive, manipulative women, but not with Swedenborg's belief in providential design. He knew that Swedenborg identified males with understanding and females with will. Throughout his work he struggled with a need to scapegoat "Female Will." From Swedenborg, as from Boehme and Milton, Blake received mixed messages about marriage. Wives secretly manipulate men and marriage causes burning jealousy, but marriage is the ultimate vehicle of eternal happiness, on earth as it is in heaven. He and Catherine approved a list of resolutions at a 1789 meeting of the Swedenborgian society, two of which emphasized the importance of marriage: "That good conjugal love is better than any other," and "True conjugal married love is good."[84] He was equally afraid of being a naive victim of married love and a guilty, deficient lover.

Blake expresses these complications in several passages about Los and Enitharmon, loose counterparts of Adam and Eve. He first narrates the creation of a separate female in *The Book of Urizen*. Although Boehme's Adam and Milton's Satan are obvious influences, Blake alters both sources by dividing the male role into two parts. Urizen initiates the fall from eternity through what Boehme called egocentric thinking, but Los creates the separate female. The first female, Enitharmon, emerges as an externalization of Los's self-pity. It may seem as if Los is more a victim than a cause of the fall, but like Boehme's Adam, he pities himself as a weakened Eternal who can remember but not retrieve his magical potency. Los (like Adam) then tries to fill the void with lustful pursuit of the female.

As Blake repeats this scene in later works, he replaces the doubled role of Urizen and Los with a new doubling of Los and the Spectre. Several times he narrates a separation of Enitharmon from Los that occurs simultaneously with a separation of the Spectre from Los. The triple schism of Los, Enitharmon, and the Spectre represents Blake's most important revision of the scene of Eve's creation. Los relies on the Spectre as protection from Enitharmon's female will. Because he is separate from Los, the Spectre also serves as a scapegoat, preserving the innocence of the character most closely associated with Blake himself. If the marriage is finally going to work the Spectre must be cast away, but within the world of *The Four Zoas, Jerusalem*, and the poem "My Spectre round me night and day," he keeps reappearing alongside Los and Enitharmon to make a marriage triangle.

A scene near the end of *Jerusalem* provides a good example of the triangle at work. This may in fact be the last such scene Blake wrote. As W. H. Stevenson notes, it comes as "a rather strange reversion to the theme of Los's own troubles"[85]—strange because the Spectre has been absent for quite a while, and the poem will soon reach its apocalyptic climax without resolving the interposed conflict. In the middle of the passage Blake refers to Enitharmon quarreling with Los "on Sussex shore," which suggests biographical relevance (Felpham in Sussex was the site of troubled times for William and Catherine).[86] The scene begins with the familiar creation of the female: Enitharmon "separates in milky fibres agonizing," "Filling with Fibres from his loins which reddend with desire / Into a Globe of blood beneath his bosom trembling in darkness" (86:51–2). The Spectre as usual hovers nearby, simultaneously separating from Los as the female emerges. This time, however, Los tries "Hiding his Spectre" from her, as if he wants to give his reborn desire one more chance. Los and Enitharmon now present an odd mixture of early hope and jaded resignation:

> She separated stood before him a lovely Female weeping
> Even Enitharmon separated outside, & his Loins closed
> And heal'd after the separation: his pains he soon forgot:
> Lured by her beauty outside of himself in shadowy grief.
> Two wills they had: Two Intellects: & not as in times of old.
> Silent they wanderd hand in hand like two Infants wandring
> From Enion in the deserts . . . (86:57–63)

Despite signs of a fresh beginning, Los and Enitharmon resemble Adam and Eve at the end of *Paradise Lost,* wandering hand in hand with the fallen world before them. They now have "two wills" and "two intellects." The unified state that came before could mean something like Boehme's hermaphroditic Adam or perhaps Milton's and Swedenborg's gendered harmony. The separation into sexual craving recalls Boehme; "will" and "intellect" suggest Swedenborg. Los tells Enitharmon that his "wild fibres" of desire must find some answering embodiment in her. She responds angrily, translating his plan for harmonious collaboration into the usual script for male domination.

> Enitharmon answerd. No! I will sieze thy Fibres & weave
> Them: not as thou wilt but as I will, for I will Create
> A round Womb beneath my bosom lest I also be overwoven
> With Love; be thou assured I never will be thy slave
> Let Mans delight be Love; but Womans delight be Pride. (87:12–16)

When Los responds by complaining of her refusal to accept his "Fibres of dominion," Enitharmon seems to have a good case. Los's love dominates women. His idea of paradise is "Brotherhood of Man with Man." Enitharmon's speech reads like an insecure man's caricature of assertive women. Los interprets her resistance to love as stubbornly willful. However, despite the obvious antifeminist elements in such passages, Blake's poetry reaches beyond its simplest meanings. Words like "create" and "slave" enrich Enitharmon's defense, especially for readers conversant with the rest of Blake's work. She may appear less a caricature of selfishness and more a person trying to create her own system to prevent being enslaved by someone else's.

The design facing this scene (plate 85) contributes significantly to the meaning of their quarrel. Enitharmon tends the fibres growing out of Los's body (from his loins, as the poem says, and others nearer the heart and navel; all the vines look vaguely umbilical). The vines bear grapes as they emerge from Los, but after Enitharmon's tending they turn into brownish leaves. Blake adds a subtle detail that may suggest a breakdown in the usual collaboration of William and Catherine. In a vine running across the middle of the page, the leaves on Los's side are colored, but those on Enitharmon's side are not; because Catherine was normally responsible for coloring the plates, this could represent a moment of resistance on her part.

The whole design invites comparison with an earlier design on plate 25, one of the most striking in *Jerusalem*. A kneeling male figure, presumably Albion, receives similar vinous-umbilical ministration by three females. The females of plate 25 seem more sinister than Enitharmon, and Albion is worse off than Los: his head droops back on one woman's lap, apparently because she has mesmerized him.[87] Albion and Los nonetheless resemble each other closely enough. Both kneel and turn away from the sight of females drawing out their blood-filled vines. Both are pictured among emblems of sun, moon, and stars, evidence of a disrupted cosmic unity now undergoing some sort of therapy in the Matrix that is indistinguishable from punishment.

In the design for plate 85 and the poetry that follows, Blake worries about women's manipulation of men's emotions. Swedenborg appreciated wives' secret knowledge and control of "affections"; Los suffers in their visceral grip. Enitharmon says that women "create secret places" as a strategy for making males subservient. Blake refers to "female spaces" as a psychological or cosmological con game. A female space leads man to think he is small and impotent in the face of an infinite, inaccessible, but attractive entity (like the vast Newtonian universe, or the mysterious desires of female sexuality). Enitharmon is secretly manipulative like Swedenborg's wives, and like Boehme's Eve she strips men of their creative powers. The Spectre accordingly shares Boehme's disgust over female sexual organs—"their places of joy & love" are "excrementitious."

Predictably, jealousy also plays a prominent role in this final quarrel between Los and Enitharmon. Even as they wander hand in hand at the start of the passage, Blake has them "envying each other yet desiring" (a nice insight to subvert sentimental pieties); envy quickly becomes jealousy as they develop a sense of possession. The jealousy is mutual, although Blake as usual emphasizes Enitharmon's jealousy. The narrator mentions how she unwittingly empowers "her objects of jealousy," and Los's Spectre punctuates the scene with a closing moral:

> Continually building, continually destroying in Family feuds
> While you are under the dominion of a jealous Female

> Unpermanent for ever because of love & jealousy
> You shall want all the Minute Particulars of Life. (88:40–43)

This last line hints at the problem of narrowed pleasure that afflicted Milton's Adam. Los and Enitharmon come together in "all devouring Love." Through jealousy and related psychological effects, husband and wife regress from magical, polymorphous pleasures into the dull track of normal possessive love.

Los's Spectre is the Blakean patron of conjugal resentment. He yearns for prelapsarian pleasure and settles into permanent disappointment. He sees only the knotted ironies of normalized love. The Spectre always joins Los whenever Enitharmon appears, to protect him by means of cynical triumph—cynicism being the only pleasure that survives the wreckage of Spectral desires. As newborn Los and Enitharmon quickly reach their old impasse,

> A sullen smile broke from the Spectre in mockery & scorn
> Knowing himself the author of their divisions & shrinkings, gratified
> At their contentions . . . (88:34–36)

In view of this depressing ending, Harold Bloom's commentary on the scene is notably peculiar: Bloom applauds Los's "mature insistence on sovereignty" as a sign of impending redemption.[88] In fact Los and Enitharmon have merely reenacted all the old torments of shrunken pleasure.

If this scene provides little help toward imagining an alternative to fallen conjugal love, Blake elsewhere suggests a few possibilities. The most obvious would be free love—that is to say, the usual sort of sexual gratification but with possessive restrictions removed. Blake's most ambitious treatment of this topic comes in *Visions of the Daughters of Albion*. The heroine Oothoon, after being raped, attempts to revise the clenched jealousy of the man she loves. Toward the end of the poem she develops a theory of free love as the most effective therapy for both of them.

> I cry, Love! Love! Love! happy happy Love! free as the mountain wind!
> Can that be Love, that drinks another as a sponge drinks water?
> That clouds with jealousy his nights, with weepings all the day:
> To spin a web of age around him. grey and hoary! dark!
> Till his eyes sicken at the fruit that hangs before his sight.
> Such is self-love that envies all! a creeping skeleton
> With lamplike eyes watching around the frozen marriage bed. (7:16–22)

Oothoon's first line sounds almost parodic in its rhapsody, but the rest of the passage is more interesting. She envisions a jealous, Urizenic patriarch spinning "a web of age around him," followed by a hint of the fall according to Boehme and Milton (fruit that sickens, envious cravings of self-love), and finally a Spectre-like figure "watching around the frozen marriage bed." ("London" with its "marriage hearse" was probably written about the same time.) Against this nightmare Oothoon proclaims herself "a virgin fill'd with virgin fancies / Open to joy and to delight where ever beauty appears." Her notion of virgin delight may not be limited strictly to sexual pleasures—in the lines just quoted she seems to suggest a broader sense of imaginative freshness; but clearly she emphasizes sexual freedom.

Oothoon's free-love therapy is notably unsuccessful. Her lover remains in despair, and she "wails every morning," unable either to change him or to change herself and break away from him. Thomas Vogler concludes that her therapy is ill-conceived at its foundation: her voice, after all, has been constructed by a male, and free love traps her in a network of desires defined by males.[89] In any case Oothoon increasingly imagines only male gratification in her scheme of free love:

> But silken nets and traps of adamant will Oothoon spread,
> And catch for thee girls of mild silver, or of furious gold;
> I'll lie beside thee on a bank & view their wanton play
> In lovely copulation bliss on bliss with Theotormon:
> Red as the rosy morning, lustful as the first born beam,
> Oothoon shall view his dear delight, nor e'er with jealous cloud
> Come in the heaven of generous love; nor selfish blightings bring.
> (7:23–29)

Her vision of "generous love" seems ironically Urizenic: note the "nets and traps" calculated to achieve consistent pleasure. If Oothoon's willingness to settle for vicarious gratification might be construed as an act of resistance to normal sexuality—perhaps even an alternative, voyeuristic pleasure—her need to please Theotormon gives the poem a decidedly androcentric shape. In *Jerusalem* and other late works, Blake tends to blame female jealousy for shrunken pleasure, and he offers a male-dominated version of free love as the eternal paradigm. Fallen women "refuse liberty to the male," thereby undoing a better state,

> Where every Female delights to give her maiden to her husband
> The Female searches sea & land for gratification to the
> Male Genius . . . (*Jerusalem* 69:15–17)

Once again Blake claims to understand female pleasure as a function of male gratification. The delights of Eternity he writes about should not be reduced to sexual acts alone; indeed, the passage just quoted contains hints of an alternative to normal sexuality, having to do with the polymorphous imagination. Still, when we consider Blake's struggles with jealousy in his marriage, and his remark to H. C. Robinson about "community of women," the literally sexual meanings cannot be ignored. The literal version of free love never seems very promising in Blake. Jealousy is too deeply rooted, and his androcentric bias too exposed.

A second Blakean alternative to normal love would involve homoerotic desire. With Locke this possibility was a fairly distant inference, but Blake offers more clues to work with. The most noticeable hints come in *Milton*, a poem closely associated with Blake's residence at Felpham under William Hayley's patronage. One speech in the poem suggests that Hayley might have felt a sexual attraction to Blake, at least in Blake's mind. The speaker is Leutha, Satan/Hayley's emanation, who tells of his feminization and consequent attraction to Palamabron/Blake:[90]

> . . . entering the doors of Satans brain night after night
> Like sweet perfumes I stupified the masculine perceptions
> And kept only the feminine awake. hence arose his soft
> Delusory love to Palamabron . . . (12:4–8)

S. Foster Damon concludes that "Hayley was unconsciously a homosexual."[91] This reading clumsily reifies Hayley's sexuality, but Blake apparently did associate Hayley with gender reversal, as in this notebook couplet:

> Of Hs birth this was the happy lot
> His Mother on his Father him begot (506)

Blake's fear of gender confusion accompanies some hints of homoerotic desire, also within *Milton*. Most striking is a full-plate design showing Blake receiving the inspiration of Los. Blake, kneeling in the foreground, turns backward to face the standing Los. Their position intriguingly suggests fellatio. Another plate nearby shows Milton and Urizen in a similar position, although the effect there is not as striking. Interpreters have been reluctant until recently to raise the subject—presumably out of some notion of politeness rather than failure to notice the effect. Erdman, for example, observes that Blake's head "reaches to Los's loins—as Urizen's head touches Milton's loins in the preceding large plate," but he does not finish the thought.[92] W. J. T. Mitchell first discussed the "direct evocation of homoerotic overtones" in these designs, and related them to themes of brotherhood and prophetic influence.[93] Margaret Storch mentions them as "evidence of a homosexual interest in Blake," which would fit within her psychoanalytical reading (an unresolved Oedipal attachment to the father figure). Storch also suggests "a homoerotic feeling in the relationship with Robert Blake."[94] She does not elaborate, but two matching designs from *Milton* might be cited as evidence. "William" and "Robert" show full-plate figures of the brothers arching backward as they receive inspiration; the context is therefore similar to the design of Los and Blake, even if the sexual implications are less obvious.[95] These clues taken together suggest not that Blake "was a homosexual" but that his imagination participated in more than one kind of sexual desire.

A third alternative to fallen sexuality might be called the therapy of polymorphous imagination. More ethereal than the first two alternatives, it is also the safest, because its practical implications do not obviously threaten cultural norms. Blake gave particular emphasis to this alternative—not because it was safe, but because it was more fundamental than any specific vehicle of heterosexual or homosexual love. The polymorphous imagination finds erotic moments everywhere. Unfallen eros lives in "mental delights" that are neither disembodied nor confined to acts of sexuality as conventionally defined. Cleansing the doors of perception makes every minute particular attractive. Our fallen "Religion of Chastity" sets up "False Holiness" within a restricted, privileged center, the mystified site of sexual and spiritual fulfillment:

   . . . a False Holiness hid within the Centre
For the Sanctuary of Eden is in the Camp: in the Outline,
In the Circumference: & every Minute Particular is Holy:
Embraces are Cominglings: from the Head even to the Feet;
And not a pompous High Priest entering by a Secret Place. (*Jerusalem* 69:40–44)

Blake's polymorphous cominglings update a Neoplatonic tradition of angelic or magical sexuality. Swedenborg wrote that "the angelic love of the sex . . . is perfectly full of inmost delights; it is a most pleasing expansion of all things of the mind."[96] Milton's Raphael explains angelic sex to Adam in terms that must have influenced Blake:

Whatever pure thou in the body enjoy'st
(And pure thou wert created) we enjoy
In eminence, and obstacle find none
Of membrane, joint, or limb, exclusive bars;
Easier than air with air, if spirits embrace,
Total they mix, union of pure with pure
Desiring; nor restrained conveyance need
As flesh to mix with flesh, or soul with soul. (8:622–29)

Angelic embraces are "total," unlimited by "restrained conveyance." Milton was drawing on Cambridge Platonist Henry More, who described sexual delights among aerial spirits. For them "the Body is wholly obedient to the imagination of the Mind, and will to every Punctilio yield to the impresses of that inward Pattern; nothing there can be found amiss."[97] For Boehme's unfallen Adam, sexuality and reproduction were "Magicall, his Conception moving in the Matrix through Imagination."[98]

Blake tried to conquer his visions of willful, jealous, shrunken love with a similarly imaginative regeneration of the Matrix. In *Urizen* he casually attributes this power to the Eternals, who expand or contract their "all flexible senses." In *The Four Zoas* these Eternals momentarily comfort Orc (the Zoa who suffers continually from sexual restriction) by bringing "the thrilling joys of sense to quell his ceaseless rage" (61:17). But it is Los whose renewal becomes most urgent for Blake. Los and Enitharmon's marriage quarrels punctuate and threaten his longest poems. The last of these quarrels interrupts *Jerusalem*, as we have seen, when the Spectre presides over a bitter impasse. One such quarrel ends differently, however. In Night 7a of *The Four Zoas*, after the marriage trio of Los, Enitharmon, and the Spectre reach their usual mutual resentment, something different happens. They retrieve a version of Boehmian magical creativity that restores their feeling of conjugal rapture. The Spectre and Los agree to give up the original sin of "domineering lust." Together with Enitharmon they work to create "embodied semblances in which the dead / May live before us," in order to "comfort Orc in his dire sufferings." It is difficult to give an adequate translation of this moment, but one thing is clear: Los and Enitharmon use their artistic cooperation to satisfy desires that seemed hopelessly withered. True, the old division of labor remains in place (Enitharmon says to Los, "Thy works are all my joy, & in thy fires my soul delights"), but Enitharmon's work receives unusual emphasis:

> And first he drew a line upon the walls of shining heaven
> And Enitharmon tincturd it with beams of blushing love
> It remaind permanent a lovely form inspird divinely human. (98:35–7)

"Tincture" obviously refers to Catherine's coloring of designs, but a more exalted meaning also enters: Boehme often used tincture in its alchemical sense of quintessence or soul of a material thing. Throughout the passage their work yields what might as well be called erotic pleasure, full of "embraces," "blushing love," "delights," and "rapture."

This scene of marital rapture makes a nice ending—something to set alongside the happy quasi-marriage of Locke and Damaris Cudworth. But it isn't really an ending; and such moments were rarer, at least in Blake's poems, than their spectral counterparts. Locke and Cudworth worked out an alternative to ordinary marriage that offered the comforts of a settled household and minimized the awkward demands of conjugal love, which both of them were reluctant to embrace. If they felt that some higher passion was missing, they did not show any obvious signs of frustration. William and Catherine suffered from the demands of visionary passion in pursuit of lost paradise. Rather surprisingly, though, they preserved within the Matrix something that looked like a happy marriage.

Chapter 3

Two English Physicians

Both Locke and Blake had a calling to heal sick English bodies. Locke was actually a practicing physician. Medicine and surrounding scientific studies became his earliest vocational passion, and although he gradually accumulated many other professional and intellectual interests, he continued throughout his life to keep track of Enlightenment theories of disease. His medical successes set the stage for a career of broader public service. Blake's work was more loosely and imaginatively medical, but his therapeutic vocation—to challenge, in many key elements, Locke's representation of the body and its discontents—was no less serious. Both physicians were also patients whose nervous symptoms resisted simple therapy.

Enlightenment Elixir

Toward the end of his part-time but absorbing career as a physician, Locke complained about the persistent foolishness of doctors. They "lay the Foundation in their own phancies" of theories that amount to "waking Dreams": "I wonder, that after the pattern Dr. Sydenham has set them of a better way, men should return again to that romance way of physick."[1] Among "romance" physicians he no doubt meant to include mediocre Galenists, overly speculative iatrochemists, and medical thinkers who clung to mystical or supernatural explanations. All these versions of romanticized medicine hindered Enlightenment progress toward natural health, to be approached gradually by means of empirical reasoning.

Locke the physician-philosopher can easily be held up as an exemplary Enlightenment figure. More than once he was urged to take holy orders, in order to secure his place at Christ Church; but he rejected this advice and tried the much more difficult course of holding an Oxford position solely by virtue of a medical degree. This substitution of a medical for a theological credential fits nicely with some of the prominent Enlightenment themes for which Locke is known. Although he did not abandon belief in an immaterial soul, he effectively preempted many of its functions with a tabula rasa brain-nerve complex. He had much sympathy for an emerging Christianized atomism, which was displacing older systems of knowledge based on microcosm and analogy. A young Locke became acquainted with his most important patron, Lord Ashley, as they sat together and took the healing Astrop waters: an alternative baptism, in a sense, at the beginning of his exemplary Enlightenment career.

It would appear that Locke's medical goal was characteristically liberal: to deliver the body from entrapping systems of unenlightened belief. But a study of his medical career shows that this obvious plot hides as much as it reveals. To begin with, vestiges of pre-Enlightenment systems such as astrology and alchemy can be found within his medical writings. More significantly, his career suggests a new version of the microcosm, mapping a route from the body to the body politic. One effect of this medical and political intersection can be seen in Locke's debunking of the old "sacred diseases" (nervous disorders, such as epilepsy, hysteria, and melancholy); but he participated in a new mystification of these conditions, transcribing them into codes of social and political definition.

Despite his allegiance to experimental modernism, Locke's medical journals show more traces of the "romance way of physick" than one might expect. He can still be called a representative Enlightenment figure—but only if one understands Enlightenment medicine as a confusing arena of competing approaches to the body. He recorded many chemical theories of disease that sound fairly modern; but he also wrote down, and apparently did not discredit, many remedies that look bizarre to a modern eye. A few examples drawn from his notes should convey this intermittent strangeness. "Take the nail of horse shoe that was flung off of a suddaine, beaten into a cold ring, i. e. without putting it in the fire. Wear this and it will cure haemorrhoids."[2] "A little cutting of the haire of the head and other parts, the pareings of nailes cornes and other callous flesh of the feet; put these all into a paper bore a hole in a growing oake with an Augur put them in and then stop up the hole with a pin made of a piece of the same driven in as hard as you can till it breaks. This cures the sciatica."[3] For treating mania: "[Boil] either common redish Horse redish or Spanish redish . . . to a pulp and therewith fil a roule such as children wear to defend their heads. Let patient wear it nights about his neck, when he finds himself begin to be disturbed, and it will allay the disorder."[4] These and similar entries have an almost magical specificity that coexists with Locke's more modern attempts at chemical remedy. One intriguing note mentions a way to "make a person return by natural Magic."[5] Elements of more systematic older paradigms also appear, particularly alchemy and astrology. The astrological residue can be seen easily enough, as in the following note from 1679: "Cinque-foil gathered in the hower of Jupiter with some other necessary observations astrological becomes a good specific [for fever] . . . whereas the cinquefoil carelessly gatherd is unsuccessful and has rarely any sensible operation."[6] In another journal entry he cites Dr. Godefroy's observation "that in the plague that was in 1666 at Orleans most people were taken sick, either in the conjunction, opposition, quadrature etc. of the moon with Jupiter."[7] Locke's interest in alchemy is just as visible. He read Paracelsus and Basil Valentine, as well as J. B. Van Helmont, the Swiss alchemist. It is not particularly surprising that Locke should be interested in such writings. Paracelsus, for all his alchemical flair, set his medical knowledge against official Church Galenism and demonology. Van Helmont provided a bridge between alchemy and iatrochemistry. Still, Locke's records suggest that he had something of a romantic enthusiasm for "archaic" alchemy, not just an academic appreciation of "modern" alchemy. In early laboratory work he made efforts to prepare the alkahest and the *elixir vitae* of Paracelsus. Much later in his life he was still attracted by alchemical dreams. At the age of sixty, he wrote to Isaac Newton about an elixir-like formula left by Robert Boyle, which Boyle had believed would multiply gold. Newton wrote back skeptically; and his letter indicates that Locke was taking the formula seriously: "In diswading you from too hasty a trial of this Recipe I have forborn to say any thing against multiplication in general because you seem perswaded of it: tho there is one argument against it which I could never find an answer to, and which, if you will let me have your opinion about it, I will send you in my next."[8] We do not have Locke's reply to this letter, but Cranston suggests that "Newton seems to have succeeded in curing him of his faith in Boyle's alchemy."[9] This may be so, but an entry in Locke's commonplace book a year later refers to Van Helmont's secret of "transposing metals."[10] Evidently Locke was so taken by the idea of elixir—both as the formula for changing metals into gold and as the *elixir vitae*, supposed to prolong life indefinitely (alchemists imagined the two elixirs to be identical or closely related)—that he was intermittently willing to suspend his disbelief of romantic science.

These traces of older systems do not draw Locke strikingly closer to Paracelsus, however much they may complicate his reputation as a modern scientist. Paracelsus believed in the analogies of a microcosmic worldview. According to his doctrine of "signatures," conditions of individual human bodies correspond to cosmic conditions, in their complicated mixtures of matter and spirit. A microcosmic event such as, for example, an epileptic fit, corresponds to a macrocosmic event—in this case, to earthquake.[11] Paracelsus' medical elaborations of microcosm were carried into the eighteenth century less by physicians than by visionaries, including Swedenborg and Blake; and Locke showed no inclination to share these visionary correspondences. His liberal goal as a physician, again, was to free the individual body from networks of enchantment in which it had been trapped. But Locke's career suggests that, as he discarded the old microcosm, he did not so much liberate the body as situate it within a new microcosmic network. The meaning of the body would again be mediated by correspondences, now muted and implicit. Specifically, the body would take its place as a signifying element within Locke's political theories of labor and property.

In his *Second Treatise of Government,* Locke founds his assertion of human equality on God's labor-based property rights. Humans are equal because they are "all the workmanship of one omnipotent and infinitely wise Maker . . . they are his property whose workmanship they are" (5–6). A human being is God's property, but Locke later grants a second ownership essential to his theory of private property: "Though the earth and all inferior creatures be common to all men, yet every man has a property in his own person; this nobody has any right to but himself. The labour of his body and the work of his hands, we may say, are properly his. Whatsoever then he removes out of the state that nature hath provided and left it in, he hath mixed his labour with, and joined to it something that is his own, and thereby makes it his property" (17). From these passages, two principles may be inferred. First, the body is a product of labor (God's, at least initially); and second, the body is implicated in, not separate from, property relations. Locke's sociopolitical discourse thus begins to link up with his medical theory and practice. Work on the body corresponds in interesting ways to work on the body politic. Locke's political writings suggest an ideology of development, which several scholars have described as a philosophical foundation for capitalism. Although the *Second Treatise* contains inconsistencies and competing values, it is susceptible to a fairly stable reading in support of capitalist development. For Locke, virtue resides in productive labor toward the improvement of nature's capacity to support human life. He argues that waste land—that is, land not inhabited or not put to proper use by native inhabitants—should be developed by more capable hands. This notion of virtuous development fits Locke the physician as well as Locke the political philosopher. A physician, for Locke, is someone of virtuously productive intelligence, who can improve the body-property by means of scientific intervention. The ultimate testimony would be his fascination with *elixir vitae* and "return by natural magick"—little hints of Locke as Frankenstein. But less dramatic evidence can be found throughout his medical writings. Of particular interest for this discussion is the story of Lord Ashley's tube.

Locke took his first step toward political influence by working on the body of Anthony Ashley Cooper (later earl of Shaftesbury and prime minister). Ashley had been suffering from serious abdominal pain and swelling—as a result of "suppurating hydatid liver abscess" (probably indicating tapeworm problems), according to a modern diagnosis.[12] Locke arranged for Astrop waters to be brought for Ashley. Since Locke himself was not in the best of health, Ashley invited him to take the waters as well. The Astrop waters may have done little to improve the condition of either man, but the occasion did much to advance Locke's career: Ashley was so impressed with their conversation that he invited Locke to stay at his London house. When he arrived, Ashley's condition had worsened, as a result of a treatment recommended by Charles II's physician. Ashley turned the case over to Locke, despite his lack of experience and credentials. Locke had a surgeon barber open the abdomen and drain the abscess. He then inserted a six-inch silver tube so that drainage could continue after the operation. As Cranston summarizes, "He wore the silver, then a gold tube for the rest of his life, and although the wits of the time found it a subject for mirth Ashley did not mind. He was well again; and he believed that he owed his life to Locke."[13] Ashley not only tolerated his tube, he seems to have been proud of it: as a sign of successful intervention, an improved property. Seventeenth-century medicine pictured a brain-nerve complex composed of hollow tubes, carrying fluids and spirits. Now Locke had supplemented the given body with a simulated tube. He had not achieved "return by natural magick" exactly, but this was something like an *elixir vitae*. His tube preserved the life of his patron, by means of a silver, then gold, transformation of base nature.

The tube's success against the worm fit nicely within Ashley's and Locke's outlook on natural properties and enlightened development. This scene of healing set up a new version of microcosm, as Ashley urged Locke to turn from the body to the body politic. Ashley's grandson makes this clear: "After this cure, Mr. Locke grew so much in esteem with my grandfather that as great a man as he had experienced him in physics, he looked upon this but as the least part. He encouraged him to turn his thoughts another way . . . He put him upon the study of the religious and civil affairs of the nation with whatsoever related to the business of a Minister of State."[14] Locke's new studies resulted in works on economics, colonial development, political organization, and toleration, all written during the next five years at Exeter House. Although he was "turning" Locke's thoughts to religious and civil affairs, Ashley must have sensed correspondences between work on his body and political work. First of all, he treated medical success as a credential for public ministry. Furthermore, in both medicine and government, he and Locke assumed that the noblest work was to improve natural properties, by intervening as God's stewards. Locke liked to imagine nature in figures of pure potential. The mind became tabula rasa, in need of proper education; the body, "an extended solid Substance" (*Essay* 2.23.22) full of chemical processes to be improved by scientists; America, a waste land, awaiting the enlightened energies of European developers—like Locke and Ashley, both quite active in shaping colonial policies and making American investments.

For Locke the physician and political theorist, reason was a key to managing all these promising but vulnerable properties. "Reason" might be defined, for these purposes, as the state of mind in which subjects comport themselves as normal human beings. The chief threats to reason came from people imagining that they were either more or less than that. Some imagined that they were infused with new revelation and became unmanageable enthusiasts; others metamorphosed into brutes. Locke wanted to police body and society in the name of reason. For society, enthusiasts posed a problem, but brutes were more obviously dangerous. The *Second Treatise* describes serious crime almost as a change of species. The criminal, "varying from the right rule of reason . . . so far becomes degenerate and declares himself to quit the principles of human nature and to be a noxious creature" (7). He goes on to say that a murderer "may be destroyed as a lion or a tiger, one of those wild savage beasts with whom man can have no society nor security" (8); and a little later, that thieves and aggressors in war may also be killed, "for the same reason that [one] may kill a wolf or a lion, because such men are not under the ties of the common law of reason" (110).

Locke's beastly humans in these passages might seem no more than rhetorical flourishes. But his medical notes showed a substantive interest in brute-human combinations; enough so that the animal imagery in the *Second Treatise* begins to look more fundamental than decorative. In medical journals from various times in his life, he made note of a mole-man (who was given mole's blood as a cure for epilepsy and took to running his nose along the ground); "a man, woman, and cat who after eating pig's blood take on the habits of those animals"; exotic island men with tails "as long as a dears"; a French dog-woman (who was bitten by a rabid dog and later bit her mother, who was asked to execute her by strangulation); and this strange literalization of a woman's "wolf" (folk term for a breast tumor): "D. W. much afflicted with a wolf in her breast, for some time swaged the pain of her sore by batheing it with strong malt beer which it would suck in greedily as if some living creature. When she could come by no beer she made use of Rhum with which it was lulled to sleepe. At last (to be rid of it all together) she put a quantity of Arsenick to the Rhum & batheing of it as formerly, she utterly destroyed it, and curd her self."[15] Dewhurst apologizes for this "extravagant," "bizarre" entry, but it entertains a topic—the crossing of human and brute—that Locke apparently found very interesting. When he attended the Oxford lectures of Thomas Willis, an important early influence, he noted a reference to melancholic wolfmen: "There remains to speak about lycanthropy and those melancholy conditions associated with the imagination of a metamorphosis, examples of which occasionally occur. But as it is a lengthy inquiry it should only be mentioned here that these conditions do not seem to consist so much in the contraction or dilation of the *anima sensitiva* [nerve center of the corporeal soul] as in the changing and deterioration of its shape."[16] Willis elsewhere warned against the dangers of melancholic metamorphosis. If melancholics "are permitted to follow and dwell long on their Phantasms and aereal speculations, the soul subsides within, and leaving the Body, and undergoing a certain metamorphosis, induces a new species, and often contrary to the state of Man; wherefore the Affected ought to be continually disturbed by the Discourses of their Friends and Acquaintances, to wit, that the animal Spirits being call'd outward from their bye ways, be brought again into their former and usual Tracts."[17] These notes convey a telling combination of discursive realms: lycanthropy is an imaginative delusion, but its cause is situated within the body's chemistry and its effects and cure within society. Whether they are seen as dysfunctional bodies or as agents of social disruption, brute-humans must be brought back to the "usual tracts" of reason.

Lycanthropy, as Locke noted, was a rare, exotic version of melancholy. But the more common forms of melancholy and related "nervous" disorders were highly interesting to Locke and his colleagues. Thomas Willis and Thomas Sydenham, the two most prominent English physicians of the time, both wrote at length on nervous disorders. They certainly influenced Locke's interests. His surviving papers include extensive notes from each doctor[18] as well as other journals containing many entries on these topics. Seventeenth- and eighteenth-century doctors grouped melancholy, hysteria, hypochondria, epilepsy, and various other disorders into a cluster of nervous conditions. They considered the major disorders to be very similar. Hypochondria was commonly regarded as a male version of hysteria, and both were listed under the rubric of melancholy; hysteria and melancholy were often closely linked with epilepsy in their causes, manifestations, and treatments. The old name for epilepsy, "the sacred disease," is appropriate for the whole cluster, since all of these conditions lent themselves to supernatural explanations. Enlightenment physicians were proud of themselves for improving on Hippocrates' original debunking of the sacred diseases. Locke made a few notes that expressed contempt for accounts of possession.

But Enlightenment diagnoses were mediated by social contexts and political purposes. Nervous disorders were remystified through codes of gender and class. The gender codes have become well known, mainly from studies of hysteria. By Locke's time, the most sophisticated physicians had de-emphasized (but not entirely discarded) simple theories of womb vapors as the primary cause of hysteria.[19] They recognized that men also suffered from hysteria (although in men they tended to call it hypochondria), and they saw things from a more modern neurophysiological perspective. Still, they were sure that women suffered from nervous disorders much more than men; and they had a neurophysiological explanation ready. "The female head is weaker than that of the male, and their nerves, moreover, are not as strong and tense. Furthermore their spirits are not as robust; terror, sadness and other trivial emotions drive their spirits into fugues and distractions" (from Locke's notes to Willis's lectures).[20] Sydenham agrees and adds the providential design: "[Hysteria] seizes many more Women than Men, because kind Nature has bestowed on them a more delicate and fine habit of Body, having designed them only for an easy Life, and to perform the tender Offices of Love."[21] Locke's views on nervous women showed the influence of his two teachers. Writing to a colleague about his patient Mrs. Beavis, he says that she "is not yet got soe far either from her French melancholy or English malady . . . You know how soft she is in this part of her soul, too apt to receive and retain such uneasy impressions."[22] When he treated Lady Northumberland's neuralgia (a case of considerable importance to him), he strove to "harden and strengthen the nerves" of his "tender" aristocratic patient.[23]

Class along with gender played a significant role in his thinking about the nervous cluster. "Idle and delicate women who haveing little business to take up their time and thoughts give way to their imaginations and phansys, have more longings & more marked & monstrous children than women either of strong mindes or constant imployment. Therefor the lazy dames of Citys are more subject to the inconveniencys than the strong country labourers . . . To women that are much liable to this it may prove a rational remedy to finde some constant imployment for them that may keepe them busy."[24] Locke distinguishes between a robust lower class and the delicate women of privilege (who made up a good portion of his practice). Two groups, then, are particularly vulnerable to nervous disorder: women and the affluent. Locke's class distinction became more entrenched during the eighteenth century. By the end of the century, Thomas Beddoes felt a need to warn the "middling and affluent classes" about their great risk of nervous illness.[25] G. S. Rousseau spells out the neurophysiological reasoning that guided this class affiliation: "a) Soul is limited to brain; b) brain performs the entirety of its work through the nerves; c) the more 'exquisite' and 'delicate' one's nerves are, morphologically speaking, the greater the ensuing degree of sensibility and imagination; d) refined people and other persons of fashion are usually born with more 'exquisite' anatomies, the tone and texture of their nervous systems more 'delicate' than those of the lower classes."[26]

In all, three main groups make up the nervous population: women, the affluent, and people with especially acute intelligence. This last group was mentioned by all the major theorists of Locke's time, including Sydenham, his favorite mentor, who noted that men with nervous constitutions "excel in deep thought and wisdom of speech."[27] The phenomenon of nervous disorder presented a strange jumble of social messages. Refined females had the privileged purpose of love objects, but as their refinements exceeded proper purpose, their delicacies became nervously deviant. Intellectual males became more useful to an enlightened age as their nerve fibers approached feminized delicacy; but the sensitive fibers of intelligence could lead to a disastrous substitution of imagination for reason. The more sensitive the brain, the greater the reach of reason, but the more likely a "change of species" away from rational normality.

Locke was troubled by this knot of assumptions. Several notes show him pondering reason, imagination, and madness:

> This at least is the cause of great errors and mistakes amongst men even when it does not wholy unhinge the braines and put all government of the thoughts into the hands of the imagination as it sometimes happens, when the Imagination by being much imploid and geting the mastry about any one thing usurps the dominion over all the other facultys of the minde in all other, but how this comes about or what it is gives it on such an occasion that empire how it comes thus to be let loose I confesse I cannot guesse. If that were once known it would be no small advance towards the easier cureing of this maladie and perhaps to that purpose it may not be amisse to observe, what diet, temper, or other circumstances they are that set the imagination agog and makes it very active and imperious.[28]

His choice of words hints at the intersection of medical and political: government, dominion, empire, usurpation. Locke seems to be probing for a medical solution to a problem with obvious social and political significance, the deviant behavior of irrational subjects. He first mentions diet, and he almost always tried new diets for his nervous patients. But he also mentions "temper," and here he must be thinking of moderating the passions. Locke learned from his mentors that passion was the primary external cause of nervous fits. "The antecedent causes of this fermentation or boiling are anything tending to agitate that matter; the most fertile agent being an error or excess . . . for example, anger, sudden passions, terror, joy, intemperance, drunkenness" (from notes to Willis's lectures).[29] According to Sydenham, "Virulent perturbations of the mind" bring on fits, and hysterical women entertain "in their restless and anxious Breasts, upon small Occasions, and perchance for none at all, Fear, Anger, Jealousies, Suspicions, and worse Passions of the Mind . . . They never keep a Mean . . . Sometimes they love above measure, and presently hate the same, without any Reason."[30] It is interesting to note that one cause of hysteria is too much sexual activity (intemperate passion) and another is too little (fermented fluids build up). Science conveniently supports a sexual norm. When diet and drugs have little effect, there will always be the physician's appeal to rational temper. Here is Locke's final advice to Mrs. Clarke: her health so much follows her "temper of mind" that "half your cure depends on the Doctor's prescriptions, the other half is in your own mind. Cheerfulness will have a greater efficacy towards your recovery than anything the apothecaries' shops can afford."[31] Be content, in other words, and your neurophysiology will cooperate. A feminist reader will see the frustration of the patient and the circularity of the advice; but it fits our ordinary picture of Locke that he should continue to believe in rational recovery, even for recalcitrant patients and symptoms.

There is one more twist, however, to this story of Locke the enlightened physician. Locke suffered all his adult life from asthma. It curtailed his activities, dictated changes of residence, and so thoroughly vexed his medical intellect that he consulted a host of physicians in search of relief, to little effect. Asthma, it happens, was often listed as one of the distempers in the nervous cluster. Sydenham mentioned that nervous convulsions could sometimes be seated in the lungs. Van Helmont called asthma a form of epilepsy—"the falling sickness of the lungs."[32] According to Willis, for treating "Fits of the Asthma . . . we must use Anti-Convulsive and Anodine Remedies, for Medicines wont to be given in Hysterick passions, are also proper in a Convulsive Asthma."[33] Sydenham (among others) saw in Locke the symptoms of a nervous constitution—his "more than ordinary both naturall tenderness and delicacy of sence."[34] Locke could not cure his own version of a (possibly) nervous distemper. He did not suggest anywhere that his illness may have been aggravated by rational acuity gone to nervous excess. But one of his colleagues did hint, in a gentle way, that Locke's reason was effecting a kind of imaginative transformation: "I am much inclined to believe your apprehensions of your condition in relation to your present distemper, are but the same which most of thinking men (Physicians not excepted) have of themselves when indisposed: viz, they make too close reflection on their own diseases eyther magnifying them, or not so distinctly perceiving them through their immediate and great concernes which generally makes men forme dreadfull Ideas of things; as the Eye does an object brought too neare it."[35] This condition of reflective dread may not be all that serious, of course. It causes no metamorphosis away from "the common law of reason," by which Locke judged the most serious threats to bodies and societies. It is nowhere near the disturbing nervous malady of his friend Isaac Newton. But Blake would have appreciated it nonetheless: a gentle hint that reason might be exposed as a distemper.

NERVOUS IMAGINATION

Blake reversed the primary terms of Locke's prescription for health and sanity. He diagnosed a modern England in which reason had overthrown imagination, rather than the other way around. The body became a very important site in Blake's imaginative counterattack. But Blake, too, suffered from a "nervous infirmity" (as one of his friends called it); and like Locke, he was determined to diagnose and treat it and liberate himself from this version of a sacred disease. The parallel with Locke extends further: Blake's scene of infirmity took place during a three-year period when he made a concerted effort to please a patron and thereby gain much greater public influence. Blake, like Locke, set out to deliver body and society from oppressive ignorance or malice. He liked to represent England as a single body (Albion), whose health and freedom would be restored when the public finally replaced the false religion of empirical reason by means of renovated senses.

The story of Blake and the body looks as if it might have a simple plot. Locke's philosophy had turned the body from "the human form divine" into an atomized material object. Blake's renovated imagination would undo the damage.

> And every Generated Body in its inward form,
> Is a garden of delight & a building of magnificence,
> Built by the Sons of Los in Bowlahoola & Allamanda. (*Milton* 26:31–33)

When he says that every body is "built by the sons of Los" he means that bodies are continually created by desires, beliefs, interpretations, and all the other acts of human imagination, not by soulless natural causes.

> And every Natural Effect has a Spiritual Cause, and Not
> A Natural: for a Natural Cause only seems, it is a Delusion
> Of Ulro: & a ratio of the perishing Vegetable Memory. (*Milton* 26:44–46)

Locke, according to Blake, could not see beyond the superficial powers conferred by a grasp of natural causes. He looked to disenchant such things as nervous disorders by locating their causes in fermenting fluids, nerve tubes, and so on. Blake wanted to reenchant the body by finding primary spiritual causes. When he read a treatise on insanity which emphasized organic causes, he wrote this note in the margin: "Cowper came to me & said. O that I were insane always I will never rest. Can you not make me truly insane. I will never rest till I am so. O that in the bosom of God I was hid. You retain health & yet are as mad as any of us all—over us all—mad as a refuge from unbelief—from Bacon Newton & Locke" ("Annotations to Spurzheim's *Observations on Insanity*," 663). He thus redefines madness as a spiritual rather than a natural effect, and more than that, he identifies Lockean science as a perverted normality, which any healthy human must try to resist.

Blake's effort to renovate the body can be seen most clearly in two poetic works. In *The Book of Urizen* he looks at what happens to the body when it falls under the power of tyrannical reason. In *Milton* he demonstrates a new approach, with an imaginative tour de force aimed at reenchanting the body and liberating it from Enlightenment chains.

The Book of Urizen mixes materials from many religious, philosophical, and literary texts, but most obviously it presents Blake's revision of Genesis. The godlike creator (Urizen) cannot tolerate the complexities of eternity, so he withdraws in self-contemplation, creates the limited world we know as "nature," and invents rational laws to keep his subjects under control. An extended passage shows Los creating the fallen human body. (In the context of *Urizen*, Los can best be described as a victim of Urizen's actions who finds himself suddenly disoriented and anxious in a fallen world. He tries to counteract Urizen's depressive collapse by creating fixed entities for the new world in which they now find themselves.) Los creates the parts of the body in seven stages. Some readers oversimplify *Urizen* by attributing to Blake a Gnostic revulsion from the body. In some parts of his work he does express some such disgust, especially over the sexual body, or a milder lack of interest. But in *Urizen* the revulsion should properly be attributed to Los and Urizen and not necessarily to Blake. Blakean redemption is better described as a "reorganization, rather than a transcendence" of the body.[36] The fallen body of *Urizen* reflects the disenchanted rationality of Locke's world. The first stage of creation, appropriately, produces the brain-nerve complex, the primary feature of Locke's body.

> Till a roof shaggy wild inclos'd
> In an orb, his fountain of thought.
> In a horrible dreamful slumber;
> Like the linked infernal chain;
> A vast Spine writh'd in torment
> Upon the winds; shooting pain'd
> Ribs, like a bending cavern

And bones of solidness, froze
Over all his nerves of joy. (10:33–41)

The last line is one of several in *Urizen* that refer to nerves. Together, they present a fairly consistent picture of Blakean neurology. Unfallen Eternals thrive on sensitivity, with their "nerves of joy." Nerves make a nice vehicle for suggesting prelapsarian monism, since they were said to communicate between spirit and matter. But nervous sensitivity also brings anxiety: "In harrowing fear rolling round, / His nervous brain" (11:10–11). Fallen nerves harden into bones or congeal into opaque, knotted webs, "twisted like to the human brain" (25:21). Just after Los is seized with "a nerveless silence" (13:38), his confusion about nerves evolves into a myth of gender difference. As he begins to weep in pity, his nervous system is projected outward as a separate entity:

The void shrunk the lymph into Nerves
Wand'ring wide on the bosom of night,
And left a round globe of blood
Trembling upon the Void. (13:56–59)

This globe of blood branches into nervous fibres[37] and turns into "the first female," "trembling and pale" (18:10, 7). Blake's poem thus appears to join the tradition of feminizing the nervous system. One could argue, of course, that he is only parodying the Lockean perceptions of his characters. This sort of caveat about dramatic context should never be ignored; but Blake elsewhere shows enough vulnerability to conventional antifeminism when he is writing in his "own" voice that the *Urizen* nerve-female may signal at least a partial convergence of Locke and Blake on this subject. By the time of *Milton*, it should be remembered, Blake will be creating the categories of "Female Will" and "Female Space" as one attempt to name the spiritual cause of the body's fall away from (masculine?) health. Even if Eternity's healthy body is more hermaphroditic than masculine, as various passages and designs suggest, Blake and his visionary precursors liked to give males a controlling priority in the politics of undifferentiated gender.

In *Milton*, written several years after *Urizen*, Los has developed into an exemplary creator (although he still struggles with contrary desires, self doubt, and difficult relationships), and interpreters receive more encouragement to take him as Blake's primary representative among the Zoas. Los in *Milton* does not project and separate a nervous female; in fact, he resides within the nerves.

And in the Nerves of the Ear, (for the Nerves of the Tongue are closd)
On Albions Rock Los stands creating the glorious Sun each morning.
(29:40–41)

The "Optic vegetative Nerves" have come under Satan's control, Blake says, and the "Nerves of the Nostrils," apparently, under Bacon/Newton/Locke's:

> But in the Nerves of the Nostrils, Accident being formed
> Into Substance & Principle, by the cruelties of Demonstration
> It became Opake & Indefinite . . . (29:35–37)

Nerves become opaque when they are simplified into material entities. Los's work is to transform the body continually from Lockean opacity toward redemptive translucence. Los and his sons try to revise Enlightenment misconceptions about time, space, and causality. The body can be redeemed only when human imagination shakes off the lethargy of empirical reason. Locke was thrilled when he first studied blood through Van Leeuwenhoek's microscope. As he saw for the first time the "globules of blood," he appreciated anew how "wonderful" and "regular" were the works of nature.[38] For Blake, microscopes merely "alter / The ratio of the Spectators Organs but leave Objects untouchd" (29:17–18):

> And every Space smaller than a Globule of Mans blood opens
> Into Eternity of which this vegetable Earth is but a Shadow.
> (29:21–22)

A globule of blood was the smallest unit Locke and Leeuwenhoek could see. As hard as modern scientists try to find the microscopic truth, Blake suggests, the only valuable answers continue to elude them, always just a little smaller than their instruments can detect. The redeemed, eternal body is something that humanity will have to "touch" with more intimate faculties than atomistic rationalism. Microscopes and telescopes leave "Objects untouchd" and humans mere spectators.

In *Milton* this new body takes shape within the spiritual regions he calls Bowlahoola and Allamanda. These names obviously have to do with the digestive system—Blake says at one point, "Bowlahoola is the Stomach in every individual man" (24:67)—but he expands their definition into a microcosmic plenum. Bowlahoola, for example, besides being the stomach, is also "nam'd Law by mortals" (24:48) and then is linked with science. This whole section of the poem ranges freely from the dance of the tiniest gnats to cities, historical epochs, and the regions of eternity. Los announces that "Every scatter'd Atom / Of Human Intellect" is being retrieved, and ancient wisdom "sought out from Animal & Vegetable & Mineral" (25:18–21). Even some sympathetic readers of the later Blake lose patience with his exotic terminology and his enthusiasm for archaic microcosm. But one must be careful not to equate Blake's poetry with, for example, Swedenborgian arcana. (Blake refers to Swedenborg in this part of *Milton* as a promising but unsuccessful precursor.) Swedenborg wrote in great detail about spiritual regions that correspond to the foot, the liver, and so forth and whom he met in each place. Blake shares Swedenborg's affinity for the microcosmic body, but in *Milton* he does not cleanly separate the earthly and spiritual realms as Swedenborg does. Blake's approach is more directly conversant with Enlightenment "normal" perception, even though he places unusual demands on a reader so conditioned.

In *Milton* and various other works, Blake is trying to show that Locke's version of the body is far from being the only or the most obvious construct available; that its preemptive normality is an effect of political power rather than intellectual progress; and that disenchanted, atomized bodies fit more easily than enchanted ones into Enlightenment plans for the development of properties. Even though he probably did not know about Locke's investments in the slave trade, Blake was convinced that the Enlightenment was more about slavery than about liberty. *Visions of the Daughters of Albion* provides a good illustration. He invents a character named Bromion, whose intellectual affiliation is with Enlightenment empiricism. Bromion rapes a young woman and then addresses her as a slave:

Bromion spoke. behold this harlot here on Bromions bed,
And let the jealous dolphins sport around the lovely maid;
Thy soft American plains are mine, and mine thy north & south:
Stampt with my signet are the swarthy children of the sun . . .
(1:18–21)

Blake is alert to the implications of property theories by which bodies and continents alike are made subjects of enlightened development. The raped woman, Oothoon, sees her oppression quite explicitly in bodily terms: she attributes her suffering to a Urizenic or Lockean interpretation of her body.

They told me that I had five senses to inclose me up.
And they inclos'd my infinite brain into a narrow circle.
And sunk my heart into the Abyss, a red round globe hot burning
Till all from life I was obliterated and erased. (2:31–34)

In *Milton* Los and his sons deliver similar laments. The "Woof of Locke" has woven a body so shrunken and impotent—a "narrow doleful form / Creeping in reptile flesh" (5:19–20)—that humanity cowers in the face of an infinite, atomized universe.

Sometimes it appears that Blake is giving up his conversation with Locke's version of the body altogether and simply replacing it with a Neoplatonic model:

> The Souls descending to the Body wail on the right hand
> Of Los, & those deliver'd from the Body on the left hand. (*Milton* 26:16–17)

Some interpreters of Blake consider his Neoplatonic strain to be a preeminent element of his thinking, perhaps the dominant one.[39] At various moments in his work he does suggest that the body is a prison from which one's spirit will eventually be delivered. But Blake at his most interesting does not surrender to this sort of dualism. He tries to bring Neoplatonic forms and Lockean bodies into a therapeutic play of contraries. *Milton* begins with an invocation of (loosely) Neoplatonic muses, but Blake then asks them to descend

> ... down the Nerves of my right arm
> From out the Portals of my Brain, where by your ministry
> The Eternal Great Humanity Divine planted his Paradise ... (2:6–8)

This invocation, in other words, draws as much from the body of Locke as it does from the soul of Neoplatonism. Generated bodies and eternal forms belong to the same imaginative process:

> And every Generated Body in its inward form
> Is a garden of delight & a building of magnificence ... (26:31–32)

But now we turn from the visions of *Milton* to a particularly difficult part of Blake's life, when he suffered from his version of a nervous affliction. In 1800 he set out to take advantage of favorable circumstances that promised to advance his artistic career. He became involved with William Hayley, a well-connected man of letters who believed that Blake had unusual gifts. Hayley moved Blake to a cottage in Felpham and planned to collaborate with him on various literary projects. Their collaboration bears some structural resemblance to that of Ashley and Locke: a public man takes in a talented protégé to improve his own work and to offer the protégé a better living and greater influence. But Hayley and Blake made a very bad team. After three of what he called "the Darkest Years that ever Mortal sufferd" (767), Blake moved away from Hayley and slipped into greater obscurity and poverty. In "The Bard's Song" of *Milton* Blake gives a poetic, mythologized account of the failure. But his letters from the Felpham period offer just as interesting an account, and surely an appropriate one: in these letters, after all, he was trying to equip Blake the inspired prophet with an acceptable public voice. He could not simply repress his convictions, but neither could he afford to ignore their public effect. He had to converse.

Shortly before his move to Felpham, Blake confessed to a friend, "I begin to Emerge from a Deep pit of Melancholy, Melancholy without any real reason for it, a Disease which God keep you from & all good men" (706). A little later he asked another friend "to forgive [his] Nervous Fear" (708). Blake was diagnosing himself in the language of Enlightenment neurophysiology. In using the word "disease," he implied a natural more than a spiritual cause for his nervous condition. At the start of the Felpham period, it would appear, he was ready to normalize his vision of the body, in preparation for the public work ahead. When the work did not go well, his patron began to make his own diagnosis of an acute nervous problem. Hayley wrote in 1802 to Lady Hesketh, who had become displeased with Blake's engraving work for Hayley's life of her cousin, the poet William Cowper. Blake reminds him of Cowper, Hayley says, in his "nervous Infirmity" and "in the Tenderness of his Heart, & in the perilous powers of an Imagination utterly unfit to take due Care of Himself,— with admirable Faculties, his sensibility is so *dangerously acute*, that the common rough Treatment which true genius often receives from *ordinary minds* in the commerce of the World, might not only wound him *more than it should do*, but really reduce Him to the Incapacity of an Idiot without the consolatory support of a considerate Friend."[40] This diagnosis comes straight out of Enlightenment conclusions about nervous diseases. Blake has admirable but overly acute faculties, a feminine "tenderness of heart," and a liability to substitute imagination for reason. Hayley uses nerves both to elevate and to disable Blake; and certainly to enclose him within Hayley's commerce of genius. Hayley continued to express concern about Blake's mental health during the Felpham years. By 1805, he considered Blake a pitiable case. He is "very apt to fail in his art" because of "nervous Irritation," and often he appears to be "on the verge of Insanity."[41] Hayley's opinion was shared by others within the mainstream, including better-known poets (such as laureate Robert Southey, who found Blake "so evidently insane, that the predominant feeling in conversing with him... could only be sorrow and compassion")[42] and more disinterested friends (such as Henry Crabb Robinson). Blake must have seen his marginalization as a necessary effect of the dominant Lockean perspective. Visionaries demand "a refuge from unbelief—from Bacon Newton & Locke," but the Enlightenment exposes that refuge as nervous incapacity. By treating the rebellious artist as an invalid, a patron like Hayley can disable or at least control him and still get the benefit of his aberrant sensitivity.

During the Felpham years, Blake at first resisted all suggestion that he was unhealthy; but after a year or so he submitted and started diagnosing himself. He saw himself as either physically or mentally unhealthy, or both, in some confusing mixture of natural and spiritual causes. Often he blamed the damp weather of Felpham and minimized his unhealthiness as the effects of a persistent cold. Sometimes he treated this cold as a more serious problem: he wrote his brother that the Felpham air was unhealthy, that he had been "really very ill," and that "illness makes all uncomfortable & this we must prevent by every means in our power" (726). In this same letter, however, he complained that Hayley and other supposed friends were misusing him out of jealousy and that he was trying not to "feel depress'd." In other letters he admitted to being "very Unhappy" and mired in "despondency." One letter mixed natural and spiritual unhealthiness in a telling way: "When I came down here I was more sanguine than I am at present but it was because I was ignorant of many things which have since occurred & chiefly the unhealthiness of the place" (723). "Sanguine" carries both a literal or natural and a figurative or spiritual meaning. The flexibility of this word allowed Blake to convey two levels of unhealthiness at once. Apparently he did not wish to discard either version or to keep them strictly separate.

When Los creates his visionary body in *Milton*, he puts in "Cabinets richly fabricate . . . / For Doubts & fears unform'd & wretched & melancholy" (28:8–9). He also takes care to warn fearful melancholics away from "the four iron pillars of Satan's Throne— / Temperance, Prudence, Justice, Fortitude" (29:48). Satan's therapy sounds like Locke's, with its emphasis on emotional restraint. Blake had no intention of regaining his nervous health in this way; but he had to do something. His letters convey two kinds of Blakean therapy for nervous infirmity. The first kind is a miraculous influx of confidence, in which Blake suddenly feels healthy and whole again. Writing to Thomas Butts in 1803, for example, he thanks his patron for helping to "lift me out of despondency." Ultimately it is not Butts but divine intervention that he thanks for his recovery. He feels the touch of God giving "a blessing to all my works," and he rejoices in imminent "Glory & Honour" (728–29). In an 1804 letter to Hayley he announces that he has been suddenly "reenlightened with the light I enjoyed in my youth," which has brought an end to his nervous "distress" and returned his "strength." Earlier in the letter, interestingly, he makes a hearty concession to medical science and natural causes: his wife is now surprisingly recovered from her Felpham ailments, and "Electricity is the wonderful cause" (756). We do not have Hayley's response to this letter. If Locke had read it, he would no doubt have focused on the following sentence: "[My friends] knew my industry and abstinence from every pleasure for the sake of study, and yet—and yet there wanted the proofs of industry in my works." Locke would have recognized symptoms of nervous distemper in the artist's immoderate dedication to his work; checked his diet; prescribed a mild nerve medication; and (above all) urged him to seek distraction in the company of genial, stable friends.

But Blake never had much patience with this sort of therapy. When he could not sustain his miraculous feeling of unification, he resorted increasingly to another kind of therapy. In the Felpham letters (and later poetic works), he frequently righted himself by declaring a severe dualism between spiritual and corporeal phenomena. He cured his nervous infirmity by shucking off the body. Back in *The Marriage of Heaven and Hell,* the attractive "voice of the devil" called it a pernicious illusion to separate soul from body and to privilege the soul. But in the Felpham letters Blake increasingly resorts to some such strategy. He says he cares not "a Fig for all Corporeal [distress]" (716). He condemns any art based on nature as "idolatry" (730). He says that "if a Man is the Enemy of my Spiritual Life while he pretends to be the Friend of my Corporeal, he is a Real Enemy" (728). (In *Milton* he tightens this into an aphorism: "Corporeal Friends are Spiritual Enemies" [4:26].) A later letter to Hayley, from 1805, with its uncompromising, boastful dualism, shows that the Felpham project has certainly come to an end: "I speak of Spiritual Things. Not of Natural. Of Things known only to Myself & to Spirits Good & Evil. but Not Known to Men on Earth . . . Excuse this Effusion of the Spirit from One who cares little for this World which passes away. whose Happiness is Secure in Jesus our Lord. & who looks for Suffering till the time of complete Deliverance . . . Would to God that [men] would Consider their Spiritual Life Regardless of that faint Shadow Calld Natural Life" (767).

Blake's severe dualizing, whatever its therapeutic value to him, may be his least effective means of resistance to Lockean domination. Eventually it bored even patient, admiring H. C. Robinson, who complained after a visit of "the same half crazy crotchets about the two worlds—the eternal repetition of which must in time become tiresome."[43] With this sort of dualism he plays into the hands of Enlightenment diagnosis. When he is unwilling to engage the Lockean body in a play of contraries, his effusions are too easily dismissed as thin romance—the false sublimities of an unhealthy nervous system. Imagination becomes merely a "refuge from unbelief," a nervous simulation of deliverance.

Interpreters should be careful about Locke's as well as Blake's most dogmatic pronouncements on therapy for bodies in distress. It is convenient and often instructive to make Blake's medical case against Locke or Locke's medical case against Blake. But if these two physicians are not exactly corporeal friends, neither are they the purest of spiritual enemies. There is less rational freedom and more romance to Locke's body than he knew, and Blake was not always able to replace Locke's body with something effectively different. This is not necessarily bad news for those who seek history or therapy between Enlightenment and Romance.

Chapter 4

Slavery

Locke's condemnation of slavery in the *Second Treatise* and, more generally, the liberal principles of his political theory gave eighteenth- and nineteenth-century abolitionists a valuable philosophical resource. However, every modern scholar who takes him seriously has had to confront an embarrassing fact: Locke actually participated in the slave trade. Blake's antislavery resolve offers no comparable surprise. He became friends with John Gabriel Stedman and helped illustrate his book critical of slavery; in his own works he consistently deplored slavery. But even Blake's work fails to shake off some of the surrounding effects of empire. In each case the topic of slavery poses some difficult questions for interpreters. How can we explain Locke's apparent inconsistency? To what extent can a stable antislavery reading of Blake be undermined by analysis of cultural codes?

Three Approaches to Locke and the Slave Trade

Interpreters of Locke have responded to his involvement with the slave trade in three different ways. A first group treats it as an unfortunate but minor lapse in the public conduct of a man deservedly known for adherence to liberal principles. Locke's conduct here, according to this first mode of explanation, constitutes a deviation from his theory. A second group would agree that his participation in slave trading seems to contradict his basic principles; but instead of merely dismissing his conduct as a deviation from theory, these interpreters draw out of Locke's writings an elaborate, unworthy justification of the kind of slavery in which he participated. For this second group, then, Locke did manage to accommodate theory to practice, but only by an embarrassingly tortured logic. A third group concludes that Locke's accommodation of slavery does not proceed from the violation or torture of his basic theories. Instead, these interpreters argue, his treatment of slavery should be seen as part of the fabric of Lockean philosophy, however embarrassing that might be for modern admirers of one of the founding liberals.[1]

Two difficulties hinder any final judgment about the relative validity of the three approaches. First, the evidence by which they may be evaluated has flaws and ambiguities. It would be unproductive, however, simply to declare the material undecidable and abandon the project to a premature indeterminacy. Second, the conclusions reached by various interpreters appear to depend as much on critical predisposition as on evidence. The deviation approach emanates from a kind of tempered idealism: theory will govern practice, except in certain obvious cases of temptation and lapse. The torture approach recognizes a specific area in which practice governs theory, rather than vice versa; but a seam remains visible, where something different intruded on the theory and was joined to it. The third approach recognizes no such seam. Theory and practice are inseparable, a seamless text of power relations. The three approaches can thus be situated—and, at least to some extent, ask to be validated—as different (but complementary) responses to familiar questions of idea and act.

Locke participated in the institutions of slavery in two basic ways. First, he invested in slave-trading companies. Second, he acted as secretary and, to some degree, policy advisor to three different groups involved in the affairs of the American colonies, including the provision and regulation of slaves.

Facts about the investments are solid enough, if not complete. (Investment records in the seventeenth century were often discarded after a transaction was finished.) Locke put money in two companies whose commercial activities depended on slavery: the Royal African Company and a company of adventurers formed to develop the Bahaman Islands. The first of these was explicitly a slave-trading enterprise. Locke invested six hundred pounds in the Royal African Company, shortly after its formation in 1672.[2] Ashley had invested two thousand pounds, which made him the third largest investor.[3] Locke's investment, then, was no inconsequential matter, either to the company or to Locke, who was always careful with his money. The Royal African Company was formed in 1672 to trade along the West Coast of Africa and primarily to provide the slaves considered indispensable by planters in America. It was chartered to replace the Company of Royal Adventurers into Africa, which had proved unsuccessful in its ten years of operation. The new company included more businessmen and fewer nobles and was determined to attend more to profits than to subtle affairs of state. Certainly Locke was the sort of investor they sought; and Ashley, despite being a nobleman, had a great interest in the mercantile practicalities of American plantations. Ashley as a young man had owned acreage and slaves in Barbados, as well as a fourth share in the *Rose,* a slave-trading ship.[4] The new Royal African Company named him sub-governor, a post which he held through 1673, and until 1677 he served in its Court of Assistants. No doubt Locke and Ashley looked carefully both at the company's charter—which granted a monopoly for the trade of "Gold, Silver, Negroes, Slaves," and any other minor Guinea goods—and at a report of its first year's activities, which mentions gold, elephants' teeth, and a few other items but places by far the greatest emphasis on slave shipping and slave factories. The slaves, this report assures, "are sent to all his Majesty's American Plantations, which cannot subsist without them."[5] The Royal African Company fared better than its predecessor, although it was never successful enough to justify its monopoly, and it had trouble meeting the considerable demand for slaves.[6] Ashley sold his stock in 1677 for a reasonable profit, and no doubt Locke did likewise, although not necessarily at the same time.

Locke also invested in a company of Bahamas adventurers. Here again he was collaborating with Ashley. Ashley and five other Carolina proprietors had been granted the Bahaman Islands, and in 1672 they formed a company with eleven "Adventurers to Bahamas" to pursue development. Locke was one of the eleven adventurers. He initially invested one hundred pounds; before long he doubled his share by taking over the hundred-pound investment of his friend John Mapletoft. Fox Bourne calculates that Locke thus "became altogether responsible for a ninth" of the project and guesses that he actually spent much more than two hundred pounds.[7]

We know only a few details about Locke's Bahamas adventure, but some historical background can help. In *A History of the Bahamas*, Michael Craton explains the terms of the proprietors' grant: they were to stimulate planting and trading of profitable crops, in a colony that had been struggling under Spanish and then English rule. The plantations supported by Locke and the other adventurers were using slaves, of course. Craton cites a 1671 census of the islands recording 443 slaves out of a total population of 1,097.[8] Another document has been found, from about the time of the adventurers, computing the "expense of settling and improving the Bahama Islands for the first three years." According to this estimate, three hundred families would need to bring along six hundred slaves (costing thirty pounds each) and to "trade for 4,000 negroes per annum, being 8,000 for the first two years . . . at 25 pounds per head."[9] The adventurers were evidently not up to these stakes, and planters in the Bahamas complained that the proprietors and their company provided insufficient support. Locke and his patron, however, remained interested in the Bahamas. Shaftesbury tried to bolster planters' confidence with plans for new crops and a hereditary nobility. Locke attended to Bahamian matters for some years, and apparently at one point he was considering a more active involvement in planting. This can be inferred from a letter to Locke from his friend Sir Peter Colleton, a West Indies planter: "I find I am your partner in the Bahama trade which will turn to accompt if you meddle not with planting, but if you plant otherwise then for provizion for your factor you will have your whole stock drowned in a plantation and bee never the better for it . . . If other men will plant there, I mean the Bahamas, hinder them not, they improve our province, but I would neither have you nor my lord ingadge in it."[10] Fox Bourne interprets the letter as Colleton discouraging Locke from managing a full plantation at a great distance; Craton reads it differently and infers that Locke had inquired about moving to the Bahamas as a planter.[11] Either way, Locke apparently entertained notions of increasing his moderate but serious participation in American planting and trade.

His second kind of participation in the institutions of slavery called for investments of time rather than money. Locke held three relevant administrative positions: secretary to the Lords Proprietors of Carolina, secretary to the Council of Trade and Plantations, and commissioner of the Board of Trade.

In the first of these positions he helped Ashley and seven other noblemen who had been granted proprietorship of Carolina in 1663. Locke acted as a secretary for them and probably as an advisor—but to what extent remains uncertain. The most significant document in the Carolina papers is the *Fundamental Constitutions of Carolina*, which sets out an interesting mixture of liberal policies and restrictive social hierarchies. A scheme of nobility was invented; Locke was granted the second highest rank of "Landgrave" and forty-eight thousand acres that came with the title. Most relevant to our discussion is a provision that "every freeman of Carolina shall have absolute power and authority over his negro slave of what opinion or religion soever" (*Works*, 10:196). The proprietors thus clarified that the religious freedom granted Carolina slaves did not imply another sort of freedom. Scholars have variously proposed that Locke (a) authored the entire Carolina constitution (there is a manuscript in Locke's hand, and many editions of his work include it); (b) had no part in it, except as amanuensis; and (c) effectively coauthored it with Ashley. Most recent scholars have argued for this third conclusion, which seems the most plausible, given the two men's respect for each other. But did Locke endorse the slavery clause? There is evidence that he disagreed with at least one other clause, establishing the Church of England;[12] so some would like to assume a similar objection to the slavery clause. Such an objection seems unlikely, however. Not only did he go on to make the slave investments already described, but in the much later commentaries to St. Paul, Locke carefully restated the distinction between religious and civil freedom articulated in the Carolina constitution. According to the constitution, slaves are free to attend the church of their choice, "but yet no slave shall hereby be exempted from that civil dominion his master hath over him, but be in all other things in the same state and condition he was in before." Here is part of Locke's paraphrase of St. Paul, 1 Corinthians 7:20–24: "Christianity gives not anyone any new privilege to change the state . . . which he was in before. Wert thou called, being a slave? . . . In whatsoever state a man is called, in the same he is to remain, notwithstanding any privileges of the gospel, which gives him no dispensation, or exemption, from any obligation he was in before"; to which he adds this commentary: "The thinking themselves freed by Christianity, from the ties of civil society and government, was a fault, it seems, that those Christians were very apt to run into" (*Works* 8:116). Apparently Locke could endorse the Carolina slavery clause without qualms, even if he did not himself compose it.

Locke's other two offices were government appointments. In 1673 he became secretary to the Council of Trade and Plantations, a position he held for over a year. As secretary he had to correspond with proprietors, governors, planters, merchants, and anyone else connected with the colonies who brought a complaint, made a proposal, or held useful information. Much of the council's work went toward expediting the triangular trade of slaves, sugar, and manufactured goods. One of the council's directives was to oversee the provision of slaves and to investigate disputes between the chartered slaving company and the American plantations. (As we have seen, Locke held investments on both sides of such disputes; putting him in an interested but neutral position.) For over a year, then, Locke spent much of his time immersed in these matters. But it is difficult to say how actively he contributed to the council's decisions: "In all the voluminous correspondence . . . [there is nothing] to show how far he acted merely as a secretary, and how far he initiated the proceedings that he had to direct."[13] There is no such uncertainty about Locke's second stint as colonial administrator. In 1696, he took office as a commissioner of the new Board of Trade, created to solve problems such as poor colonial government, piracy, and abused or ineffective trade regulations. In this position he was unquestionably an active policy-maker. Cranston concludes that "documents of the Board of Trade make abundantly clear, that Locke was the leading Commissioner in nearly everything which was undertaken."[14] This opinion has been reinforced by Peter Laslett, who emphasizes Locke's contribution to the board's formation and early policies.[15] He served until 1700, when he became too ill to continue.

Given all this evidence, scholars must account for the incongruity between Locke's actions in these matters and his place in the ordinary history of ideas. There are three main approaches, as set out above: practice as deviating from theory, as torturing theory, and as fulfilling theory. In the deviation approach, no one, to my knowledge, has accused Locke of blatant hypocrisy. Influenced primarily by idealist histories, most deviation theorists have privileged theory over practice (even for a man known as "the practical philosopher") and taken

Locke's participation in slavery as an embarrassing but insignificant lapse—an effect of local negotiations of personal interest. The importance and influence of the grand theory overwhelms such lapses. Historians of slavery such as Craton, for example, will pause to note the lapse, but as a parenthesis to the main fact of Locke as antislavery theorist. A more extreme version of deviation idealism is to discount the actions so drastically as to consider them unworthy of mention. Kathy Squadrito's 1975 essay does mention them, but only to judge them irrelevant: defending Lockean empiricism against a charge of racism, she will "consider irrelevant any references to Locke's supposed involvement in, or support of, the slave trade."[16] Ruth W. Grant, in a more recent book, is not squeamish about admitting his involvement; but she argues for practice as deviation from theory, "which can in no way support that institution [slavery]."[17]

It would be useful here to highlight some antislavery passages from the *Two Treatises of Government*. Source books of abolitionist thinking like to quote the beginning of the *First Treatise:* "Slavery is so vile and miserable an Estate of Man, and so directly opposed to the generous Temper and Courage of our Nation; that 'tis hardly to be conceived, that an *Englishman*, much less a *Gentleman*, should plead for't" (1). Snobbishness aside, this sounds like a clear, spirited denunciation. Context alters the message, however. This is Locke's exordium to his attack on Filmer's theory of patriarchal monarchy. The slavery he refers to in this first sentence is the condition to which Filmer would reduce all English subjects. Locke is thus using slavery in a general rather than a specific sense, more figuratively than literally. This does not simply disqualify the sentence as an abolitionist text; but it does suggest that Locke's antislavery theories need careful reading. Near the end of the *Second Treatise* he returns to his opening theme and attacks Filmer-like tyrannists who would resolve "all Government into absolute Tyranny, and would have all Men born to, what their mean Souls fitted them for, Slavery" (239). Here the rhetorical flourish again complicates an apparent repudiation of slavery. By suggesting that a "mean soul" makes a person fit for slavery, Locke slips toward two ancient traditions justifying slavery: the classical model of natural inferiority (accepted easily enough by Plato and Aristotle) and the Judeo-Christian model of slavery as divine punishment.[18] But this is only a rhetorical flourish, one might argue. And even if some traces remain of antique paradigms, Locke fought against the old assumptions. Men are not born into or fitted for slavery, according to the real Locke. "No body can give more Power than he has himself; and he that cannot take away his own Life, cannot give another power over it" (23). Everyone is naturally free "from any Superior Power on Earth" (22), and anyone who attempts to enslave a person "puts himself into a State of War" with that person (17).

There is one technical exception within this antislavery doctrine, but deviation theorists can discount its importance. Locke allows that captives taken in a just war may be kept as slaves: "This is the Perfect condition of *Slavery*, which is nothing else, but *the State of War continued between a lawful Conqueror, and a Captive*" (24). He uses here the primary justification of slavery from the Justinian Code—and a principle written into, among other things, the 1641 Laws and Liberties of Massachusetts. But deviationists can observe that Locke adds a liberal condition to the old justification. Once victor and vanquished have made a formal "agreement for a limited Power on the one side and Obedience on the other, the State of War and *Slavery* ceases, as long as the Compact endures"(24). Clearly, they would argue, Locke did not expect the old slavery to impinge on modern government, with its sophisticated diplomatic machinery. Furthermore, Locke denies to conquerors any claims on the children of captives (189). In no way can Locke's theory be said to support chattel slavery as practiced on the American plantations.

Interpreters of a second kind agree that Locke deserves his reputation as an opponent of slavery, but they regretfully explain how he tortured his basic theories in order to accommodate American slavery. Advocates of the torture approach are not as confident about the integrity of Lockean theory. The theory is vulnerable to contamination by misjudged practical interests. Still, this second approach recognizes a clear distinction between normal and intruding elements.

Locke's tortured justification of American slavery has been set out most thoroughly by Martin Seliger.[19] Seliger finds in the *Second Treatise* a special defense of colonization and slavery, two pillars of the first British empire. The justification represents an "inane" and localized (but still systematic) affirmation of territorial annexation and enslavement, elsewhere so forcefully repudiated in the *Second Treatise*. Seliger begins with the admission of slavery for captives in a just war. A just war, for Locke, was a war fought in defense of one's possessions against an aggressor. One society cannot legitimately use war to subjugate another society by attacking the lives, liberties, and possessions of its citizens. Locke's principles of just and unjust war are not among his more sophisticated ideas. Even if his simple distinction between offensive and defensive war will admit some complications (e.g., the matter of justifiable preventive war), the *Second Treatise* insists on defensive motivations. Locke appears confident that he can distinguish between an aggressor and a defender in a given set of circumstances. His confident principles of just and unjust war serve to disqualify one possible defense of the African slave trade. As Craton observes, "most English writers believed that the majority of slaves were captives in the wars that were endemic to West Africa."[20] It was commonly thought (if not scrupulously verified) that Africans taken as slaves would be worse off as war captives in Africa than as slaves in America. But even if Locke held this view of the origin of enslavement, he could not, on these grounds alone, justify the Royal African Company slaving. Only captives taken in a just war deserve to be enslaved. All the English buyers could be sure of in an African war—if they gave it any thought at all—was who had superior force. The *Second Treatise* grants no privilege to conquerors with only this claim to superiority.

But Seliger identifies another line of thinking by which Locke appears to justify colonial slavery. Again it begins with the legitimate enslavement of war captives. The real torture comes in the next link of the logical chain: native Africans and Americans can be considered aggressors in a war against the Europeans who would colonize and develop their lands. Hence, Peter Laslett says, "Locke seems satisfied that the slave raiding forays of the Royal African Company were just wars."[21] Laslett uses "seems" because Locke never actually drew such a conclusion. Seliger has to put together premises culled from the *Second Treatise* and find the "unavoidable implication" about colonizers as just conquerors. Deviation theorists object that he is putting words into Locke's mouth, but Seliger's case should not be dismissed lightly.

The difficult link, the one about natives being aggressors, needs more inspection. This idea seems an absurd violation of *Second Treatise* principles. In the chapter on war, Locke asserts that "he who makes an *attempt to enslave me* thereby puts himself into a State of War with me" (17), and the aggressor-enslaver deserves to be punished or killed. How can the African and American victims of such aggression be turned into the aggressors themselves? The answer, according to Seliger, is Locke's theory of waste land, in which he may have been influenced by More's *Utopia*.[22] According to this principle, people occupying (or claiming as property) land that they either cannot or will not develop may become aggressors against those who can and would develop that land. In Utopia, when the population rises above fixed quotas, Utopians colonize a nearby mainland area where "the natives have much unoccupied and uncultivated land." Ideally, the natives will agree to live under Utopian laws; but those who refuse, "they drive from the territory which they carve out for themselves. If they resist, they wage war against them. They consider it a most just cause for war when a people which does not use its soil but keeps it idle and waste nevertheless forbids the use and possession of it to others who by the rule of nature ought to be maintained by it."[23] Locke's version of this thinking resides in two *Second Treatise* passages. As part of his analysis of property, he mentions that "there are still *great Tracts of Ground* to be found, which . . . *lie waste*, and are more than the People, who dwell on it, do, or can make use of" (45). (In a journal entry from 1677, he defined the West Indies as such a waste land: natives of "that large and fertile part of the world" have "lived a poore uncomfortable laborious life ... scarce able to subsist.")[24] Later, in a discussion of war reparations, Locke explains that no victor may justly seize possession of a defeated enemy's land—except that, "where there being more *Land*, than the Inhabitants possess, and make use of, any one has liberty to make use of the waste" (184). Thus, if a native population should "resist conquest of their waste land, they become aggressors in war,"[25] and the developers may justly kill them and enslave captives.

Squadrito, following Seliger, has had to supply this last piece of reasoning: Locke nowhere says that those who would develop a waste land may justly kill or enslave those who resist. Indeed, the principle is clearer in *Utopia* than in the *Second Treatise*. Ashley preferred, where possible, to purchase land from Indians (although Haley cynically points out that this method was cheaper as well as more humane than combat).[26] It seems a reasonable surmise that Ashley and Locke wanted to think of plantations in the benign way of Bacon: "I like a Plantation in a Pure Soile; that is, where People are not Displanted, to the end, to Plant in Others." Bacon is nevertheless alert to problems of planting "where Savages are." These natives should be treated "justly and gratiously"; but even before the Virginia massacre of 1622, he advises colonists to keep "sufficient Guard."[27] Locke, coming after this massacre and consequent changes in English policy, can adjust his liberal principles to suit colonial realities. Here is a minor but revealing passage from the *First Treatise:* "A Planter in the *West Indies* ... might, if he pleased (who doubts) Muster [a personal army] ... against the *Indians*, to seek Reparation upon any Injury received from them" (130). Locke is engaged in an entirely different argument (against Filmer), but this casual illustration shows that he assumes native resistance in the waste land and that he takes for granted the justice of a developer's "resistance" to such "aggression." The wastes of Africa were less promising to the developer's eye than those of America, but the justification would have applied well enough to Africa and hence to Africans, who were of course so useful to American development. However tortured and incomplete this chain of logic, it is not simply an illusion conjured up by imaginative interpreters. Locke the opponent of slavery cannot entirely suppress Locke the Landgrave, eager to make his mark on the tabula rasa of American waste land.

Locke must have entertained complications to any *vacuus locus* model of a new world, as he did for his tabula rasa model of a new mind. In 1671 he was asked to write a description of Carolina to accompany publication of a map; although he never wrote it, he did sketch a bibliography and a list of topics, which included "Inhabitants—Number, Bodies, Abilities of Mind, Temper and Inclinations, Morality and customs, Religion, Economy."[28] His notes from reading reveal a lively curiosity about what would now be called anthropological topics, especially matters of cultural difference. He frequently cited passages about dress, habits, and rituals among peoples of the Americas, Africa, and Asia. Still, he never lost confidence in his own definition of development, embedded in reasonings about labor and property. Virtue resides in productive labor toward the replenishment of the earth, and only through this labor do people earn title to lands and goods. Such thinking, as well as his actions in support of colonial slavery, would suggest that he sympathized with the Utopians on matters of waste and development. And at least one American Puritan, a Connecticut minister, used Locke's arguments about waste land to justify the dispossession of native inhabitants.[29]

Seliger considers this line of thinking a torture rather than a fulfillment of basic liberal theories, because elsewhere Locke shows such respect for self-determination and such sympathy for the dispossessed. Theorists of the final group instead see the justification of slavery as an integral part of Lockean theory. Three very different versions of this approach can be isolated. One sees Locke as an advocate of capitalism above all other considerations; another finds in Locke's empiricism a foundation for racism; and another concludes that his justification of slavery depends upon the same assumptions as his defense of natural liberties.

The first version comes from C. B. Macpherson, Leo Strauss, and their followers. They have proposed a bourgeois Locke, whose political philosophy rationalizes capitalist appropriation. For Macpherson, the primary confusion in Locke derives from his holding two contradictory conceptions of human nature and society, both of which originate in bourgeois ideology: "A market society generates class differentiation in effective rights and rationality, yet requires for its justification a postulate of equal natural rights and rationality ... Most of Locke's theoretical conceptions, and most of his practical appeal, can be traced to this ambiguous position."[30] Strauss's Locke is more devious than Macpherson's—Strauss accuses Locke of being a crypto-Hobbesian, whose efforts to conceal unpleasant premises left a trail of inconsistencies—but his purposes are similar: "To say that public happiness requires the emancipation and the protection of the acquisitive faculties amounts to saying that to accumulate as much money and other wealth as one pleases is right or just ... Locke's followers in later generations no longer believed that they needed 'the phraseology of the law of nature' because they took for granted what Locke did not take for granted: Locke still thought that he had to prove that the unlimited acquisition of wealth is not unjust or morally wrong."[31] Macpherson's and Strauss's conclusions have been challenged over the years by a number of scholars who have charged them with neglecting evidence, misreading intention, and oversimplifying historical context. One recent challenge proposes an extreme counterversion: James Tully's Locke is egalitarian and anticapitalist. But the bourgeois theory has remained respectable. Ashcraft's recent work, which criticizes the bourgeois Locke, nevertheless upholds Macpherson's approach as substantially useful.[32] To those who believe wholly or partially in this version of Locke, his participation in slavery comes as no surprise. Protections against enslavement are less fundamental to his theory than provisions for capitalist growth.

According to a second argument, Locke's empiricism opens the door to racism and hence to an acceptance of slavery. Leon Poliakov claims that the *Essay* promoted, beneath its explicit arguments, an Enlightenment myth of white superiority.[33] H. M. Bracken is more attentive to Locke's acceptance of slavery, and he argues that Locke's theory of substance and nominal essence "has been crucial as an ideological bulwark behind which racially biased pseudo-science continues to flourish."[34] Although some scholars have defended Locke by pointing out mitigating passages from the *Essay* or contrary tendencies in the *Second Treatise*, the charge is far from being dismissed. Eugene Miller says that he "can find no basis in Locke's account of substances for criticizing someone who chooses to define the essence of man in such a way as to exclude Negroes or any other racial group."[35]

In brief, Locke's argument about nominal essence goes as follows. He admits into his empiricism the terms "substance" and "essence" to convey what might be called the inner constitution of a thing. But he wishes to revise radically the Aristotelian discourse of substance. Although real substances may be assumed to exist, we cannot know them. What we call substances are in fact abstract and variable inferences collected from particular sensory ideas. Thus we categorize things not by real substance but by nominal essence. Applied to ideas of human essence, this theory disrupts scholastic and rationalist assumptions about what constitutes a human being. We delude ourselves into believing that nature has established strict boundaries between humans and other species, but this is not so: "Wherein then, would I gladly know, consists the precise and *unmovable Boundaries of* that *Species*? 'Tis plain, if we examine, there is *no* such thing *made by Nature*, and established by her amongst Men . . . *The boundaries of the Species, whereby Men sort them, are made by Men*" (3.6.27, 37). One person's or one society's idea of human essence, therefore, may differ significantly from another's. And there is no convenient distinction between essential and accidental human properties.

Interpreters like Poliakov and Bracken see this as a foundation for racism. Bracken suggests that Locke's involvement in slavery fits easily inside such a theory. Critics of this approach have argued that in the *Second Treatise* Locke does establish—but within moral rather than epistemological discourse—identifying characteristics of a human being. Some have looked to the *Essay* for counterevidence. One reply to Bracken cites a passage in which Locke warns against taking "the measure of a Man only by his out-side" (4.4.16).[36] Neal

Wood observes that Locke's "view of natives and tribesmen was not marked by the negative attitude and anti-primitivism to be found in much contemporary and later literature on the subject."[37] These defenses certainly have merit. But they cannot remove all suspicions. In a passage about nominal essence, Locke composes the following example to clarify his argument: "[A] Child having framed the *Idea* of a *Man*, it is probable, that his *Idea* is just like that Picture, which the Painter makes of the visible Appearances joyned together; and such a Complication of *Ideas* together in his Understanding, makes up the single complex *Idea* which he calls *Man*, whereof White or Flesh-colour in *England* being one, the Child can demonstrate to you, that *a Negro is not a Man*" (4.7.16). Obviously Locke is not arguing in favor of the child's construction, which is supposed to violate the common sense of readers. But his point is to show the constructed quality of all definitions of a man and hence to entertain the validity of this one. Locke's convenient child also appears earlier in the *Essay*—"The Child certainly knows, that the *Nurse* that feeds it, is neither the *Cat* it plays with, nor the *Blackmoor* it is afraid of" (1.2.25)—as well as in Draft A: "A child unused to that sight & haveing had some such descriptions of the devil would call a Negro a devil rather then a Man & at the same time call a dryl a man."[38] Locke's choice of examples can make modern readers uneasy, especially those aware of his slavery connections. To Poliakov, they "suggest a prejudice already well rooted in English society" and compatible with Locke's empiricist theories.[39]

Because these two references decorate rather than undergird Locke's argument, strict readers will dismiss them as accidents of convention. With David Brion Davis's version of the integral approach, no casual dismissal is possible. Davis reasons from the very foundation of Locke's argument:

> It was precisely the same opening in Locke's theory of social contract that allowed both a justification of slavery and the preservation of natural rights. For in Locke's view, the origin of slavery, like the origin of liberty and property, was entirely outside the social contract. When any man, by fault or act, forfeited his life to another, he could not complain of injustice if his punishment was postponed by his being enslaved . . . [Locke] had turned the traditional Stoic and Christian conception of slavery upside down, for instead of picturing bondage as a product of sinful society, he found its origins and justification outside the limits of a free and rational society. It followed, though Locke did not press the point, that slavery was in conformity with natural law and was as universally valid as private property.[40]

In contrast with general arguments about capitalism and racism, Davis attends to the specifics of Locke's slavery for war captives. Unlike torture or deviation theorists, Davis sees this provision as a coherent part of his system. Locke wants to authorize natural, presocial individuals, whose rights and property precede social contract. With complementary reasoning he asserts that some individuals, by a willful turn against natural rights, can forever lose those natural rights. He creates a zone outside of social agreements, which acts both as the repository of natural rights and as a kind of detention area for unnatural criminals.

I would like to extend Davis's argument by looking at how Locke uses the word "common" in the *Second Treatise* to define these criminals who deserve slavery. A man may kill an aggressor or a thief "for the same Reason, that he may kill a *Wolf* or a *Lyon;* because such Men are not under the ties of the Common Law of Reason" (16). This "Common Law of Reason" defines a community of those who respect natural rights of self-preservation and property. Locke calls these rights natural, but he also calls them common; and with this word he drifts away from the absolute law of nature and toward contingent laws of specific human communities. One of the main reasons men form societies is to put themselves under a "common Judge" (19). When Locke builds his justification of slavery by turning enemies into beasts of prey, he reduces a conflict of social interests into a simple difference of natural type. Humans become beasts become slaves, by means of community judgments held up as natural.

"Common" again plays a crucial role in the waste land extension of justified slavery. As Seliger has noticed, Locke defines waste landers as people who have not "joyned with the rest of Mankind, in the consent of the Use of their common Money" (45). These are not beasts outside of common reason, then, but a new version of the outsider, undeveloped in their failure to use common money. Here the common values are more obviously conventional rather than natural. Money and other symbols of wealth, Locke explains elsewhere, "are none of Natures Goods, they have but a Phantastical imaginary value: Nature has put no such upon them" (184). The waste landers may have their "Wampompeke," but they have not joined the communal imaginings of "European silver money," with its specific codes of property, exchange value, and development.[41] Hence *"great Tracts of Ground . . . lie waste,* and are more than the People, who dwell on it, do, or can make use of, and so still lie in common" (45).

Waste land is common land, according to this logic; and it awaits the virtuous energy of European developers, who may find themselves killing, enslaving, and philosophizing in the interests of development. But earlier in Locke's discussion of property, he uses "common" with a different inflection: "'Tis very clear, that God, as King *David* says, *Psal.* cxv.16 *has given the Earth to the Children of Men,* given it to Mankind in common" (25). Here "common" implies a community of all humans, with no exclusions. Tully looks at this passage and this version of community to articulate his anticapitalist Locke. In such a community, people live as small-holders, tenants in common under God, in an egalitarian golden age.

But Tully's Locke is just one of many available to the shapers of intellectual history. The interesting trail left by "common" shows how his justification of slavery can lead back to his abhorrence of it. Perhaps one useful message to draw from all of this would be a caution against totalizing interpretations. Interpreters who wish to choose one of the three approaches—or finally to uphold or subvert a body of liberal theory—are apt to find what they look for. The same might be said of an analysis like this one, which expects indeterminacy and ends up producing a variety of competing claims to truth. Such an analysis, whatever its inherent limitations, can help to show how Locke has written himself into the histories of both slavery and abolition. His treatises, essays, constitutions, and notes are sufficient to place him but insufficient to confine him in either camp. Locke has built in too many confusions of theory and practice, too many defenses against either being caught in the act or missing the boat.

If one were tempted to improve on this valuable but frustrating message and to distinguish one approach as most useful, it would probably be a modified version of the third or integral group. The first two approaches cannot be refuted conclusively, but they tend to imply too simple a distinction between "disinterested" theory and the personal interests of John Locke. Locke's investments, friendships, and practical habits should neither be dismissed as irrelevant nor elevated above theory to a domain of privileged causes. Locke's work with slavery consists of theory interwoven with practice. It would be misleading, however, to assume that the resulting "integrated" texts should cohere under the authority of one resolute purpose or value. The integral approach will be helpful only to the extent that it recognizes within Locke's work a destabilizing competition of values. Underlying Locke's involvement in slavery is a difficult marriage of development and natural rights.

HEART-FORMED AFRICA

For Blake, there was no such conflict. He spoke out against the tyrannical moral virtue of developers in the name of the underdeveloped, the exploited, the enslaved. The freedom of Enlightenment developers depended on the slavery of an underclass: "You cannot have Liberty in this World without what you call Moral Virtue & you cannot have Moral Virtue without the Slavery of that half of the Human Race who hate what you call Moral Virtue" (*A Vision of the Last Judgment*, 564).

Blake uses the term slavery here rather broadly, but he certainly showed specific concerns about American slavery. By the time of Blake's early work, abolition had become such a common public theme that a huge number of writers had produced something on the subject. Readers were offered so many accounts of the horrors of American slavery that the accounts were in danger of becoming routine, and the readers in danger of being satirized as frivolous. In William Combe's *Devil Upon Two Sticks in England* (1790), Asmodeus points out a "genteel man reading assiduously" on the subject of Jamaican slavery. This man is no scholar, the devil notes; but he has been invited to dine with some clever people, and he wants to bone up on the most likely topic of conversation.[42] The widespread and genteel popularity of antislavery literature did not, for a number of reasons, translate into immediate political effect: although parliamentary debates over slavery were well begun by 1790, it would take nearly two decades to end the slave trade and still longer to free the slaves altogether. It is no surprise that Blake participated in the popular expression of disgust over slavery. Blake like Locke has earned a place in the history of abolition. But some fault lines also run through the antislavery texts of Blake. Certainly Blake made no investments or political associations in support of slave institutions. Nevertheless, the abolitionist meanings embedded in some of his works need to be complicated beyond their obvious antislavery virtue. The prophet works against but within an imperial culture's constructions of the African Other.

Blake must have read about slavery in quite a number of places, including works by Thomson, Young, Blair, Erasmus Darwin, and Cowper—to name just a few poets well known to Blake who contributed to antislavery literature. But his richest source of information was undoubtedly John Gabriel Stedman. Stedman went to Surinam in 1772 as part of an expeditionary force sent by the Dutch to protect plantations against runaway slaves, now organized into rebel camps. He eventually settled in England and wrote a long narrative of his five years in Surinam. Blake was one of several artists engaged by Joseph Johnson to engrave Stedman's drawings; the finished book contained sixteen plates by Blake, which he worked on from about 1790 until 1794. As Keynes discovered, Blake and Stedman became good friends.[43] Stedman's journal indicates that from 1794 through 1796, he and Blake corresponded frequently, entertained each other (Stedman sometimes staying at Blake's for visits of three days), and treated each other with casual, friendly confidence. In light of their friendship, as well as their collaboration on the *Narrative*, it is tempting to assume that Blake and Stedman held identical opinions about slavery. I think, for reasons to be offered shortly, that such an assumption is too simple. But we can safely assume that Blake had a fundamental respect for Stedman. Because the *Narrative* is commonly taken as an antislavery text that "helped to build up moral resistance to slavery,"[44] it seems to fit easily within Blake's career as a champion of human liberation. Stedman's *Narrative* is no simple antislavery text, however. In fact, although modern readers might easily understand its appeal among abolitionists—the book gives numerous lurid accounts of torture by masters and drivers, as well as familiar denunciations of European barbarism and greed (which by that time had become conventional, almost formulaic)—they would be surprised at the defenses of slavery Stedman offers and at some of the more unfortunate effects of the *Narrative*'s ethnocentrism.[45]

To begin with, Stedman's laments over European barbarism do not mean that he has forsaken the ideology of development as articulated by Locke in the *Second Treatise*. Stedman praises the richness of Surinam soil "particularly in those parts which are cultivated by European industry" (23),[46] and he often conveys the advantages of European development for both the Europeans and the people whom they have mastered. He was certainly not alone in this combination of revulsion over slavery and praise of European commercial success: Thomson and Cowper, for example, wrote enthusiastic celebrations of British commerce, as well as indictments of heartless slave merchants and masters. Stedman resolves the apparently contradictory messages of his book by defending slavery, but only as practiced by the most enlightened and humane of owners. He offers several arguments against the oversimplifications of abolitionists. To those who consider sugar and rum as grotesquely unworthy ends to justify such terrible means, he replies: "Take care, lest, under the enthusiasm of humanity, you do not, at the expence of your neighbour, and perhaps of your country, inconsiderately give up *your* advantages, without the least chance of benefiting or improving the condition of those, whom I most heartily join with you in calling our brethren" (112).

Stedman is not callous enough to let the advantages of sugar and rum stand alone against abolition. He offers a set of weightier (and fairly typical) arguments. One is the traditional legal justification cited by Locke and many others that prisoners of war may be enslaved. Stedman says that slavers do trade, though not exclusively, for prisoners of African wars. But he does not seem to regard this argument as a particularly strong one, and he passes over it quickly. Next comes a sociological approach. He has observed that some slaves are treated abominably, but others are treated with great kindness. His survey is impressionistic and suspiciously patriotic: English masters are less likely to treat slaves barbarically than are masters of other nationalities. The ethical conclusion is obvious: a sudden emancipation will simply turn slaves over to more cruel masters, serving nations who will be unable to temper their desire for sugar. Stedman's next argument, a biological one, follows from this last point about implacable European desires. "The quantum of sugar, &c. will be had, and must be provided by negroes, natives of Africa, who alone are born to endure labour under a vertical sun" (112). To supplement his biology he turns to an analysis of "national character." The displaced but free Africans have shown Stedman no "marks of civilization, order, or government ... but, on the contrary, many examples of ungovernable passion, debauchery, and indolence": they are "perfectly savage" (112–13). Stedman, of course, shows little inclination toward temperance in drinking, fighting, and sexual activity; but he does not comment on this complication. He sees only two kinds of Africans, each an extreme deviation from a human norm. At one extreme he sees the savage African, brutally violent, aggressive, ungovernable, lascivious. Hence the necessity of European intervention. Is it "possible to keep the African negroes in habits of obedience and industry without the strictest and often the severest discipline?—No" (35). Stedman worries primarily about their capacity for violence and resistance to work, both of which he construes as racial characteristics rather than political effects. He also shows some discomfort over apparent inversion of gender codes: he is slightly alarmed by women who, at various moments in the *Narrative*, make sexual advances, fight duels, smoke pipes, and win swimming races.

At the other extreme he sees blacks as helplessly virtuous—victims of their noble simplicity. This is a version of the African slave well established in sentimental antislavery literature of the eighteenth century. The "noble negro," usually of aristocratic lineage, lived in such a pure state of guileless, vulnerable innocence that he or she was defenseless before normal Europeans. They made perfect victims, well suited to a kind of literature that depended on remarkable sufferers. The noble negro has several incarnations in the *Narrative*, but most prominent is Joanna, the slave who became Stedman's lover. Joanna has all the credentials. She is "by birth a gentleman's daughter from Holland; and her mother's family were most distinguished people on the coast of Africa" (267). Her virtues make her "singular amongst her caste" (62). She suffers undeservedly, but inborn virtue leads her to stoical (but still passionate) heroism, in the form of self-sacrifice. Stedman says that he pleaded with her to let him purchase her freedom, marry her, and take her to Europe; but Joanna argued eloquently against his degrading himself, and against her elevation beyond the condition to which fate had appointed her.[47]

In addition to all her other virtues, Joanna has a physical beauty that pleases Stedman's ethnocentric taste. Stedman finds Joanna attractive to the extent that her features differ from the African and approach the European. Although her lips are "a little prominent," her nose is "perfectly well-formed" (i.e., not flat and broad); and through her cheeks "glows, in spite of the darkness of her complexion, a beautiful tinge of vermilion, when gazed upon" (52). Altogether she has "the countenance of an angel" (267). Stedman obviously has trouble appreciating the beauty of darker coloring, which he tends to see as more or less obstructive to the expression of inner light (or "freshness" or "bloom"), depending on the degree of darkness.

In a grotesque passage toward the end of the *Narrative,* Stedman implies a theory of white skin as primary. He gives a conventional theory of color as caused by climate and then adds: "The epidermis or cuticle of the negroes I have seen dissected more than once; it is clear and transparent, but between this and the real skin lies a thin follicle, which is perfectly black, which being removed by severe flagellation, or by scalding, exposes a complexion not inferior to that of a European" (358). Stedman does not notice the grotesque, repulsive effect of this scientific interlude, with its blend of torture and supercilious observation. His theory of skin follows the anatomical studies of that time, which had used dissections, chemistry, and Newton's optics to build a model of three-layered skin. Theories differed in various details, but by the 1790s a basic agreement had been reached: between the interior or "true skin," which is always white, and the outermost cuticle, which is transparent, lies a middle layer responsible for secretions that cause coloration. This model was put to liberal purposes because, in suggesting that color did not signify any essential difference among races, it tended to support a monogenetic theory of origin. But as Stedman's passage makes clear, even this three-layer model can encode a message of white primacy.

Michael Craton remarks that Blake "portrayed the tormented Surinam blacks as tinted Europeans," in a manner consistent with prevailing images of the noble savage, who was "considered as a European *philosophe* in blackface."[48] Craton's generalization needs to be corrected, although not discarded altogether. First of all, it is difficult to say how closely Blake's engravings follow Stedman's original drawings (which have not been found) and consequently how much invention to attribute to Blake. When Bartolozzi engraves a very European Joanna (plate 8), we know at least that he is following Stedman's prose image of his lover. With Blake, who did most of the human subjects, it is harder to say. Both Keynes and Essick have suggested that the plates were probably not very close copies of the Stedman drawings.[49] Still, even if we assume for Blake some inventive authority, not all of his Surinam blacks are "tinted Europeans." Blake pictures a variety of black features. Not even all of his "tormented" blacks, in the plates depicting nobility under torture, wear European features.

A few of Blake's plates, moreover, seem to complicate the messages of Stedman's prose. Plate 71 shows a black criminal being beaten and dismembered on a rack. Stedman's prose offers some "relief" to readers shocked by this "dreadful spectacle" by noting that the man was a "desperate wretch" who deserved punishment (383). But Blake's plate shows no hint of the wretch: only a dignified, Christlike sufferer. The book's final plate, an "emblematical picture" of three women representing "Europe supported by Africa & America," illustrates Stedman's hope that "they may henceforth and to all eternity be the props of each other" (435). But as Erdman has noticed, Europe is doing none of the propping in this picture, and Africa and America are wearing slave bracelets instead of pearls.[50]

In two other plates, Stedman's own image is at issue. "Flagellation of a Female Samboe Slave" (plate 35) illustrates the story of a "beautiful girl" of about eighteen, who, having refused the sexual advances of an overseer, was tied naked to a tree and severely whipped. Stedman then enters the story: "Turning to the overseer, I implored that she might be immediately unbound . . . But, to prevent all strangers from interfering with his government, he had made an unalterable rule, in that case, always to double the punishment, which he instantaneously began to put in execution: I endeavoured to stop him but in vain. Thus I had no other remedy but to run to my boat, and leave the detestable monster" (177–78). Stedman gives a virtuous account of himself, but the plate does not flatter him. He is pictured in the background and to the left of the suffering woman; in the right background stands the overseer, and behind him, two black drivers with whips. From this perspective the overseer appears puny—an effect Blake emphasizes with an averted face and blustery pointing. Stedman is also fairly small, although slightly closer to the woman. He has turned his back to her and begun his retreat. Only the woman's face remains in full view. The design makes Stedman seem something less than heroic: even with a sword at his side and against such a puny enemy he runs away from the tortured, imploring woman. His left hand covers his face, and his right arm points upward in a gesture of helpless resignation. Virtuous Stedman and monstrous overseer, as background figures flanking the sufferer, have more similarities than differences in this visual account. Stedman's story reads a little like a warning to abolitionists about the unfortunate consequences of well-meaning but naive intervention; but Blake may have been less impressed by the warning than by Stedman's weakness in the face of evil.

In "The Sculls of Lieut. Leppar, & Six of his Men" (plate 25), the plate again adds an edge to Stedman's self-portrayal. Here he leans dejectedly on his rifle, temporarily letting it point at his own head, rather than in the direction of the rebels (unlike his comrade, who points his finger and bayonet outward). The design he gave Bartolozzi for a frontispiece is somewhat similar, with a downcast Stedman standing over a fallen rebel. But the Blake plate is more interesting. Stedman's face, propped up on the rifle, adds an eighth skull to the picture: the other seven sit on top of branches made into stakes—grotesque substitutes for human bodies in the corporeal wars underwritten by European development.

Georg M. Gugelberger has recently applauded Blake's Stedman plates for their unequivocal revolutionary message: "[Blake] chose to illustrate exclusively scenes of torture and oppression. These choices signal Blake's class affiliation perhaps more than many of his literary works. There is no doubt about interpreting these etchings. Multiple interpretation has no place. The other illustrators opted for maps, pictures of flora and fauna, in short: exoticism. Blake subverts this exoticism by what the eye really sees if it is not closed by the tactics of an exploiting system."[51] In his appreciation for Blake's sensitivity to the oppressed, Gugelberger oversimplifies somewhat. Blake did not illustrate "exclusively scenes of torture and oppression." Only about half of his plates could be so classified. He depicted, among other subjects not obviously revolutionary, a happy Loango family thriving in slavery, two versions of monkeys, an aboma snake, and a group of fruits native to Surinam. Despite evidence of Blake complicating Stedman's vision, his engravings cannot be cleanly separated from the exoticism of the *Narrative*.

With Blake's Stedman, as with Locke's *Fundamental Constitutions of Carolina*, it is difficult to distinguish his authorship within a collaborative text. And even where it might be possible to separate Blake's vision from Stedman's, there remains the delicate problem of evaluating mythic enrichment against hegemonic ethnocentrism. A good test case would be plate 71, the man being executed on the rack. Blake's plate more than Stedman's prose tends to Christianize the scene. As noted above, Stedman tempers sympathy for the man by calling him a "desperate wretch": the reader will be relieved to know that this punishment was "not inflicted as a wanton and unprovoked act of cruelty, but as the extreme severity of the Surinam laws, on a desperate wretch, suffering as an example to others for complicated crimes" (383). Blake's mild, clear-eyed sufferer on the cross shows none of the irreverent toughness of Stedman's wretch. The black man doing the beating has a look of horror on his face. In one sense, of course, Blake's scene "corrects" Stedman's interpretation. Stedman, distracted by a specific set of laws surrounding a local event, has neglected the larger myth. Blake saw in the story a mythic plot of exemplary suffering. The man had been a carpenter; his crime was killing a slave overseer who had come to kill him, over a sheep taken by the carpenter as a gift to his lover. The story also contains a hint of Prometheus as well as Christ, with a vulture making regular visits to the man's remains. Blake used a similar suffering figure as a vehicle for Orc in the first plate of *America*.

Most of Blake's modern readers appreciate his mythic synthesis as a process of discovering universal patterns. But African intellectuals have become increasingly wary of the universalist perspective. As Felix Ekechi summarizes, many African writers find "something sinister lurking behind it [universalism]; hence its rejection in African literary circles. In the opinion of some, the universalist approach to, say, African literature, is but a code word for Euro-

American intellectual 'hegemonic control.'"[52] Decolonization advocates warn of "being conned into pseudo-universalism."[53] For Third World criticism, as for feminism, distinguishing the pseudouniversal from the universal becomes a subtle but politically volatile act; and it would be misleading to pretend that such acts of reading can be separated from their political and methodological presuppositions. Gugelberger, looking for a European double of a Third World writer, finds in Blake's design a message of universal class consciousness. A reader wary of universalism might see the Christian overlay as an appropriative misunderstanding of the actual event—as an example of what Mary Louise Pratt has called the "reductive normalizing" of the alien.[54] The black sufferer has been converted for use by readers sympathetic to his cause: readers who are conditioned to translate worldly suffering into spiritual benefit, both for the sufferer and for the readers themselves.

Suspicions of "intellectual hegemonic control" and "reductive normalizing" lead to provocative questions about Blake's other work associated with American slavery. To what extent does Blake's work participate, against its own best intentions, in a tradition of racial prejudice too deeply imprinted to be erased? How effectively does his work make contact with real conditions, as opposed to ethnocentric and pseudouniversal disguises?

When Blake adapts the man on the rack for *America,* he makes him white, using a code of universality that one would expect. Although the daughter of Urthona calls Orc "the image of God who dwells in darkness of Africa" (2:8), Orc's image on the plates is European. There is little to gain by questioning *America* about its exclusion of blacks—or more precisely, its assimilation of blacks into a family of exploited humanity. After all, *America* does not make African-American slavery its primary focus; and to the extent that slavery does enter the poem, it adds an enriching layer of meaning. If slavery in *America* can seem more directed at Anglo-Americans in the mill than at African-Americans in the field—"Let the slave grinding at the mill, run out into the field / Let him look up into the heavens & laugh in the bright air" (6:6–7)—its messages of bondage and liberation apply to many different versions of enslavement. The situation is somewhat different with *Visions of the Daughters of Albion*. As Erdman was the first to make clear, slavery is one of "the two poles of the poem's axis" (the other being love), with the enslavement of blacks in America particularly at issue. Despite its greater emphasis on slavery and the themes of English debate on the subject, *Visions* contains only one small design of a black figure. The poem is dominated by Oothoon, who represents all enslaved people. If Oothoon is supposed to stand for slaves, why isn't she black? The question is worth taking seriously, even if scholars accommodate the white Oothoon as a universal code. Erdman suggests that Blake has combined into one the three women of his final plate for Stedman—the emblematical design of "Europe supported by Africa and America": "Pictured in chains she [Oothoon] is the female slave, but she does not have the black skin and tight ringlets of the Africa of the emblem . . . Allowing for differences in media, Oothoon is the American Indian of the emblem, with the same loose black hair, sad mouth, and angular limbs."[55] Erdman wishfully overstates the resemblance between Oothoon and the Amerindian woman. He even qualifies his idea in two ways: sometimes Oothoon looks much more like the European woman, and in the poem she refers to herself as "snowy" white: "I am pure because the night is gone that clos'd me in its deadly black" (2:29).

As Oothoon uses imagery of black and dark with the traditionally negative associations, one wonders whether a black Oothoon ever had a chance in a poem whose very name conveys whiteness. Blake's imagery elsewhere participates in this pejorative figuration of black. He repeats Oothoon's "deadly black" several times, and he routinely associates black with pains and lapses of human spirit such as depression, anxiety, jealousy, and despair. With images of illumination and translucence counting for so much in his work, black becomes a convenient figure for antiredemptive phenomena: black means opaque, as in "opake blackening Fiend" (*Jerusalem* 7:8), and hence ignorance or spiritual debasement, whether propagated by spectres, churches, or antichrists. When the Little Black Boy regrets his black color at the beginning of that poem, he can be pitied as a victim of symbolic conventions; and as he attempts to revise the traditional associations of white with spiritual privilege, he more effectively upholds them. Elsewhere, a few passages subtly imply, as in Stedman's *Narrative*, that white is the primary human color. The Chimney Sweeper of Experience has turned black as a result of damage to his white body. In *The Song of Los*, "black grew the sunny African" (3:10) during a traumatic fall into abstraction.

As they address the subject of Africa and Africans, Blakean voices tend to conform to distorting stereotypes of British eighteenth-century convention.[56] In *America*, when the daughter of Urthona calls Orc "the image of God who dwells in darkness of Africa," she participates in a well-established tradition of imagery. Africa as the dark continent, Philip Curtin observes, can be taken both as "an expression of geographical ignorance" (even though the British actually knew a great deal about the geography of coastal Africa) and of "cultural arrogance."[57] Orc's association with Africa fits into a conventional view of Africans as ruled by elemental emotions. Stedman's Africans were either gently, helplessly loving or passionately violent. When Blake refers to "heart-formed Africa" (*The Song of Los* 3:3), he probably refers not only to geographical shape but to a continental character, thus reinforcing European convention by giving to Africa Orc's territory of the heart.

Orc is also associated with heat, now separated from Urizen's light. With this state of separation Blake delivers a version of Milton's Hell, where flames give off heat but no light. Blake in one passage identifies "the desarts of Africa" as the place of "the Fallen Angels" (*The Song of Los* 4:20). Blake's work thus hints at an image of Africa and Africans that is expressed more fully in the poetry of others. A good place to look for developing poetic conventions about Africa is Thomson's "Summer" from *The Seasons,* a work with which Blake was undoubtedly acquainted. Sypher calls Thomson "the earliest poet of pseudo-Africa."[58] In "Summer" he conjures up the passionate Africans; and despite a sentimental tenderness he feels for them, he also focuses on their pointedly un-British ignorance and brutality:

> Ill-fated Race! the softening Arts of Peace,
> Whate'er the humanizing Muses teach;
> The godlike Wisdom of the temper'd Breast;
> Progressive Truth, the patient Force of Thought;
> Investigation calm, whose silent Powers
> Command the World; the LIGHT that leads to HEAVEN;
> Kind equal Rule, the Government of Laws,
> And all-protecting FREEDOM, which alone
> Sustains the Name and Dignity of Man:
> These are not theirs. The Parent-Sun himself
> Seems o'er this World of Slaves to tyrannize;
> And, with oppressive Ray, the roseat Bloom
> Of Beauty blasting, gives the gloomy Hue,
> And Feature gross: or worse, to ruthless Deeds,
> Mad Jealousy, blind Rage, and fell Revenge,
> Their fervid Spirit fires.[59]

Like fallen angels, Africans have heat but no light. They commit satanic transgressions of "Mad Jealousy" and "fell Revenge," motivated by what he later calls "selfish fierce Desire" and "the wild Fury of voluptuous Sense." Although "Summer" includes antislavery sentiments, Thomson imagines the Africans to be pre-enslaved, as it were, by a tyrannical "Parent-Sun." "Europe's cruel Sons" have not, therefore, altered the essential African state, although they have in some cases aggravated the conditions of their natural enslavement. Thomson thereby positions himself for a typical double attitude: he criticizes the cruelties of the slave trade at the same time he celebrates the "HEAV'N-inspired" commercial genius of his nation.

Pseudo-Africans of the eighteenth century, for all the deprivations caused by absence of light (which damages physical features as well as character), have genuine souls. The Little Black Boy is following a popular tradition when he takes comfort in a white soul beneath his black skin. If anatomists can offer only a white "true skin" underneath the black surface, theologians, metaphysicians, and poets offer something more. Swedenborg, for example, praises Africans as the most spiritual of heathens.[60] A popular poem by Day and Bicknell (1773) illustrates the sentiment upon which the Little Black Boy draws:

> What tho' no rosy tints adorn their face
> No silken ringlets shine with flowing grace?
> Yet of etherial temper are their souls . . .

Historian Philip Curtin quotes the first four lines of "The Little Black Boy" and concludes that "even so Christian and humanitarian a poet as William Blake could couple a belief in spiritual equality with pejorative reference to the dark skin of the Africans."[61] Literary scholars, more attentive to dramatic context, are less likely to identify the Little Black Boy's voice with Blake's. Blake's conventional figurations of black and dark, however insensitive they may now seem, cannot be construed as a low opinion of the black race. One brief passage from "A Song of Liberty," however, might trouble some readers: "O African! black African! (go. winged thought widen his forehead)" (44). Taken by itself, this hints at some degree of participation in contemporary theories of restricted black mental capacity. This passage has not attracted any attention, no doubt because of its context: Blake begins by urging Londoners to "Look up! look up! . . . enlarge thy countenance"; so that his appeal for expansion goes out not just to blacks. Still, "widen his forehead" gives a more specific physical reference than "enlarge thy countenance." Both forehead and countenance suggest a physiognomic subtext at work here. Blake did some engraving work for an English edition of Lavater's *Essays on Physiognomy;* and various remarks elsewhere suggest Blake's interest in this version of eighteenth-century semiotics, so hospitable to painters. His call to widen African foreheads fits easily within the speculative physiognomy of the eighteenth century, which was gradually turning toward a more "scientific" phrenology.

According to Lavater, "How different are foreheads . . . and how expressive may these differences be! I imagine nature cannot speak more decisively, in the skull, alone, or in any part of the skull, than she does here." When Lavater mentions African foreheads, he urges a realistic assessment of black intellect. Ethiopian foreheads, "high and narrow," have inherent limitations. "What care of education can arch the skull of a negro like that of a star-conversant astronomer?" In another section, Lavater cautions a liberal enthusiast: "Why not the soul of Newton in the head of a negro? Why not an angel mind in a fiendlike form? . . . We do not speak here of what God can do, but of what is to be expected, from the knowledge we have of his works. Could the mind of Newton have invented the theory of light, residing in the head of a negro?"[62]

Blake was influenced by physiognomy but did not restrict human freedom so simply. His is a song of liberty, and he calls for thought to widen the African forehead. In this sense he shares more with the new phrenology than the old physiognomy. Phrenology, as pioneered by Gall and developed by various eighteenth-century followers, substituted biomechanics for semiotics. It explained head shape as the result of mechanistic causes. The act of thinking physically shaped the head, at least to some extent. As Samuel S. Smith summarizes, "The brain . . . will, by its dilatations and contractions, contribute, in some degree, to mould the interior cavity in which it is embraced . . . The accumulated result of an infinite number of the slightest touches becomes very perceptible in a long course of time."[63] In this system, therefore, a gift of thought can actually widen a forehead. But there are limits to such renovations. Smith says that African heads begin with a natural disadvantage: because their foreheads are not as broad, their mental "freedom" is restricted, so that one should expect from them a "paucity of ideas." Once again, as with Thomson's tyrant sun, Africans are seen to be pre-enslaved by natural conditions, before any interventions of imperial development.

It would be grossly misleading to align Blake with the pre-enslaving ideologies of empire. The evidence presented in this discussion cannot support anything like a radical revision of his antislavery reputation. Evidence does suggest, however, that Blake's vision of human liberation does not enable him to challenge ethnocentric systems as effectively as one could hope. Instead of reimagining the conventions of pseudo-Africa and Africans, his works tend to slide away from a specific focus on American slavery in pursuit of a universal myth of liberation. This becomes, rather peculiarly, the poetic counterpart of abolition's greatest political problem: the linkage of the antislavery movement with a host of other radical causes. Supporters of slavery were eager to package abolition with Jacobinism, opposition to all private property, and leveling theories of many varieties, so that black slavery became just one part of a conglomerate political idea. The more black slavery became incorporated into a total discourse, the less an antiabolitionist had to worry about antislavery sentimentality being translated into political and economic effects.

The poetic version of this process can be glimpsed in Wordsworth as well as in Blake. When Wordsworth returned to England in 1792, he noticed how enthusiastically the public had roused itself against slavery; but his own feelings on the subject were muted:

> For me that strife had ne'er
> Fastened on my affections, nor did now
> Its unsuccessful issue much excite
> My sorrow, having laid this faith to heart,
> That if France prospered good men would not long

Pay fruitless worship to humanity,
And this most rotten branch of human shame
(Object, as seemed, of superfluous pains)
Would fall together with its parent tree.

Characteristically, Wordsworth turns a diminution or absence of feeling toward some greater power. Here, the diminished feelings come from his commitment to a total alteration of human spirit, to a grand theory that dwarfs the particular cause of "traffickers in Negro blood." With Blake, at about the same time, an antislavery poem like *Visions of the Daughters of Albion* incorporates so many themes of liberation that the specific problems of black slaves in America become absorbed. Slavery in *Visions* merges with several radical themes, such as the manipulation and subordination of women, the oppression of the English working class, and the neuroses of tyranny.[64] My point here is not to demean Blake's synthesis as superficial or illusory but to place it within a context of similarly enthusiastic but distracted antislavery discourse. When Locke, a century earlier, condemned slavery as a "vile and miserable Estate of Man," he used "slavery" in such a general, figurative sense that he could simultaneously outlaw it and include it within the political systems of his Enlightenment. When Blake slides away from the minute particulars of black slavery and reaches toward universal synthesis, he may diminish his chances of altering received opinion on this subject.

Blake's one poem which focuses specifically on a black subject, "The Little Black Boy," provides an interesting example of this process of sliding. The poem seems to originate in a reflection on discrimination against blacks, but it becomes a poem about all bodies and souls. Interpreters have taken three basic approaches to the poem. I want to conclude this discussion by examining the three briefly, but in enough detail to establish a loose parallel with the three approaches to Locke and slavery.

In the first approach, "The Little Black Boy" is primarily a poem about the flaws of dualistic perception. This approach was nurtured within the methods of New Criticism, with its sensitivity to dramatic context, its penchant for irony, and its displacements of intention and historical context. The boy is attempting to think his way out of an imprinted feeling of inferiority. His mother comforts him with a well-meaning, but much too simple, symbolic explanation of racial difference; the boy then adds something of his own, but the lesson remains crippled by dualism. This first approach is loosely comparable to the first or deviation approach to Locke and slavery. "The Little Black Boy" appears to offer a sentimental and otherworldly solution to the problems of racial difference, but this solution so clearly deviates from Blake's own position that the poem must be out to subvert the adequacy of its speaker's formulations.

Howard Hinkel typifies the first approach when he says that the boy "has subscribed to a doctrine of salvation which the poet rejects."[65] The boy and his mother fall into a Urizenic trap by treating contraries as opposites. Interpreters variously emphasize the dualistic themes of body and soul, human and divine, present and hereafter, literal/natural and figurative/spiritual; but in each case, complications within the poem's imagery show the poet's distance from his speaker, who does not recognize the inadequacies of his dualistic perception. For example, take the theme of body and soul. The boy and his mother depend on the comfort of a soul entirely separable from the body. Souls are all white and will soon enough be freed from bodily containment. But the boy also imagines a function for his (now white? or still black?) body in heaven. The boy's color in heaven differs from copy to copy. Several versions of the second plate show the black boy turned white in heaven. Others show him still dark or somewhere in between.[66] Interpreters of the first group might explain the variation—although I have not seen this question addressed—as further indication of the boy's confusion about body and soul. He is only able to alternate between a body-reading and a soul-reading of his situation, each of them inadequate to the true complexity of contraries.

This first approach, then, recognizes the problems inherent in the thematic slide of "The Little Black Boy"—from a specific question about race and social relations to universal metaphysical abstractions. But because Blake's own opinion is nothing like the boy's, this slide toward transcendence does not implicate the poet in a tacit cooperation with ideologies of empire. A second approach is not as confident that it can isolate a stable, integral meaning for the poem or penetrate to the poet's underlying opinion. Thus it resembles, if only in this limited sense, the second approach to Locke: those interpreters were not as confident in the integrity of Lockean theory.

I am depending on Myra Glazer's reading for this second approach.[67] Glazer carefully differentiates her approach from the established antidualism. The poem is not "about a misguided lesson, nor is it ironic"; these are effects more or less dictated by New Critical method. Her own method follows Mitchell's theory of Blake's composite art. The poem becomes primarily "a dramatization of the process, intricate and involved, by which symbolic form comes into being." It "neither validates, nor actually portrays a dualistic reality, but rather creates an artistic expression before which dualisms falter." Glazer's method might be described as a conservative version of poststructuralism. She works with two fairly stable texts—the poem as it appears in copy B of *Songs of Innocence* and in copy Z of *Songs of Innocence and of Experience*; but with her emphasis on "intricate process" and an "artistic expression" hard to reduce, she introduces elements of instability and multiplicity to the older readings.[68]

As Glazer reads the two poem-design composites, she finds not a single author and message but a double set of messages, both of them fertile with complexities. Copy B presents the boy and mother enclosed within a protective, gentle nature (signified by the paler, milder sun of the first plate); copy Z shows a much more powerful sun, hence a more threatening natural environment, something to be overcome by exertions of spirit. B emphasizes the "beams of love" emanating from the mother, whose presence seems so important and benevolent within the gentler shade of this copy; Z emphasizes the more awful beams of divine love, conveyed by the powerful sun/son of the design. (The sun in the first plate carries over to the halo over the son of God in the second plate. B has the milder sun and no halo.) In B the mother's lesson becomes a valuable rite of passage from the natural to the spiritual world, and God's love becomes "a metamorphosis of mother-love, not in conflict with it." In Z the boy is "less tied to the mother of his mortal part": the mother, "seeking to protect, yet by that very act keeping us from the divine (which itself thereby becomes more searing, more remote), prepares us not for a God of Love, but for a God who embodies yet surpasses all conflicting human desires." Although Glazer's B more than Z conveys positive associations for the color black (mainly because of the gentle sun and shade), the black boy in both copies turns just as white as the English boy in the heaven of the second plate. Here Glazer might have acknowledged the differences in the black boy's color from copy to copy: it varies, as noted above, from white to black. This would disturb the symmetry of difference in her reading, because B and Z share the white version. A more radical poststructuralist could use the color variations to destabilize even further the poem's and Blake's positioning on race.

A third approach to the poem is much less sophisticated. It has, in fact, only a ghostly presence in recent readings of "The Little Black Boy." This approach takes the poem as primarily a contribution to antislavery literature and as Blake's answer to the problem of racial prejudice. This approach appears outdated in its interpretive methods: it does not respect the difference between Blake's voice and the voice of his characters, and it relies on a prefabricated historical context to determine the poem's meaning. Prefabricated or not, the historical context looms large enough that sophisticated readers still nod in its direction, usually as they announce another focus and a richer network of themes. Geoffrey Keynes conveys with his qualifiers this move away from the antislavery poem: "The poem probably was to some extent inspired by contemporary indignation against slavery and the supposed inferiority of black races, but it also teaches that the creation of the world was an act of divine mercy, by which man might become accustomed to endure the heat of divine love."[69] Keynes apparently sympathizes with unsophisticated assumptions about Blakean voice and meaning; but he carries enough sophistication to deemphasize the antislavery element. Hazard Adams elevates his New Critical first approach above an unsophisticated third approach: "Van Doren's assumption that Blake is trying to prove both boys 'equal under the skin' is somewhat off the point. Blake probably does believe this, but the poem is primarily concerned with exploring a particular state of mind."[70]

The third approach, to put it briefly, treats "The Little Black Boy" as Blake's wholehearted effort to counteract racial prejudice with an assertion of equality. Like the third approach to Locke, it recognizes no separation between the "authentic" voice of the author and an imposter. By calling it unsophisticated I do not mean to assign it to less perceptive readers, but only to place it within a different interpretive community. Coleridge's reading, after all, belongs in this third group: he gave "The Little Black Boy" higher praise than any of the other *Songs*, with a gushing enthusiasm probably not due to ironic discrepancies and subtle contradictions within the poem.[71] Among readers nurtured in New Critical times, Erdman is one of the few who show no embarrassment in making straightforward antislavery links: "'The Little Black Boy' assists the philanthropic agitation of the Society for Effecting the Abolition of the Slave Trade, which was formed in 1787."[72]

It is possible, however, within the third approach to criticize as well as to praise Blake for his poem's racial implications. Recall the unsophisticated reading of Philip Curtin: "even so Christian and humanitarian a poet as William Blake could couple a belief in spiritual equality with pejorative reference to the dark skin of the Africans." I cannot, after conducting this discussion of Blake and slavery, dismiss Curtin's unsophisticated remark quite as comfortably as I could before. Let me return to a piece of evidence from "The Little Black Boy" to which I have referred in explaining both the first and the second approaches: the varying color of the boy when he joins God and the English boy in the second plate. An interpreter of the third group might see this variation of color as supporting Blake's message of equality. Here, for example, is Erdman's comment, from *The Illuminated Blake:* "The black boy is as light of skin as the English boy in some copies, quite black in others—different ways of making the same points" (51). Erdman is presumably suggesting something like the following: Blake changes the boy's skin color from copy to copy to emphasize that only the soul really counts, not the body. Bodies are like clouds, the boy says in the second plate, whether they are white or black. But only the black boy's color varies. Why doesn't the English boy become black in some of the copies? To answer this question, one can examine the relevant traditions of ethnocentrism and look at the poem—where the black boy knows that souls and angels are white and that God is best conveyed by images of light. If "The Little Black Boy" is taken (by third group interpreters) as Blake's antislavery, proequality message, other third group readers might plausibly complain that he has collaborated with the forces of European cultural hegemony; albeit against his vigorous anti-imperial intentions. The little black boy is actually enslaved by the universalist transcendence designed to liberate him.

I will not conclude by embracing or rejecting the unsophisticated third approach. As in the analysis of Locke, I want to grant the three approaches some measure of validity and suggest that it may be worthwhile to suspend a resolving evaluation. Blake much more than Locke has written himself into a history of resistance to empire. But in the matter of slaves and slavery, the prophet against empire was not able to expunge imperial designs as well as one might have hoped.

Chapter 5

Seditious Plots

The most obvious biographical parallel between Locke's life and Blake's is that both were accused of sedition. The law that both allegedly broke—subverting public confidence in the king—was defined essentially the same way in 1685 and in 1803, despite the political changes that the intervening century produced. Blake, of course, was challenging the curtailed monarchy put into place by Locke et al. in the seditious success of the Glorious Revolution. Given the operative definitions of the crime, both men were guilty; but both found ways to maintain their innocence, and neither was convicted. Full details of the two cases will never be known. Locke went into exile and successfully kept much of his activity secret. Blake was not ordinarily very good at keeping things secret, but in this case he made a much better effort. If Blake's case was nothing of particular importance for the larger society—merely a local incident involving an eccentric artist—his trial raised issues of law and innocence that deserve comparison with Locke's more influential political activities and writings.

Who Shall Be Judge?

Unlike Blake, Locke was never formally indicted and brought to trial for sedition. But his name was included on a 1685 list of treasonous or seditious radicals whom the king wanted to have arrested and extradited from Holland, where they were living in exile. Charles Middleton, one of James II's under secretaries of state, sent a list to the English envoy in Holland, Bevil Skelton. This first list did not include Locke's name, but Skelton was asked to add any names that might have been inadvertently omitted. He added Locke, among others. Some scholars have assumed that the accusation was a flimsy one and merely the work of Skelton. But as Richard Ashcraft points out, Middleton sent a second list of names before he had received Skelton's addendum, and apparently this raised to that degree," were it not for the leniency of the court. One of the two writings for which he was convicted expressed many opinions similar to those in Locke's *Two Treatises*. For example, he says that a king "is made and ordained for the defence or guardianship of the law of his subjects, and of their bodies and goods, whereunto he receiveth power of his people, so that he cannot govern his people by any other power."[3] The official information against Johnson declared that he "maliciously and designedly published two pernicious, scandalous and seditious libels, to raise and stir up sedition and rebellion in his Majesty's liege subjects." The government produced a few informants and a handwriting sample to make their case. Johnson tried two tactics in his defense—both of which Locke might also have tried. First, he "hoped, that seeing he was indicted for a seditious and scandalous libel, the jury would consider whether those papers they had heard read, were so or no?" But the court made clear that the jury must only consider "the matter of fact" whether he was the author of the writings, which the court had already deemed seditious libel. Then Johnson pointed out that his manuscript had been discovered in a box nailed shut, which showed that it was not intended for publication. (Locke had kept his work manuscript similarly private.) But this defense was ineffective: the 1661 act had outlawed writing as well as printing. The jury stayed out only fifteen minutes before bringing their verdict of guilty. Johnson received the following punishment: "To pay 500 marks to the King, and to lie in prison till it was paid; to stand three times in the pillory; on the Monday following, in the Palace-Yard, Westminster; on Wednesday, at Charing-Cross; and the Monday after at the Royal-Exchange; and to be whipt by the common hangman from Newgate to Tyburn."[4]

We can only speculate that Locke's trial and punishment might have been similar. Perhaps his poor health might have led the court to minimize the whipping; Samuel Johnson, we are told, "had a quick sense of every stripe which was given him, with a whip of nine cords knotted, to the number of 317." After 1688, Johnson was pardoned and compensated for the injustice done him. But the 1686 verdict was technically just, given the Restoration legal context.

Had Locke actually been indicted and tried, the charge would have been sedition at the least, and the king's prosecutor might have tried to prove high treason. The charge of treason could have had to do with Locke's possible connections to the Rye House conspiracy or with his role in Monmouth's Rebellion. It is hard to say what success the prosecutors might have had in proving these charges, given the doubtful evidence surrounding these two Whig attempts against the crown.

The Rye House conspiracy refers to an unsuccessful plot of 1682–83 to assassinate Charles II and his brother James. Apparently this attempt was linked with plans for a general uprising against the Stuart government. Because the victorious Whigs were writing history after 1688, they were inclined to dismiss Rye House as a government exaggeration, provocation, or outright fabrication. More disinterested historians have had trouble establishing solid facts. Much evidence has been destroyed. Even the available evidence is hard to evaluate: when it comes from official informants it cannot be trusted, and alleged participants communicated in code to protect themselves.

Until fairly recently, historians and biographers had refused to believe that Locke was involved in any serious way with the alleged Rye House conspiracy. Macaulay wrote that Locke's temperament as a philosopher "preserved him from the violence of a partisan."[5] Fox Bourne went to great lengths to protect Locke's innocence, selecting and perhaps even inventing evidence. Cranston corrected Fox Bourne's distortions with a much better informed (but still fairly cautious) account of Locke's involvement in radical activities against the crown: Locke was not as active and dangerous as his government enemies suspected, but neither was he the scrupulous innocent portrayed by Fox Bourne et al. More recently, Ashcraft has presented a strong case for an activist Locke, substantially involved in the important plots and councils against the king. Ashcraft traces Locke's involvement with a network of radicals, including several "dangerous" friends with whom he stayed in contact while in exile, despite his claims to the contrary. The case for Locke's activism is rarely straightforward because he was so adept at covering his tracks. He destroyed most of his relevant letters. Those few that remain seem innocent unless they are translated, as Ashcraft thinks they should be, from their disguised "canting" language into secret political meanings. Locke, like other radicals, may have encrypted his references to plots with metaphors of gardening, medicine, business, and so forth. Ashcraft's case is engaging and plausible, if not airtight. Locke had a wonderful poker face and made himself hard to read. This is a condition that scholars have learned to live with, just as the king's spies did in the 1680s. Humphrey Prideaux, assigned to watch Locke at Oxford, reported that "John Locke lives a very cunning unintelligible life here."[6]

In the case of Monmouth's Rebellion, the basic facts are not as much in dispute as with the Rye House conspiracy, but Locke's participation is no clearer. The Duke of Monmouth, the King's illegitimate son, led an invasion of western England in 1685 that failed miserably. He was executed and his supporters were severely punished. Depositions by two plea bargainers mentioned that "Mr. Lock(e)" (spelled differently in the two depositions) contributed about one thousand pounds to the cause. Once again, Locke's biographers have gradually come to take the charge more seriously. Fox Bourne, who knew the account of only one deponent, considered it a contemptible fabrication. Cranston looked at both depositions and found them credible; but he argues that the "Mr. Lock(e)" to whom they refer was probably a different man, a tobacconist named Nicholas Lock. Part of his reasoning has to do with John Locke's tightness with money. Cranston can "readily imagine [Locke's] taking part in the deliberations which led to the rebellion," but "I should not have expected the philosopher to give money to the rebel funds: he was not a giving man."[7] Ashcraft dislikes this argument ad hominem and doubts the tobacconist theory. After tracking financial transactions as carefully as possible, he concludes that, of the two Locks, John was more likely to have been a major contributor than Nicholas.

If conclusions about Locke's political activities in the 1680s must remain somewhat speculative, Ashcraft's account is more thickly documented and persuasive than Fox Bourne's. Locke was possibly treasonous and certainly seditious. The best evidence we have for sedition, of course, is the *Second Treatise*. Even with the evidence in plain sight, the case of Locke's sedition has a number of complications. Most relevant for this discussion are those concerning law and innocence.

The *Second Treatise* puts kings in jeopardy. Here Locke and Blake share a seditious cause, however different their seditious styles. Blake's sedition was much more blunt than Locke's—he allegedly said "Damn the King" as he shoved a soldier from his garden—and at the same time more abstruse: much of his political criticism is expressed in densely allusive, polysemous narratives that need an alert commentator like David Erdman to recover their political sting. Locke held his poker face, nimbly avoided confrontation, and eventually published a (formerly) seditious treatise that was received as common sense. Locke's common sense was successful enough to help redefine what law means, for his time and beyond. But his discussion of law in the *Second Treatise* is not as simple or stable as his seditious common sense makes it appear.

Four versions of law can be detected in the *Second Treatise*, although Locke does not always acknowledge the differences among them.[8] These variations in his ideas about law complicate his argument, especially in passages where distinctions blur. The first two versions are God's law and the law of nature. They are not identical, but both are versions of absolute law, promising a foundational, universal justice. A third can be called positive law: these are the laws of commonwealths to be upheld by governors. The fourth (and least obvious within the explicit argument) is not named in the *Second Treatise*, but it might be called willful law. In a simple analysis, these four versions can be arranged on a ladder from highest to lowest—God's law, law of nature, positive law, willful law—with the highest carrying the greatest authority and the most orderly, desirable regulation of human behavior, and the lower stages gradually slipping toward doubt and instability.

At the beginning of the *Second Treatise* Locke emphasizes the second stage, the law of nature. He summons the law of nature to provide a foundation for the important arguments to come. The law of nature must not be confused with "natural laws." The plural refers to a constantly changing and expanding set of causal relations articulated by empirical science; in the last two centuries this term has effectively eclipsed the other, singular term. In Locke's time the two were about equally in circulation, although the "laws" had already begun to push aside the "law." The law of nature is deductive and prescriptive, as opposed to the a posteriori inductions that bring forth the laws of nature. For Locke the law of nature is discovered through the proper use of reason. Once it is found and clearly articulated, it becomes the measure of all "laws of countries, which are only so far right as they are founded on the law of nature, by which they are to be regulated and interpreted" (12). At this point, the distinction between the law of nature and the positive law of commonwealths is clear: the former is a paradigm to which the latter struggles to conform.

Early in the *Second Treatise,* Locke wants to describe the original or natural human state as a starting point for his theories of political power. Underlying this "state of nature" is the law of nature: men began in "a state of perfect freedom to order their actions and dispose of their possessions and persons as they think fit, within the bounds of the law of nature, without asking leave or depending upon the will of any other man" (4). He then needs to define more precisely these "bounds" of the law of nature:

> But though this be a state of liberty, yet it is not a state of license; though man in that state have an uncontrollable liberty to dispose of his person or possessions, yet he has not liberty to destroy himself, or so much as any creature in his possession, but where some nobler use than its bare preservation calls for it. The state of nature has a law of nature to govern it, which obliges every one; and reason, which is that law, teaches all mankind who will but consult it that, being all equal and independent, no one ought to harm another in his life, health, liberty, or possessions; for men being all the workmanship of one omnipotent and infinitely wise Maker—all the servants of one sovereign master, sent into the world by his order, and about his business—they are his property whose workmanship they are, made to last during his, not one another's, pleasure; and being furnished with like faculties, sharing all in one community of nature, there cannot be supposed any such subordination among us that may authorize us to destroy another, as if we were made for one another's uses as the inferior ranks of creatures are for ours. Every one, as he is

bound to preserve himself and not to quit his station wilfully, so by the like reason, when his own preservation comes not in competition, ought he, as much as he can, to preserve the rest of mankind, and may not, unless it be to do justice to an offender, take away or impair the life, or what tends to the preservation of the life, the liberty, health, limb, or goods of another. (6)

This influential account of the law of nature suffices for Locke's purposes. But the passage is open to many complications. Most notably, there are difficulties with his assertion of equality. He first posits equality as a consequence of God's labor-based property rights. Because God made us, we belong to him; we do not own ourselves and cannot dispose of ourselves with the rights of an owner. Locke can make the argument for equality only by positing an original hierarchy: in effect, we are all equally inferior to our "sovereign master." The argument has an old-fashioned feel to it, with its rebuke of human pretension and its a priori, almost catechismal logic. Perhaps Locke is not entirely satisfied with this sort of argument, because he supplies a second one: we are equal because we are "furnished with like faculties." He says no more about this matter (in the *Second Treatise*, that is; the *Essay* and various informal writings will have more to say, not all of it supportive of equality), but he has now introduced a very different sort of argument from the first one. This second foundation for equality suggests a thesis that should be investigated not by moral but by natural philosophers. As we have seen in "Slavery," some recent philosophers blame Locke's empirical methods and his theory of nominal essence for providing a foundation for "scientific" Western racism. This criticism is drawn from the *Essay* rather than the political writings. But in the quoted passage the *Essay* leaks into the *Treatise* and slightly alters it.

Even if we ignore this complication and concentrate on his (apparently) straightforward thesis, the argument remains unstable. Let us assume that when he refers to "faculties" he means nothing more than a fundamental ability to reason. The passage still shows a tension between two different kinds of thinking. On the one hand he seems to hypostatize an essential, unitary faculty (reason), using a philosophical style similar to older scholastics and rationalists and to his Scottish antagonists of the next century. This kind of thinking makes possible a fairly simple definition of equality. On the other hand, he articulates a hierarchy among God's creatures with an implication that greater or lesser value may be distributed according to some proto-Darwinian scheme of competitive success. At first he evokes a peaceable kingdom where "man . . . has not liberty to destroy himself, or so much as any creature in his possession." If this sounds like the start of an argument to check anthrocentrism, he quickly changes course: another creature may be destroyed "where some nobler use than its bare preservation calls for it." His use of "noble" is vague, but it implies some as yet unspecified hierarchy of value among creatures. Because Locke wants to preserve his premise of human equality, he rejects "any such subordination among us that may authorize us to destroy another, as if we were made for each other's uses as the inferior creatures are for ours." His logic rests comfortably within the chain of being, with humans superior to animals but equal among themselves.

The new complication arises with the threat of competition among equals: a person cannot destroy another as long as "his own preservation comes not in competition." The argument is sliding now to accommodate a more Hobbesian or Darwinian world. Locke wants to bring closure to this dangerous line of thought by identifying such competitors as "offenders." As he later elaborates, these offenders are thieves or aggressors who have abandoned the "common law of reason"—i.e., the law of nature as articulated by Locke—and may be killed "for the same reason that [one] may kill a wolf or a lion" (16). In other words, they have lost their status as humans and become "beasts of prey" (16), among the ranks of God's inferior creatures. Locke doesn't worry here about the possibility of rational motivation for theft or a principled redefinition of property and ownership. Nor does he engage, as he does elsewhere, the biochemistry and neurology of aberrant behaviors. He assumes that any competition can be sorted out into a guilty and an innocent party. The act of sorting amounts to reason, which gives us the law of nature, which protects all reasonable people. The argument has a smug self-containment of the sort that made Blake loathe the words "reason" and "nature" all his productive life.

Blake disputed the Enlightenment use of reason as a foundational faculty. Reason, and the law of nature it supposedly produces, can create nothing by itself: "This is shewn in the Gospel, where he prays to the Father to send the comforter or Desire that Reason may have Ideas to build on" (*Marriage of Heaven and Hell*, 35). Locke never lost faith in "the law of nature ... and reason, which is that law" (6), but at best one can say that he always promised more than he delivered toward an articulation of natural law. This is true of his early thinking about natural law and it is certainly true of the *Second Treatise*.[9] The law of nature is curiously present and absent, essential and impossible. He begins with its principle of self-preservation, and he indicates that all laws and public policies would derive from a fully articulated law of nature. But he defers this obviously crucial task: "for though it would be beside my present purpose to enter here into the particulars of the law of nature, or its measures of punishment, yet it is certain there is such a law" (12).

At an interesting moment in these early sections of the text, Locke turns away from the law of nature to God's law—the second version of absolute law present in the *Second Treatise*. He has been addressing the general question of how to determine who is innocent and who guilty in a conflict. Where there is no common secular authority, the only appeal is to heaven. He cites the biblical example of Jephthah:

> 'The Lord the Judge,' says he, 'be judge this day between the children of Israel and the children of Ammon' (Judges xi. 27), and then prosecuting and relying on his appeal, he leads out his army to battle. And, therefore, in such controversies where the question is put, 'Who shall be judge?' it cannot be meant, 'who shall decide the controversy'; every one knows what Jephthah here tells us, that 'the Lord the Judge' shall judge. Where there is no judge on earth, the appeal lies to God in heaven. That question then cannot mean: who shall judge whether another has put himself in a state of war with me, and whether I may, as Jephthah did, appeal to heaven in it? Of that I myself can only be judge in my own conscience, as I will answer it, at the great day, to the supreme Judge of all men. (21)

His biblical example conveys a message more or less opposite to that of Job: with Jephthah, secular justice is expected to follow as a consequence of righteousness. The very fact that Locke relies on biblical material—as he does from time to time in the *Second Treatise*—suggests that inspired revelation may be more important than naked reason. Locke acknowledged the primary authority of revelation, although he set up reason (and the law of nature) as a parallel authority. In this Jephthah passage, he seems to expose a hint of doubt about law of nature. The last sentence is most telling. He slips from his simple confidence in natural law, "intelligible and plain" to any "rational creature," and invokes private conscience, with a rhetorical flourish that heightens the ominous effect: "as I will answer it, at the great day, to the supreme Judge of all men." When Locke is most confident in his premises, he implies that God's law and the law of nature are effectively identical. In the Jephthah passage above—which he reprises at the end of the *Second Treatise*—he leaves room for doubt. God's judgment of Locke's law cannot quite be taken for granted.

Locke elsewhere distinguishes between the law of nature and the positive law of commonwealths. The law of nature should be "intelligible and plain" to a rational person, plainer than "the positive laws of commonwealths": "reason is easier to be understood than the fancies and intricate contrivances of men, following contrary and hidden interests put into words; for so truly are a great part of the municipal laws of countries, which are only so far right as they are founded on the law of nature, by which they are to be regulated and interpreted" (12).

This passage serves to introduce both the third and the fourth versions of *Second Treatise* law. The laws enacted and executed by proper governments should ideally conform to the law of nature. Governments will vary in how closely they approximate this ideal; the passage above implies that most do not come very close. Positive laws have already been "put into words," and the law of nature, at least in the *Second Treatise*, goes almost without saying. It has a kind of Platonic purity that resists mundane articulation.[10] When he writes about the actual laws of commonwealths, Locke sometimes considers them respectfully, even deferentially. He suggests that positive law ought to be obeyed as a stable, coherent authority. In other moments he characterizes such laws as willful products of defective governing. They show the marks of "fancies," "interests," "desires" (all code words for this fourth and lowest version of law); they are incoherent, fragmented, chaotic. Willful law deserves sedition more than obedience.

Willful law contrasts most clearly with positive law when Locke is writing about tyrants (a major topic of the *Second Treatise*, given his intention to portray Stuart rule as tyrannical). A tyrant is any ruler who "makes not the law, but his will, the rule" (199). A "king's authority being given him only by the law" (206), he cannot transgress it without becoming a tyrant and thereby sacrificing his right to rule. "Wherever law ends, tyranny begins" (202). In these and similar passages he defines tyranny as a substitution of some willful facsimile for the law. He refers to "the law" as a monolithic, foundational entity. If positive law is not identical with the law of nature, he sometimes writes as if it were effectively the same thing. He says, for example, that a king's transgression of the law is less excusable than an ordinary constable's, because the king "is supposed, from the advantages of his education, employment, and counselors, to be more knowing in the measures of right and wrong" (202). Here fidelity to positive law converges with fidelity to "the right," which sounds tantamount to the law of nature and/or God's law. More often he keeps positive law separate from the law of nature, but he usually refers to "the law" as a stable, unitary given.

Blake reacted badly to this. "One Law for the Lion & Ox is Oppression" (*The Marriage of Heaven and Hell*, 44). For him, all three versions of law amounted to the same oppressive tyranny—"One King, one God, one Law" (*The Book of Urizen* 4:40). But Locke feared mainly a fourth kind of law, the one that Blake seemed to like: a Pandora's box of diverse, contingent laws, nourished by the energies of desire. This idea of law has more affinities with critical legal studies than with natural law (both of which are considered extreme positions within our contemporary judicial mainstream; yet one or the other "extreme" seems secretly to underwrite many of the "moderate" positions now considered practical and respectable). Willful law envisions a volatile mix of competing interests adjudicated by acts of discursive power rather than the application of neutral justice.

Locke tries for the most part to confine willful law as the special domain of tyrants. A tyrant "makes not the law, but his will, the rule" and uses power to satisfy "his own ambition, revenge, covetousness, or any other irregular passion" (199).

Earlier in the *Second Treatise* he sets up the danger of tyrannical desire as he describes the wild momentum of criminal intention: "And hence it is that he who attempts to get another man into his absolute power does thereby put himself into a state of war with him, it being to be understood as a declaration of a design upon his life; for I have reason to conclude that he who would get me into his power without my consent would use me as he pleased when he got me there, and destroy me, too, when he had a fancy to it" (17). Words like "fancy" and "as he pleased" always mark his references to willful law. He describes a kind of domino effect of desire: if a tyrant's will motivates him to get power over someone, it makes sense that he will stop at nothing, including murder, in the exercise of that power. The argument is strained, but Locke apparently needs his domino effect to justify preventive action against supposed tyrants.

Willful law does not enter the *Second Treatise* exclusively in discussions of tyrants. Recall Locke's malaise about "the positive laws of commonwealths": natural law is easier to understand than "the fancies and intricate contrivances of men, following contrary and hidden interests put into words" (12). Here he slides away from the coherent authority of "the law" that prevails in many other passages. Instead of respectable foundational principles of justice, the law offers "contrivances" driven by unsettlingly diffuse interests. It consists of treacherous, unstable words conveying "hidden" meanings. The language of law encodes a jumble of contrary desires, as if the tyrant problem were atomized and distributed throughout the social body.

Locke addresses the disturbing implications of willful law in some important passages late in the *Second Treatise*. Twice he raises the question posed by relativists: "Who shall be judge" in a case of competing interests? In answer he invokes the unimpeachable authority of divine judgment, which serves as a safety net for the other levels of law. The answer is conclusive but transcendent and hence a measure of the difficulty of the question. He anticipates another, more specific question: if, as his treatise argues, the commands of a king may be opposed, "May he be resisted as often as any one shall find himself aggrieved, and but imagine he has not right done him? This will unhinge and overturn all politics, and, instead of government and order, leave nothing but anarchy and confusion" (203). Here Locke confronts his worst fears about his own seditious theory. "Imagine" is a code word for willful law, now applied to any potentially seditious interest. His immediate answer is brief and absolute: only "unjust force" may be opposed (204), according to natural (and divine) law. Any other rebel is merely a "heady malcontent" (208). But he goes on to supplement this solution with more detailed, practical answers; as if tacitly conceding that justice is hard to discern in a willful world of competing interests. He argues, among other things, that people are basically conservative, preferring a *status quo* to innovation whenever possible. Further, people will not rise up in general rebellion as a result of isolated, private grievances. With these answers, he seems to acknowledge—but minimize—the dangers posed by willful law to a theorist of sedition.

Locke was not just a theorist of sedition, but a seditious activist. Cranston, Laslett, and Ashcraft have made too strong a case against the innocent philosopher for this portrait to remain plausible. Nevertheless, Locke did try to create a state of innocence for himself. He did this in two ways: by creating an appearance of innocence through a number of evasive tactics; and by creating a theory of innocence in the *Second Treatise* that would justify his political activity.

Many of his evasive tactics look like the resourceful, even heroic efforts of a spy. To some extent, Locke can be seen as a committed radical who disguised his authentic self in the face of enemy surveillance. He moved around and hid when necessary (in England and in Holland) to avoid danger. He used aliases, including "John Lynne," "Johnson," "Dr. Van Linden."[11] His surviving political letters (very few) are shielded by code and canting. An example of a coded letter comes from 1685, when he writes from Holland to Edward Clarke asking him to find a trunk containing books wrapped up as parcels. The first book has to do with "nuts, acorns ... and such other things of nature's production as she herself offers to human use."[12] This is evidently a synechdochal reference to the "Property" section of the *Second Treatise*, stored in manuscript somewhere Locke no longer considered safe. (Recall his derivation of labor-based property rights: "He that is nourished by the acorns he picked up ... has certainly appropriated them to himself" [28].) He also asks about a second book "relating to the animal kingdom as it is divided in the beginning of Gen[esis]." As Ashcraft points out, this must be the manuscript of the *First Treatise*, "since Locke's discussion of Filmer is the only time he ever addressed himself to Adam, the creation of the world, and the book of Genesis."[13] Locke chooses for his code the apparently apolitical subject matter of plants and animals.

Canting refers to a special set of metaphors agreed to by Whig conspirators for the transmission of messages. Locke's canting letters can be read as perfectly innocent discussions of gardening, business, or medicine; but read against the background of other known canting letters, their political messages come into view. Here is an example from 1683 having to do with plans for

Monmouth's attempt against his father. From other letters by radicals, notes Ashcraft, "we know that Monmouth was referred to as a 'Lady,' and that the metaphor of a 'child' was used for the revolution."[14] Locke is writing again to Clarke: "The child is thriven since we saw it there, but yet your Lady has resolved to put it into Nurse Trents hands tomorrow who is also come to town with Mr. Hadley to leave him here, and that for these plain reasons. First because the thriving of the child since your last seeing of it, argues some neglect in the nurse before ... 2nd Tis agreed that Nurse Edeling has very little or no milk and Nurse Trent plenty."[15] Ashcraft's decoding is persuasive. "Nurse Trent" is John Trenchard, to whom Monmouth will now trust the operation. Testimony from Rye conspirators indicated that around this time a Mr. Edeling ("Nurse Edeling") was replaced by Trenchard.[16] For Locke the physician this canting code was especially convenient. His therapeutic designs for the body politic are nicely masked as medical notes.

Other actions and writings of Locke do not lend themselves as easily to the portrait of heroic commitment. Some indicate a prudence so pronounced that it might be seen as cowardice. In 1688, for example, Locke stayed behind in Holland when William's fleet left for England. Jean le Clerc later commented that Locke was "plutot timide que courageux."[17] This may be ungenerous, given the dangers that he faced through the 1680s; but it seems fair to say that Locke waited to make sure he was on the winning side before he exposed his commitment. Locke's least impressive evasions appear in a letter he wrote to Pembroke late in 1684.[18] He wrote to his aristocratic friend in defense of his reputation (a letter had been sent to Oxford asking for his official removal from Christ Church). His letter contains lies and partial truths, which is understandable, given the dangers; but these particular exculpatory claims do not show him in the best light.

In three main points he asserts his innocence by denying free, full agency and portraying himself as a victim of circumstance. The most strained of the three might be called the Dutch Beer Excuse. He is explaining why he chose Holland instead of France (the former obviously safer for a Whig in exile) to get his supposed "change of air": "Wine ... sensibly hurts my lungs and water since my last sickness gives me the colique, and there is but little beer in France." It is hard to imagine Pembroke giving this explanation much credit. More important are two other claims. As to the king's suspicions of his having "writ divers scandalous seditious libels," he tells Pembroke, "I here solemnly protest in the presence of God, that I am not the author, not only of any libel, but not of any pamphlet or treatise whatsoever in print good bad or indifferent." This sounds clear enough, especially with the oath in front. Yet it allows for equivocation in two places. He is not the author of anything "in print," but the *Two Treatises* exist in manuscript. He is not "the author" of anything in print, but the evidence is strong for has having collaborated, to what extent remains uncertain, on Shaftesbury's *A Letter from a Person of Quality to his Friend in the Country* and Robert Ferguson's *No Protestant Plot* (debunking the idea of a Whig succession conspiracy).[19] He let Shaftesbury and Ferguson bear the responsibility and risk of authorship, although both tracts emerged from discussions of the Shaftesbury circle. This tactic seems somewhat more ignoble than his other. Locke is inclined to hold himself back, keep his options open, defer responsibility until his side comes to power. In a third excuse from the Pembroke letter, he tries to clear himself at the expense of Shaftesbury's reputation. Locke claims that "chance and not my own seeking ... threw me into his acquaintance and family" and complains as follows: "Yet some of my friends, when they considered how small an advancement of my fortune I had made in so long an attendance have thought I had no great reason to brag of the effects of that kindness. I say not this to complain of my dead master, it would be in no way very decent in me. But in this extremity I cannot but complain of it as a hard case: that having reaped so little advantage from my service to him whilst living I should suffer so much on that account now he is dead." Again he disavows agency: his association with Shaftesbury is an association in the loosest sense, a fortuitous concourse of human particles. His complaint about Shaftesbury's patronage—which occurs only here and does not fit well with other evidence—is a meaner gesture for being displaced onto "some of my friends."

In short, Locke's evasive tactics can be seen as the cleverness of a full-blooded radical gone underground or the equivocation of a man unwilling to commit himself to a cause until it came to power. The first characterization befits a theorist who is confidently absolute in his sense of justice; the second suggests the influence of willful, contingent law, with right inextricable from structures of power.

If we return briefly to the *Second Treatise*, we can observe how Locke tried to create a theory of innocence that would justify his politics, regardless of who held power. It begins, not surprisingly, with the law of nature: "for, by the fundamental law of nature, man being to be preserved as much as possible when all cannot be preserved, the safety of the innocent is to be preferred" (16). He tries to be precise about what innocence means. Innocent people do nothing to violate the basic respect for property inherent in natural law. Aggressors who violate property rights are guilty; they bring about a state of war. He goes on to characterize such aggressors as subhuman: "[O]ne may destroy a man who makes war upon him ... for the same reason that he may kill a wolf or a lion, because such men are not under the ties of the common second list did include Locke. Skelton wrote to Middleton about "the names you sent me on the second list . . . as for Mr. Lock, that was secretary to my Lord Shaftesbury, he is not mentioned in this last memorial, for before that I had any order for it, I had put him into the first list, which is printed."[1]

The question of Locke's guilt or innocence has been a matter of scholarly disagreement. He was careful and secretive in these matters (as anyone would be; but Locke was unusually good at self-concealment), and the evidence is therefore incomplete, ambiguous, and often indirect. But we know that Locke was suspected at least of having written seditious texts and at most of having conspired with traitors to depose or kill the king. There is no clear proof of the most serious charges, although they are now beginning to seem more plausible than they once did. The charge of sedition is easier to make. Locke's contributions to some radical texts is uncertain, but his manuscript of the *Two Treatises of Government* would have been sufficient to convict him of seditious libel. He was successful in keeping this manuscript secret, and even when it was published after the 1688 revolution he did not attach his name to it. If Locke had been arrested and extradited, however, and this manuscript had been discovered, he would have had a difficult time defending himself. As long as the government could prove that Locke was the author (by using handwriting samples and informers, as they usually did), the case was solid. There could be no doubt about the seditious nature of the treatises. In fact, given Charles II's broadening of the original definition of treason (from 1352, during the reign of Edward III), sedition had become harder to distinguish from the more serious charge of treason. According to the early definition, treason had to do with "compassing or imagining" the death of the king by "overt act." The broadened definition came with the 1661 "Act to Preserve the Person and Government of the King." Anyone who was found to "compass, imagine, invent, devise, or intend" the king's "death . . . or restraint" or to "deprive or depose him from the stile, Honour or Kingly Name" would be convicted of treason. The stricture of "overt act" from 1352 was thus replaced by looser criteria of intention. Further, the act specified that such treasonous intentions were culpable when expressed "by any Printing, Writing, Preaching, or Malicious and advised speaking."[2] The 1661 law blurred the traditional distinction between treason and sedition by declaring as treasonable such a wide range of expressive acts.

In order to imagine how a hypothetical trial of Locke might have proceeded, we can look at the actual trial of Samuel Johnson. Johnson, a cleric active in the Whig cause, was tried and convicted of sedition in 1686, when Locke was hiding in Holland. He was fortunate to have been charged with sedition (a high misdemeanor) rather than treason. The judge told the jury that the alleged acts were "within a small matter of high-treason; and might have been law of reason, have no other rule but that of force and violence, and so may be treated as beasts of prey, those dangerous and noxious creatures that will be sure to destroy him whenever he falls into their power" (16).

The description has an excessive feel to it. He uses a rhetoric of extremities—aggressors have "no other rule" but violence and "will be sure to destroy" anyone weaker. This passage (and others like it) beg for complication. Can innocence plausibly be defined as the very act of using reason? Or must innocence and guilt be continually constructed out of a heterogeneous mix of rational interests? Locke explicitly answers "yes" to the first question, although the specter of the second question is never entirely exorcised from the *Second Treatise*.

Perhaps this is why he adds a second, alternate foundation for his theory of innocence. The violent self-interest of beastly humans is beginning to sound too much like the world of Hobbes. He swerves away from Hobbes in a famous passage: "And here we have the plain difference between the state of nature and the state of war which, however some men have confounded, are as far distant as a state of peace, good-will, mutual assistance, and preservation, and a state of enmity, malice, violence, and mutual destruction are one from another" (19). Thus he shakes himself loose from a notorious predecessor, in a move so effective that it has been installed as the one standard fact about Locke and Hobbes to be memorized by casual students. The *Second Treatise* contains several passages that cut against this assumption of natural innocence. Beastly aggressors sometimes seem more the rule than the exception: "the enjoyment of [the state of nature] is very uncertain and constantly exposed to the invasion of others . . . the enjoyment of the property he has in this state is very unsafe, very unsecure" (123). Nevertheless, Locke's state of innocence survives these Hobbesian traces—so effectively, in fact, that it now undergirds political assumptions common enough to seem like natural law.

At this point it would be useful to place Locke's state of innocence alongside Blake's state of innocence. The *Second Treatise* describes the innocent state of nature as one of "peace, good will, mutual assistance, and preservation." In "The Divine Image" from *Songs of Innocence*, four "virtues of delight" secure the state of innocence: "Mercy Pity Peace and Love" (12). Only the word "peace" is an exact match, but the bundles of virtue are similar. Blake's poem makes it clear that these virtues are operating in a dangerous world—"To Mercy Pity Peace and Love, / All pray in their distress"—but in so doing he stays close to Locke, whose innocents are vulnerable to beastly aggressors. When Locke's innocents are overmatched in the state of nature, their only remedy is "an appeal to heaven" (20); in Blake's innocence, distress also calls for prayer, and supernatural relief of one sort or another usually seems available.

If Blake were commenting on Locke's innocence, he would probably criticize the way Locke abstractly separates the virtues of peace, good will, etc., from their contraries ("enmity, malice, violence, mutual destruction"). Blake urged his readers to make progress by engaging innocence and experience as contrary states. The point in Blake is not to choose, for example, between the selfless Clod and selfish Pebble, but to understand that neither perspective is simply "good" or "evil" (according to conventional, fallen terminology). He would chastise Locke for abstracting peace and good will as virtues and imposing them as restrictive laws. Surely Locke was one of Blake's models for Urizen, who made "Laws of peace, of love, of unity / Of pity, compassion, forgiveness / . . . One King, one God, one Law" (*The Book of Urizen* 4:34–35). Blake's Locke is no enemy of tyrants; he simply substitutes for the old tyrants a new tyranny of law.

Blake's *Songs* disturb the integrity of Locke/Urizen's virtue laws. "The Human Abstract" takes on "Mercy Pity Peace and Love" (called "peace" and "mutual assistance" in the *Second Treatise*).

> Pity would be no more,
> If we did not make somebody Poor:
> And Mercy no more could be,
> If all were as happy as we;
> And mutual fear brings peace;
> Till the selfish loves increase . . . (27)

These virtues, in other words, have vices woven into their texture. Even "preservation," the last and blandest of Locke's terms of innocence, comes into question: Blake's later, longer poems often present "Self Annihilation" as a redemptive catalyst. Blake's vision of an unfallen world is not dominated by the soft virtues. In "Great Eternity," "War and Hunting" are "the Two Fountains of the River of Life" (*Milton* 35:2). Blake's "Eternity" is something like Locke's "state of nature": these are the names they give to putatively original conditions when people are doing what they are supposed to do. If war and hunting are fountains of life in Eternity, Blake seems to be acknowledging Hobbes but altering his vision. A predatory world can be reimagined as healthy (just as the terrible tiger of the poem becomes mild or even cute in the design). Blake would criticize Locke for making an abstract, regulative distinction between Hobbes's state of war and Locke's state of nature. But in a more sympathetic mood, he might admit that Locke is doing something visionary. The *Second Treatise* shows imaginative vitality to the extent that it inverts Hobbes and loosens a mind-forged manacle. Locke was not seditious enough for Blake, but he did threaten some of the old restrictions on human energies.

ONE LAW FOR THE LION AND OX

Blake, like Locke, declared himself an enemy of tyranny. Blake, however, did not attempt a careful distinction between tyrants and proper kings. He used "king" almost interchangeably with "tyrant," as in his marginal notes to Bacon: in one place, "A Tyrant is the Worst disease & the Cause of all others" (625); on another page, "[A drawing of] the devils arse [with a chain of excrement ending in] A King" (624). If Blake's seditious ideas were more radical than Locke's, the specific charge against him involved an episode of small consequence; but he was more vulnerable and could not escape a trial. These events and the texts surrounding them raise questions of law and innocence from Blake's more marginal perspective.

On August 12, 1803, Blake quarreled in his Felpham garden with a soldier named Scolfield, who charged him with sedition.[20] Scolfield alleged that Blake damned the king and said he looked forward to a French invasion. The charge came at a particularly tense time, as Erdman points out: "Not since the days of the Spanish Armada and not again till 1940 has England suffered such an invasion alarm as in the autumn and winter of 1803. Napoleon was known to be assembling thousands of flat-bottomed gunboats and rafts to embark a vast army with ten thousand horses and a prodigious four hundred pieces of cannon. Along the shallow Kent and Sussex coasts tar-barrel beacons were erected and bomb-proof Martello towers. When the Blakes returned to London in September, their quiver laden with Intellectual Arrows, they entered a city of gunpowder and panic."[21] Blake was indicted for sedition under the severe restrictions of a 1795 law enacted in the wake of the French Revolution. The "Treasonable and Seditious Practices Act" defined as seditious any "writing, printing, preaching, or other speaking" that does "express, publish, utter, or declare any words or sentences to excite or stir up the people to hatred or contempt of the person of his Majesty, his heirs or successors, or the government and constitution of this realm, as by law established."[22] The terms of this "gagging act" were so broadly applicable that indictments were easy to get and informal accusations common. One of Blake's neighbors said that she "never heard people quarrel but they always charged each other with the offense."[23]

The incident comes down to us mainly in the accounts of the adversaries. Neither account is entirely plausible, and it seems likely that both men reshaped their plain memory of what went on in the garden. A few basic facts are not disputed. Scolfield, quartered near Blake's cottage in Felpham, came into the garden to assist or speak with Hayley's gardener. Blake became irritated with him, took hold of his elbows, and pushed him out of the garden and down the street toward the Fox Inn, where the soldiers were staying. Scolfield claimed that Blake uttered flagrantly seditious words during the quarrel, but Blake denied having said anything of the sort. Blake was indicted for sedition (with a separate charge of assault) in early October. Hayley engaged a lawyer for Blake's defense and supported him during the ordeal, despite the recent struggles between patron and protégé over work and relationships in Felpham. Blake was tried and acquitted by a jury on January 11, 1804.

Scolfield's specific charges survive in his deposition. William Blake, "a Miniature painter,"

> did utter the following seditious expressions viz. That we (meaning the people of England) were like a parcel of Children, that they would play with themselves 'till they would get scalded and burnt, that the French knew our strength very well and if Buonapart should come he would be master of Europe in an hour's time, that England might depend upon it that when he sat his Foot on English Ground that every Englishman would be put to his choice whether to have his throat cut or to join the French & that he was a strong Man and would certainly begin to cut throats and the strongest Man must conquer—that he Damned the King of England—his Country and his Subjects—that his soldiers were all bound for Slaves & all the poor people in general—that his Wife then came up & said to him this is nothing to you at present but that the King of England would run himself so far into the Fire that he might get himself out again & altho she was but a Woman she would fight as long as she had a Drop of Blood in her—to which the said Blake said, my Dear you would not fight against France—she replied, no, I would fight for Buonoparte as long as I am able—that the said Blake then addressing himself to this Informant, said, tho' you are one of the King's Subjects I have told what I have said before greater people than you—and that this Informant was sent by his Captain on Esquire Hayley to hear what he had to say and to go tell them—that his wife then told her said Husband to turn this Informant out of the Garden—that this Informant thereupon turned round to go peacefully out when the said Blake pushed this Informant out of the Garden into the Road, down which he followed this Informant & twice took this Informant by the Collar without this Informant's making any resistance and at the same time said Blake *damned the King & said the ___Soldiers were all Slaves*—[24]

The jury obviously doubted that Scolfield was telling the truth. He had a clear motive of revenge, and no one except Scolfield's friend supported his claims about Blake's words. Nevertheless, the speech attributed to Blake sounds sufficiently Blakean to make it credible, however much it might have been varnished, added to, and confused by Scolfield. Most scholars have concluded, as Erdman puts it, "that Blake is as unlikely to have said none of this as to have said all of it."[25] Perhaps the most authentic sounding part of the speech has Blake saying that the King's "soldiers were all bound for slaves & all the poor people in general." This sentence is particularly credible: it makes good sense in this context, and the sentiment is consistent with some of his earlier work.

It is harder to assess Scolfield's account of Blake and the imagined French invasion. Blake's lawyer, Samuel Rose, told the jury that he found this part of the account "unintelligible." Blake's early enthusiasm for the French Revolution had clearly waned, and he had a streak of cultural patriotism underneath all his criticism of English society. His symbolic representations of France and Napoleon convey ambiguous messages. The Zoa of revolutionary violence, Orc, is both a means to liberation and an obstruction to it. Gilchrist records Blake's theory of two Napoleons: "The Bonaparte of Italy was killed, and . . . another was somehow substituted from the exigent want of the name, who was the Bonaparte of the Empire!"[26] His painting of the "spiritual form of Napoleon" has been lost, but it was described as a "strong energetic figure grasping at the sun and moon with his hands, yet chained to earth by one foot, and with a pavement of dead bodies before him in the foreground."[27]

These ambiguities granted, Scolfield's account is not all that implausible. It is partially reinforced by George Cumberland's report of a conversation with the Blakes in 1815: "Blake says he is fearful they will make too great a Man of Napoleon and enable him to come to this Country—Mrs. B says that if this Country does go to War our K__g ought to loose his head."[28] Catherine Blake's contribution sounds more or less in the spirit of the 1803 deposition. Further, Scolfield's account of Blake calling himself a strong man—"that he was a strong Man and would certainly begin to cut throats and the strongest Man must conquer"—resonates with imagery found elsewhere in his work. In *America*, Urizen hides Orc

> Till Angels & weak men twelve years should govern o'er the strong
> And then their end should come, when France receiv'd the Demons light.
> (16:14–15)

At least in this early poem, he describes French energy in imagery of strong and weak men. In his 1809 catalogue, as Blake analyzes the picture of "The Ancient Britons," he spells out a Zoa-like mythology of the Strong Man (one of "the three general classes of men" and one of the four components of unfallen man). The Strong Man "represents the human sublime": he is "a receptacle of Wisdom, a sublime energizer . . . The Strong Man acts from conscious superiority, and marches on in fearless dependance on the divine decrees, raging with the inspirations of a prophetic mind" (545). The Strong Man has affiliations with Orc's energy as well as Los's prophecies (which complicates the attempt to match up Britons with Zoas neatly). It is possible, then, that Scolfield did hear something about a strong man; but if he did, it is hard to say whether strong Blake intended to fight for the French, for the English, or as an unaffiliated Zoa. Blake denied that he had uttered any of the words attributed to him, and he found neighbors to support his defense. Blake's memorandum in refutation of Scolfield suggested two possible motives for the soldier's action. The first was the obvious motive of revenge: Scolfield had been humiliated in public. This explanation became the foundation of Rose's defense. However, Blake suspected a lower layer, a government plot against him. Rose ignored this theory, which he must have treated as a nervous artist's fantasy; but it smoldered in Blake's memory for many years. He suspected that Scolfield had been sent to his garden—perhaps with Hayley's collusion—for the purpose of gathering intelligence or provoking him. This theory emanated from his sense of prophetic importance (the government *should* be afraid of him) as well as his bad relations with Hayley, whom he believed was deeply jealous of his greater abilities. In his bitterest and most paranoid moments, he believed that Hayley, Scolfield, and Rose were all conspirators in a plot against him. A notebook poem refers to "Billy's [Hayley's] Lawyer & Dragoon," and a passage in Blake's memorandum hints at a government plot: Scolfield came to the garden with a "bad intention."[29]

The grand jury returned two indictments, for assault and sedition. The second and important charge described him as "a Wicked Seditious and evil disposed person and greatly disaffected to our said Lord the King and wickedly and seditiously intending to bring our said Lord the King into great hatred contempt and Scandal with all his liege and faithful Subjects."[30] If one skips over the "evils" and "wickeds," the charges ring true enough for the prophet against empire.

Fortunately for Blake, his poems and drawings were not at issue, and the trial went smoothly. Scolfield and his colleague Cock testified for the prosecution. At one point Blake reportedly shouted "False!" during Scolfield's testimony, but this was the only breach of decorum. He was able to restrain himself, even if he lacked Locke's helpful poker face: one young spectator later remembered from the trial only "Blake's flashing eye."[31] Rose based his case on a complete denial of the seditious words, instead of using the other kind of defense common in sedition trials, an attempt to mitigate the sense of the words. The mitigation defense was called for if the words could not plausibly be denied or if the defendant had a radical reputation. Rose's more absolute defense depended not merely on denying the words but on establishing Blake as a gentle, peaceful artist. Rose described his client as an engraver—"an art, which has a tendency, like all the other fine arts, to soften every asperity of feeling and of character, and to secure the bosom from the influence of those tumultuous and discordant passions, which destroy the happiness of mankind."

This art tends to "render [the artist] indifferent to the factions & disputes of the world." This piece of fiction apparently held up well enough, despite its ludicrous misrepresentation of Blake. Like Locke, whose delicacy was assumed by generations of historians (recall Macaulay: Locke's philosophical temperament "preserved him from the violence of a partisan"), Blake found himself caricatured as a noble innocent. Rose, taking no chances, painted his client as a devoted subject of the king: "I am instructed to say, that Mr. Blake is as loyal a subject as any man in this court:—that he feels as much indignation at the idea of exposing to contempt or injury the sacred person of his sovereign as any man . . . Do you not hear every day, from the mouths of thousands in the streets the exclamation of God save the King:—it is the language of every Englishman's lip—it is the effusion of every Englishman's heart."[32] If this sort of thing turned Blake's stomach, he betrayed nothing to the jury, who acquitted him on both counts. The *Sussex Advertiser* reported that the verdict "so gratified the auditory that the court was, in defiance of all decency, thrown into an uproar by their noisy exultations."[33]

Despite his courtroom victory, Blake was not reconciled to the institutions of English law. He struggled against them in his later work as much as in his earlier work. In *Jerusalem* he made characters out of Scolfield and other figures from the trial, reenacting and altering the scene of judgment from his prophetic perspective. Blake's treatment of law, like Locke's, consists of a complicated mixture of ideas, however effectively these ideas have been reorganized by readers looking for stable political theory or simple virtue. Blake, like Locke, will construct both a semblance of innocence and a higher theory of innocence as he works to justify himself and to return England to justice.

We identified four versions of law in the *Second Treatise:* God's law, natural law, positive law, and willful law. Blake tends to lump the first three into a single category. For him, the distinctions that Locke tried to make among these kinds of law were insignificant compared with the overwhelming (and pernicious) effects of their convergence. Positive law is given to people as God's law, which is represented as natural truth:

> Thus the terrible race of Los & Enitharmon gave
> Laws & Religions to the sons of Har binding them more
> And more to Earth: closing and restraining:
> Till a Philosophy of Five Senses was complete
> Urizen wept & gave it into the hands of Newton & Locke. (*The Song of Los* 4:13–17)

With Blake, it is the fourth or willful version that needs the most careful attention. Willful law posits a society of competing desires and interests adjudicated by acts of power rather than neutrally rational justice. This version of law, we observed, was the most troublesome for Locke and apparently the most promising for Blake. Blake does find it attractive, most clearly in his early work. But he cannot simply embrace this view. In *Milton* and *Jerusalem* he struggles with his mixed feelings and tries to revise willful law with theories of pity, repentance, and forgiveness.

Locke feared willful law because it empowered nonrational desires (interests produced by "fancies," "irregular passions"), whether they came from tyrants or "heady malcontents." Blake's earliest comments about "will" appear in his marginal notes to Lavater's *Aphorisms on Man*. He expresses uneasiness with various aphorisms that challenge willful conviction. In a general comment at the end of the book, Blake disputes Lavater's concept of virtue and vice. Lavater treats vice as an essential "propensity" of a man, "But as I understand Vice it is a Negative—It does not signify what the laws of Kings & Priests have called Vice . . . Every mans leading propensity ought to be calld his leading Virtue & his good Angel . . . Accident is the omission of act in self & the hindering of act in another, This is Vice but all Act from Individual propensity is Virtue" (601). The term "propensity" serves more or less as a synonym for "will" without the pejorative connotations. He proposes it as a substratum of authenticity, more valid than the "laws of Kings & Priests" with their abstractions of good and evil. As an ethical theory it has obvious problems. But if his comment is read as an extended aphorism rather than a systematic theory, it shows him thinking in little bursts of antinomian insight, trying to dissolve Enlightenment common sense.[34]

A similar tendency runs through *The Marriage of Heaven and Hell*. An admirable devil persuades an angel that "The worship of God is Honouring his gifts in other men each according to his genius. and loving the greatest men best" (43). Obviously this is no egalitarianism but a meritocracy of imagination: he promotes individual "genius" as the organizing principle of society instead of the Ten Commandments or King's laws. Blake's own collection of aphorisms, the Proverbs of Hell, includes several that approve energetic desire as a self-justifying motive force. Although his messages are by no means consistent, the *Marriage* is a kind of workshop for Blake as he explores the contours of his "genius" and "individual propensity."

At the end of the *Marriage* he prints a final aphorism: "One Law for the Lion & Ox is Oppression." Beneath this he draws Nebuchadnezzar of Babylon, crawling in a bleak setting during his temporary sentence as a beast. This image was one of Blake's favorites. He sketched an early version in his notebook, used it here in the *Marriage*, issued a separate color print a few years later, and later still produced a "visionary head of Nebuchadnezzar." Scholars have generally treated Nebuchadnezzar as an archetypal tyrant, which makes good enough sense.[35] The context of the French Revolution encourages an antityranny message. The spiky crown emerging from Nebuchadnezzar's hair resembles other crowns Blake draws for oppressors. Biblical accounts of Nebuchadnezzar portray a decidedly willful king: he demands to know the shape of the future, he orders great buildings, he sets up his own gods and insists that they be worshipped. According to this reading, the crawling king has effectively punished himself in his selfish obliviousness.

However, the aphorism and drawing conclude a "Memorable Fancy" in which the devil proclaims, "Worship of God is . . . loving the greatest men best, those who envy or calumniate great men hate God, for there is no other God" (43). Nebuchadnezzar was certainly a great man in historical, legendary, and biblical narrative. He was willful but not inflexible: he changed his mind at critical moments and embraced the god of Daniel. When Blake draws Nebuchadnezzar underneath "One Law," this is not simply a warning about the fate of a willful king. It is just as plausibly a complaint about Nebuchadnezzar's punishment by a jealous, Urizenic god. The great king is a lion forced to act like an ox because a restrictive lawgiver cannot tolerate his creative will. This second reading is not precisely opposite to the first—both condemn tyranny; but in the second reading, Nebuchadnezzar becomes a Blakean hero, punished by Urizenic law for following his good angel of virtuous energy. The complication emerging from these two readings of Nebuchadnezzar is somewhat similar to Locke's problem with "heady malcontents." For both of them, the engine of "good" sedition—creative will in one case, reason in the other—slips toward precisely the wrong result: tyranny for Blake, anarchy for Locke.

Blake at his sedition trial might have felt something like the crawling Nebuchadnezzar: a great man humiliated by the one law. Even if his "flashing eye" was visible, his posture was submissive. Like Locke, Blake created not only a higher theory of innocence but a lower semblance of innocence for practical purposes of safety. Neither man chose reckless heroism.

A passage from *Jerusalem* conveys the thinking behind Blake's "deep dissimulation":

The Visions of Eternity, by reason of narrowed perceptions,
Are become weak Visions of Time & Space, fix'd into furrows of death;
Till deep dissimulation is the only defence an honest man has left.
(49:21–23)

His dissimulation took various forms. Sometimes he let himself shrink from prophetic stature, especially in letters surrounding the Felpham years, to maintain useful professional relationships. To Hayley in 1804: "I also thank you for your very beautiful little poem on the King's recovery; it is one of the prettiest things I ever read" (749). He dissimulated in letters like this one at the same time he was attacking Hayley and the King in private writings.

More significant dissimulation came when Blake either altered or suppressed work that he considered dangerous. The first such instance was probably the 1791 withdrawal of *The French Revolution* from publication. This was a poem Blake wrote in the revolutionary spirit; the first of its seven books was set in type (the page proofs survive) but never published. Blake may have canceled it for fear of a sedition charge, or Joseph Johnson, the publisher, may have pulled it for the same reason. Even if it was Johnson who withdrew the poem, Blake made no attempt to publish it elsewhere, as (for example) Thomas Paine did when his own work was censored. A few years later, when Blake annotated his copy of Bishop Watson's *Apology for the Bible*, he seems to have considered some form of publication. (He drafted a formal title on the back of the *Apology* title page.) Certainly he realized the importance of the matter. "Read patiently take not up this Book in an idle hour," he writes, "the consideration of these things is the whole duty of man & the affairs of life & death trifles sports of time But these considerations business of Eternity" (611). Elsewhere in his notes he observes that the best example of a modern miracle is "to overthrow all the armies of Europe with a small pamphlet" (617). But Blake tried no such pamphlet defending Paine against kings and priests. He explains why in a single sentence: "I have been commanded from Hell not to print this as it is what our Enemies wish" (611). Understandably he feared the sedition law, although he seems to have exaggerated the consequences. Conviction would get him a fine and some imprisonment; Blake writes that it "would cost a man his life." He ameliorates what looks like cowardice by calling it daemonic inspiration.

In works that he did publish, he made a few changes to remove the clearest markers of sedition. His notebook draft of "London" for the *Songs of Experience* read, "In every voice: in every ban, / The german forged links I hear."[36] Before engraving and printing the poem he changed "german forged links" to "mind-forg'd manacles." The new phrase has metrical advantages, but it also gets rid of the metonymic reference to the king. Blake removed a literal reference to George III from *America* when he canceled the original plate 4: "To this deep valley situated by the flowing Thames; / Where George the Third holds council. & his Lords & Commons meet" (b:8–9). From *America* forward, his work will become increasingly opaque to contemporary readers and, consequently, safe from government surveillance. In *Jerusalem* he apparently refers to his Lambeth books as carefully disguised to fool "Satan's Watch Fiends": "There is a Grain of Sand in Lambeth that Satan cannot find / Nor can his Watch Fiends find it" (37:15–16). The watch fiends, thrown off by exotic neologism, figuration, and intertextuality, cannot read the dangerous books of the prophet. (Still, he takes no chances: he decided to cover with vines a line from *Jerusalem* listing the most recent English monarchs: "Edward Henry Elizabeth James Charles William George" [73:37].) It would be silly to treat Blake's prophetic language as merely an encrypting device, like Locke's canting letters; or even to suggest that concealment was a primary motive in the development of his mature prophetic style. Still, this style did provide the dissimulation that he persuaded himself was necessary.

In the cryptic books that fooled the watch fiends, Blake struggles to articulate a higher theory of innocence, nobler and more important than any dissimulating mask. Blake's theory of innocence, like Locke's, begins in an uneasiness with willful law. To some extent, as we have seen, he welcomed this view. "Opposition is true friendship"; people necessarily impose on each other. A good society should liberate and nurture the diverse energies of its members. Blake's problems in Felpham, however—including Scolfield and the continual quarreling with Hayley—were testing the limits of this theory. "If Men were Wise the Most arbitrary Princes could not hurt them," he wrote in his notebook, but "If they are not Wise the Freest Government is compelld to be a Tyranny" (580). More and more he found himself lamenting a Hobbesian world "in which Man is by his Nature the Enemy of Man, / In pride of Selfhood" (*Jerusalem* 38:52–53).

In *Milton* and *Jerusalem* he tried to revise his ideas about liberation in order to discover not a warmed over social contract of the oppressive Enlightenment but some sort of imaginative cooperation. He tended to call this state of cooperation "Eternity" and "regeneration" the process of reaching it. Blake's version of a social contract does not have the analytical persuasiveness of Locke's; but of course he distrusted any system for regulating human behavior that laid out abstract rational guidelines. He tried several approaches in his efforts to make willful law seem workable.

One approach was to recognize but redefine "war" as essential to eternal life. Fallen humanity had corrupted "intellectual war" into "corporeal war." Eternal wars have ideas instead of bodies at stake. Fighting is fluid and expansive, not frozen into corporeal bulk. In *Jerusalem*, Albion will be restored "with the Spiritual and not the Natural Sword" (52).

This approach displays the "Romantic ideology" in a fairly pure form: Blake sublimates the material/historical world through the alchemy of imagination. This was not his only approach, of course; and because he engaged so many political and historical subjects in their "corporeal" contexts, it would be shallow to attack him as an unwittingly conservative Romantic idealist. If it is a bit disappointing to see him meek in the Chichester courtroom, reserving his battle against Scolfield et al. for "the worlds of Thought" (*Jerusalem* 5:19), the court was not a suitable arena for wars of eternity.

Even intellectual wars, however, need ameliorative theories. *Milton* and *Jerusalem* try out three terms in their efforts toward a visionary social contract: pity, repentance, and forgiveness. Blake proposes pity (or mercy, which he uses more or less synonymously) as a means of counteracting wrath and thereby making eternity emotionally practical. Los is the chief architect of this strategy. In *Jerusalem* he recommends pity to his Spectre, who has been fuming over Albion's crimes. "They have divided themselves by Wrath. they must be united by / Pity" (7:57–58). In *Milton* he tells his angry sons, "We live not by wrath. by mercy alone we live!" (23:34). The sons are "indignant" and "unconvincd by Los's arguments," which is not surprising, given Blake's critique of "Mercy Pity Peace and Love" in the *Songs of Experience*. Los even has trouble taking his own advice. "O that I could abstain from wrath!" (7:59), he says, and later he regrets a pitying judgment he had made: "Mine is the fault! I should have remember'd that pity divides the soul / And man, unmans" (8:19–20). Presumably wrath makes him feel "manly," if only temporarily. To Blake's credit, he did not yield to the simple pleasures of wrath; but pity as well seemed to give him only momentary, unstable relief. Los's sons notice "that wrath now swayd and now pity absorbd him / As it was, so it remaind & no hope of an end" (*Milton* 24:46–47). In *Jerusalem* he draws a chart of "This World," with pity and wrath posed as contraries on the east-west axis. (Reason and desire sit north-south.) Pity is not a simple virtue, but one of two contrary states. If *The Marriage of Heaven and Hell* warned against the oppressive reconciliation of contraries, *Milton* and *Jerusalem* often seem to reach for something more than mere contrary play—something like a privileged redemptive virtue.

Repentance is a second attempt at such. Repentance has more to do with moral theory than emotional therapy; it offers a version of "self-annihilation" inflected toward traditional piety. Repentance promises to relieve the guilt inevitably attending willful vitality. *Milton* emphasizes repentance more than any other Blake poem.[37] Most obviously, the character Milton returns to earth to repent of his misapprehensions and correct the harmful effects of his poetry. Besides Milton, three other major characters repent at some point. Although Milton and Ololon achieve a moment of productive repentance at the end of the poem, it remains a doubtful visionary resource. At its worst it cloaks a secret, manipulative selfishness. Even the best repentance may only repress temporarily a fundamental problem.

Alongside pity and repentance, Blake tries out a third term, forgiveness. Calls for forgiveness can be found throughout *Jerusalem*. Forgiveness differs from repentance, of course, because it is directed outward, but the goal is the same: to make a world of clashing wills livable. In *Jerusalem* the calls for forgiveness often sound like ordinary Christian piety. The voice of Joseph tells Mary,

> But Jehovahs Salvation
> Is without Money & without Price, in the Continual Forgiveness of
> Sins
> In the Perpetual Mutual Sacrifice in Great Eternity! (61:21–23)

Except perhaps for the phrase "Great Eternity," which projects an eccentric Blakean aura, this is disappointingly routine. Elsewhere in *Jerusalem* he updates the message by applying it to Rousseau: "Rousseau thought Men Good by Nature; he found them Evil & found no friend. Friendship cannot exist without Forgiveness of Sins continually" (52:prefatory prose). In Blake's view, Rousseau and Locke committed a similar error of abstracting virtue and vice and applying one term or the other to primal humanity. Locke's theory of original innocence appears to counteract Hobbes's theory of original brutishness, but they both depend on abstraction, and either theory leads to a system of oppressive regulation.

If forgiveness seems too pious or too soft for readers attracted to a riskier Blake, they might consider the (loose) contrary to forgiveness: law. A more precise contrary might be revenge, but law and revenge are closely allied, with law evolving from and sublimating revenge in civilized society. As we have seen, Blake ordinarily disparages law as a set of oppressive rules made to look like natural and divine truth. His sedition troubles in 1803 painfully reinforced that opinion. His last poems are filled with sympathy for "the accused, who at Satans Bar / Tremble in Spectrous Bodies" (*Milton* 23:42–3). A spectral underworld is "fill'd with Revenge and Law" (*Jerusalem* 36:35); Satan makes bad laws "from his own identity" (*Milton* 11:10); "Genius [is] forbidden by laws of punishment" (*Jerusalem* 9:16); Albion erects law that makes "every Act a Crime, & Albion the punisher & judge" (*Jerusalem* 28:4).

In one nice passage from *Milton*, however, he uses law somewhat differently. Los has been arguing with his sons: he sympathizes with their anger, but counsels pity and patience. Los ends up confused, feeling alternately pitying and wrathful, with "no hope of an end." Then the narrator shifts to a description of "Bowlahoola," where Los descends to work:

> Bowlahoola is namd Law. by mortals, Tharmas founded it:
> Because of Satan, before Luban in the City of Golgonooza.
> But Golgonooza is namd Art & Manufacture by mortal men.
>
> In Bowlahoola Los's Anvils stand & his Furnaces rage;
> Thundering the Hammers beat & the Bellows blow loud

> Living self moving mourning lamenting & howling incessantly
> Bowlahoola thro all its porches feels tho' too fast founded
> Its pillars & porticoes to tremble at the force
> Of mortal or immortal arm: and softly lilling flutes
> Accordant with the horrid labours make sweet melody
> The Bellows are the Animal Lungs: the Hammers the Animal Heart
> The Furnaces the Stomach for digestion. terrible their fury
> Thousands & thousands labour. thousands play on instruments
> Stringed or fluted to ameliorate the sorrows of slavery
> Loud sport the dancers in the dance of death, rejoicing in carnage
> The hard dentant Hammers are lulld by the flutes lula lula
> The bellowing Furnaces blare by the long sounding clarion
> The double drum drowns howls & groans, the shrill fife. shrieks & cries:
> The crooked horn mellows the hoarse raving serpent, terrible, but harmonious
> Bowlahoola is the Stomach in every individual man. (24:48–67)

This passage has puzzled many interpreters, and to nonspecialists it must look like free association. Damon shrugs off the connection between Bowlahoola and law as "one of Blake's riddling definitions."[38] Stevenson tries a little harder—he sees "control" as the common feature to law and stomach/bowels—but he admits that the "equation with law is confusing."[39]

It remains confusing if one assumes that Blake uses "law" in a uniformly pejorative sense (Stevenson: "Law is fierce, firm, and heavy-handed"). If we suspend this assumption, a different notion of law comes briefly into view. Law in this passage is part of Los's redemptive machinery. It was founded by Tharmas, who tends to be pitying and compassionate, because of Satan, who tends to be selfishly willful. Law, in other words, is created in response to the kind of pity-wrath problem Los has been having. It fails if it is too sensitive (it must be sufficiently "fast founded" not to "tremble at the force / Of mortal or immortal arm") or not sensitive enough (it "feels" "thro all its porches"). Law works with the violent materials of the willful world (carnage, slavery, etc.), and like the body's digestive system, it tries to sort out the most harmful elements without giving up too much of value. Interestingly, Blake also puts a lot of music into his stomach of law. He reinforces this association of music with law a little later. He names the four arts of eternity—poetry, painting, music, and architecture—and assigns each art a "profession," by means of which the arts "become apparent in Time & Space" (27:59). The profession for music is law. Perhaps he thinks of law as musical in its effort to fabricate some sort of harmony out of diversely expressive elements. Law, like music, will fail if its harmonies are stiflingly uniform or if it achieves no sense of coherence and cooperation at all.

Bowlahoola law may not be strikingly different from Locke's law, *mutatis mutandis*. If Locke could have observed Blake's sedition trial, he would have been pleased that rational, contractual English law worked the way he conceived it should—even for a nervous, unstable enthusiast, who would continue to imagine that agents of the king were bedeviling him. Blake must have felt some gratitude at the way English law delivered him from a satanic accuser. But Blake would have found Locke's complacency irritating. For a man who had government spies snooping all around him, checking his countenance, eavesdropping at dinner, Locke made disappointingly little progress against the watch fiends.

Chapter 6

Possessions

Locke's ideas about property were crucial to his overall theory of social organization. Although he tried to make his conclusions seem obvious, he was actually writing within a difficult transitional period for property theories. As Andrew Reeve points out, "Locke may reasonably be seen as providing a pivot between the exegetical or justificatory" arguments of an older tradition (including those of Aquinas) and more modern arguments focusing on self-interest and social development (like those of Adam Smith).[1] Blake reacted angrily against the new reasonings. Modern theories of property led to selfish, acquisitive identities and entrenched economic inequalities, all made to sound natural and rational. Blake could not simply escape from the grip of possessions and self-interest, but he tried to revise what these things might mean. Two loosely parallel events from their lives provide a useful focus for a discussion of property and possessive individualism. Each man had a fit of anger when he thought that a friend had stolen a picture from him: from Locke, a portrait of himself, and from Blake, a design for a picture of the Canterbury pilgrims. Because both of them reacted so strongly to the alleged (but not indisputable) theft, the topic of passions becomes a helpful supplement to this analysis of possessions.

PROPERTY AND THE LURKING PASSION

Shortly after his return to England from Holland, as he was making plans for publication of *An Essay Concerning Human Understanding,* Locke became very upset with a friend over a portrait of himself that he wanted to use for the frontispiece engraving. Appropriately, the man for whom all knowledge originates in an imprinting was anxious about which imprinted version of himself he would transmit. The portrait had been painted in 1672 by John Greenhill, who had come to do a portrait of Shaftesbury, and he ended up painting Locke as well.[2] When Locke left for France in 1675, he carefully organized his belongings for storage; in 1679, after his return, he noted one thing missing: "Found at Thanet House the things I had left with Mr Stringer at Exeter House on 12 November 1675; except my picture which he had removed to his house at Bexwells."[3] Thomas Stringer was Shaftesbury's secretary and one of Locke's friends—a good enough friend for Locke to have spent time as a guest at Bexwells, in Essex. But the picture of Locke hanging in Stringer's house eventually spoiled the friendship.

Locke decided early in 1688 that he wanted to take the portrait to an engraver for the *Essay* frontispiece. He asked Edward Clarke to get the picture from Stringer. Stringer refused to hand it over for several reasons, ranging from the facetious to the provocative. Withholding the picture would force Locke to correspond regularly with the Stringers; the portrait hung in good company; the portrait belonged to the Stringers, because Locke clearly gave it to them; and in any event, it was unsuitable for engraving, so that Locke's request must have been simply a "Colourable Excuse" for getting it back.[4] This last suggestion was the most offensive one, and Locke's reply shows his irritation: "I hope I may be allowed to be of an age enough to know if I would have print of myself what kind will please me best."[5] But it is a simpler matter for Locke to defend his aesthetic judgment than to contest Stringer's claim to ownership. He does want to contest the claim and deny that he ever gave the portrait to his friend; but his cagey reply suggests that he is hindered by some uncertainty about facts. Instead of presenting his specific recollection against Stringer's, Locke cites his general reputation for integrity and respect for private property: "For you will not finde any one who knows me, that will imagine, I deserve to be suspected of a designe to cheat any one of what is his, much lesse a friend of what I my self had given him."

In a later letter to Clarke, Locke again denounces Stringer, although he continues to write as if he cannot entirely dismiss his friend's claim. Stringer "tells me his wife has it under my hand that I gave it to him. I am afraid he strains the matter too far, for having never purposed but to have that picture in my chamber at Oxford when I came to settle there I am sure I could never give it away in a letter to anyone, or say anything like it unless I were drunk when I writ it."[6] Locke says Stringer "strains the matter too far," but he hedges his denial. The letter suggests a mild self-estrangement encroaching on Locke's common sense. He mentions the possibility of a drunken other self, although he would not expect Clarke to take this seriously. More tellingly, he is perplexed by the possibility of a document in his own hand performing a transaction that seems entirely alien to his recognizable intentions. Locke's theories of personal identity have helped germinate, in other thinkers, skeptical concepts of an unstable self. But an unstable self was not something he wanted to entertain as a practical matter; and as the portrait controversy continued, Locke tried to clarify the case with the simplest of economic claims. He paid for it: "it cost me the pains of sitting and fiveteen pounds drie money to boote."[7] Locke nevertheless continued to act as though he had doubts. He was anxious for Clarke to find the letter upon which Mrs. Stringer based her claims. And when the dispute finally moved toward a resolution, about a year later, Locke meekly asked for the Stringers' permission to use the portrait. The Stringers agreed; but oddly enough, Locke ended up not using the portrait after all. He chose instead a drawing from life done by his valet and amanuensis, Sylvanus Brownover, which was engraved in time for the second edition but not the first. Perhaps Stringer had been right in the first place about the Greenhill portrait—that it was unsuitable for engraving.[8]

One question might be drawn from this little narrative: why did Locke suffer extended discomposure over the painting, even in the face of plausible doubts about its practical value to him, and even over who owned it? Two answers might be proposed. First, he let this incident breach his serenity because he was naturally disposed to anger; and in this case his anger, and the selfishness that may have been its cause or its effect, overcame rational judgment. Second—and contrarily—he acted not out of unreasonable anger but from rational principles of private property and its protection. Both of these answers can be derived from Locke's own thinking. I would like to examine each in turn, by drawing on relevant passages from his writings.

Cranston finds evidence that Locke had a tendency toward anger. He quotes from Pierre Coste's memorial sketch: Locke was "naturally somewhat choleric." Cranston goes on to say that Coste's "criticism must surely have been just, as even Lady Masham admitted it: 'The passion he was naturally most prone to was anger.'"[9] It may seem strange that his friends both use "natural" predispositions to characterize the great opponent of innatism. Although Locke fought conspicuously against theories that privileged inborn endowments and pre-established ideas, he was actually quite far from denying the determinative significance of innate elements. One area he concedes to innatism has to do with what he calls "tempers" or "characters." He discusses this subject most carefully in *Some Thoughts Concerning Education*. Locke believes that educational methods must be adapted to the particular disposition and needs of each child. "We must not hope wholly to change their original tempers, nor make the gay, pensive and grave; nor the melancholy, sportive, without spoiling them. God has stamped certain characters upon men's minds, which, like their shapes, may perhaps be a little mended; but can hardly be totally alter'd and transform'd into the contrary" (66). He uses "character" here with its original meaning foremost (from Greek for engraving), but with the looser, figurative sense lurking behind. Surely Locke does not want to grant as innate all that the word "character" can mean, in his time as well as ours. In a later passage he switches metaphors: "for few of Adam's children are so happy, as not to be born with some biass in their natural temper, which it is the business of education either to take off, or counterbalance" (139). Here the controlling image has to do with balance rather than writing, and education seems to have better prospects for decisive intervention: it is easier to correct an imbalance than to alter a divine engraving. Still later, though, he writes as if innate temper must simply be taken for granted: "Each man's mind has some peculiarity, as well as his face, that distinguishes him from all others" (217).

Coste and Lady Masham suggest that Locke's natural temper consisted in a bias toward anger. For Locke's thoughts concerning anger we need to turn to the second book of the *Essay*, where he discusses the passions. He links passions with "tempers of mind" (the same phrase that appears in *Education*) and then lists and briefly defines the ten major passions: love, hatred, desire, joy, sorrow, hope, fear, despair, anger, and envy. All ten passions derive from pleasure and pain, and ultimately from good and evil, which he names as the respective causes of pleasure and pain. Anger and envy, the final two passions, differ from the first eight because they have "in them some mix'd Considerations of ourselves and others."

> ANGER is uneasiness, or discomposure of the Mind, upon the receipt of any Injury, with a present purpose of Revenge.
> ENVY is an uneasiness of Mind, caus'd by the consideration of a Good we desire, obtain'd by one we think should not have had it before us. (2.20.12)

His friends recognize his anger but do not accuse him of envy, the other intersubjective passion. It would certainly be embarrassing if they did, given that Locke founds his definition of virtue on the denial of desires. "And the great principle and foundation of all virtue and worth, is placed in this, that a man is able to deny himself his own desires, cross his own inclinations, and purely follow what reason directs as best, tho' the appetite lean the other way" (*Education* 33). Locke's definition of envy presents desire overcoming reason, instead of virtuous reason overcoming desire. Biographical materials do not suggest that Locke had trouble with envy. Someone eager to make a case might find one or two small hints: for example, Locke was possibly disappointed at receiving a minor post from Shaftesbury, after his patron had become Lord High Chancellor. But a more sympathetic interpreter would conclude that Locke resisted the temptations of envy well enough.

Still, that definition of envy might be altered somewhat to produce a new passion: one that Locke did not name, but of which he might more plausibly be accused. The altered definition might go something like this:

STINGINESS[10] is an uneasiness of Mind, caus'd by the consideration of a good we possess or believe we possess, when it is in jeopardy of being transferred to another.

This would be a form of ungenerous self-absorption that leads to acts or feelings that reason cannot endorse. The portrait incident comes to mind, of course, if we observe that Locke's behavior there was not as calmly rational as he ordinarily expected of himself. But Cranston notes more telling examples of Locke's ungenerous tendencies, mostly having to do with money he was owed. "Locke was often agitated by some failure or delay in the receipt of his rents. He was not the most patient of landlords, and he always kept a sharp eye on his money."[11] He once ordered the eviction of one Mary Cooke, behind in her rent.[12] His friend James Tyrrell was irritated by a letter from Locke demanding repayment of a small debt.[13] Locke looked bad on two occasions when his passion for debt collection led him to violate ordinary decency. About a month after his friend Thomas Dare had died, Locke received a letter from Dare's widow, explaining that she was trying to find a way to pay him the money her husband owed him and that she would satisfy him as soon as possible.[14] Obviously Locke, who had written to her very shortly after her husband had died, was at least as interested in having a debt repaid as in paying his respects. Some years later, after his friend David Thomas died, he again mixed grief with collection in an unbecoming way. Here is Cranston's unflattering but fair summary: "Locke wrote a letter of condolence to the son, William Thomas. He told him how 'extremely troubled' he was at the doctor's death; he recalled their 'uninterrupted friendship' of 'many years'; he said how 'sorry' he was for Mrs. Thomas. But by far the greater part of Locke's letter was taken up with a record of money David Thomas owed him and of books his late friend had borrowed and not returned."[15] In short, Locke's stingy selfishness led him at times to violate his standard of rational self-denial. This passion could trigger his natural cholera—as in the case of the Greenhill portrait—and jeopardize friendships. In *Education* he emphatically warned parents to correct children's yearning for "Propriety and Possession" (105), because such "Covetousness" seriously disrupted human relations: "As to the having and possessing of Things, teach them to part with what they have easily and freely to their friends ... Covetousness, and the Desire of having in our Possession, and under our Dominion, more than we have need of, being the root of all Evil, should be early and carefully weeded out, and the contrary Quality of a Readiness to impart to others, implanted" (110). Apparently this "root of all Evil" had not been "weeded out" of Locke in time to change his adult behavior. Still, he expected and to some degree sympathized with passionate transgressions of reason. In the *Essay*, he says that God knows "our frailty, pities our weakness"; that he will forgive us when some "violent Passion, running away with us, allows us not the liberty of thought, and we are not Masters enough of our own Minds to consider thoroughly, and examine fairly" (2.21.53).

But surely all of this can be looked at in a different way. Do Locke's bouts of selfishness show his mind as mastered or mastering? In other words, which came first, the passion of stinginess or the reasoning about private property? This is no doubt an impossible, artificial question, but it serves a purpose. In examining the case for rational possessiveness, we can observe how reason recuperates a lurking passion.

Assumptions about property undergird many Lockean positions. "The great and chief end . . . of men's uniting into commonwealths, and putting themselves under government, is the preservation of their property" (*Second Treatise* 124). The only occasion on which people may justifiably dissolve an established government is "whenever the legislators endeavour to take away, and destroy the property of the people" (222). Twice in the fourth book of the *Essay*, when he wants to give an example of an indisputable moral axiom, he uses the idea that property is the foundation of justice (4.3.18; 4.4.9). Property authorizes not only his reasonings about society but about God: "For, man being all the workmanship of one omnipotent and infinitely wise maker; all the servants of one sovereign master, sent into the world by his order, and about his business, they are his property, whose workmanship they are" (*Second Treatise* 6).

With property counting for so much, even a small matter like the portrait dispute can be significant beyond its specific boundaries. I would like to examine Locke's ideas about property according to a scheme suggested by the portrait dispute. The chief problem with this strategy comes from the nature of the property at issue. When Locke theorizes about property in the *Second Treatise*, he writes mainly of food and food-producing land; he does not go into things like paintings, the practical value of which is harder to judge. Although the Greenhill portrait seems incongruous alongside Locke's discussions of apples, acorns, and venison, this incongruity may prove as much an advantage as a liability. It may help to clarify the rhetorical choices he has made and to update his deliberately archaic setting.[16]

There are four possible answers to the question of who owns the portrait: the general public; the artist; the purchaser; and the friend. Each answer has some foundation in Locke's theories of property as set forth in the *Second Treatise*.

First, the general public. As Locke begins to address the matter of property, he has one question foremost in mind: how can private property be justified at all, when "'tis very clear, that God, as king David says, Psal.cxv.16 'has given the earth to the children of men'; given it to mankind in common" (25)? Locke quickly dismisses the notion of a universal monarch owning all, as Adam's successor. But if he summons common property as a defense against patriarchal absolutism, he immediately moves beyond it to establish the principle of private property:

> God, who hath given the world to men in common, hath also given them reason to make use of it, to the best advantage of life and convenience. The earth, and all that is therein, is given to men for the support and comfort of their being. And, though all the fruits it naturally produces, and beasts it feeds, belong to mankind in common, as they are produced by the spontaneous hand of nature . . . yet being given for the use of men, there must of necessity be a means to appropriate them, some way or other, before they can be of any use, or at all beneficial to any particular man. The fruit, or venison, which nourishes the wild Indian, who knows no inclosure, and is still a tenant in common, must be his, and so his, i.e. a part of him, that another can no longer have any right to it, before it can do any good for the support of his life. (26)

Here Locke begins his account of first things, his American idyll. Unlike his predecessor Pufendorf and his successor Hume—both of whom considered any pure, presocial state of nature a philosophical fiction—Locke reconstructs the natural origins of property from what he presumes to know about Indians. It was important for Locke to consider his original scene something more than mere fiction; and his contacts with America, despite being entirely mediated by travel literature and letters from associates, gave him some confidence against such a charge.

Several things in the passage deserve comment. He introduces reason right away, in order to transfer control from God to man. Reason in this passage stands distinct from two prerational sources of authority: nature, with its "spontaneous hand," and biblical dicta, from an inspired hand. Locke has no wish to contradict either of these, but he effectively de-emphasizes them. Filmer, after all, has his own biblical texts; and nature's hand implies nothing to distinguish Filmer's argument from Locke's. But reason allows Locke to introduce his own premises. He posits that men are meant to use the earth "to the best advantage of life and convenience" and "for the support and comfort of their being." He carefully adds "convenience" and "comfort" to "life" and "support," so as to make room for desires that reach beyond needs. In the last sentence he arrives at his intended conclusion, the inference of private ownership from an original common grant. His hypothetical Indian gives him the necessary foundation. When all doubtful appearances of private property have been stripped away, one unmistakable, irreducible fact remains: the needs of a separate self, which must appropriate pieces of nature for nourishment. Community reduces to individual, a point Locke's pronouns make insistently—"must be his, and so his, i.e. a part of him." In the next paragraph he will qualify his point by making a concession to communal welfare (which has come to be known as the Lockean Proviso). The individual has a right to property only "where there is enough, and as good left in common for others" (27). This condition causes no trouble for the nonenclosed Indian, whose world is expansively provident and whose goods are interchangeable. If the condition is applied to the Greenhill portrait, however, it makes no sense. Locke's archaic scene cannot accommodate goods that are unique, or at least noninterchangeable. Nor does it address the problems of private property in a world characterized by enclosure and scarcity, rather than vast common land and Edenic plenty.[17] His invention of presocial Indians provides a means by which he can both satisfy a humanitarian conscience and authorize the accumulation of private property.

In Locke's story of first things, ownership must be earned by labor. "The labour of his body, and the work of his hands, we may say, are properly his. Whatsoever, then, he removes out of the state that nature hath provided and left it in, he hath mixed his labour with, and joined to it something that is his own, and thereby makes it his own property" (27).[18] Whoever picks up acorns or apples can claim them as property. Conveniently, there are no competitors or landowners to worry about. Locke does ask one complicating question: "When did they begin to be his? when he digested? or when he eat? or when he boiled? or when he brought them home? or when he picked them up?" Plainly, when he picked them up, because "that added something to them, more than nature, the common mother of all, had done, and so they became his private right" (28). This is not as plain as Locke claims. At one extreme he proposes and rejects appropriation by digestion—an answer which could be defended, since only at that point has the purpose of nourishment actually been fulfilled. At the other extreme he approves appropriation by gathering. But why stop there? One could speak of mental acts of appropriation, which precede any physical acts and might plausibly be considered appropriative labor.

Locke has simplified this aspect of property to create a pristine identification of worker with product and product with value. The logic is comforting. Bring the story into the present, however, and some of the simple comfort falls away. The real owner of the painting would be John Greenhill, who painted it. Of course this answer can be easily refigured by the economics of exchange, a subject which occupied Locke in his writings on money and interest. But here a nostalgic John Locke looks back to simpler satisfactions. He grounds his theses about private property in a nostalgic scene of workers producing and consuming goods, untroubled by alienation or mediation of any sort. If his conscience ever troubled him about being a landlord of properties he simply inherited and collecting or evicting at a distance, he could take comfort in a chain of reasoning that led back to this scene.

Locke did not paint the picture, but neither did he inherit it. He purchased it. And as purchaser he has a strong claim to it; a claim so strong that it must seem natural, indisputable. Money was invented, Locke explains, so that people could take a nonperishable symbol in exchange for perishable products, whenever they were industrious enough to produce more than they could use. Before money was introduced, use constituted a natural limit to appropriation. No one could reasonably or rightfully hoard goods until they spoiled. The natural law of use that "does ... give us property, does also bound that property too" (31). But money makes it possible for men to possess more than they need. Locke's discussion of money conveys two conflicting messages. On the one hand, he sets out a basic Protestant-capitalist paradigm. Money is the logical invention of virtuously industrious people, who have appropriated ever greater amounts of land in order to improve the earth's productivity. If this system leads to different proportions of property, it justly reflects different degrees of industriousness. On the other hand, Locke also expresses a nostalgic attachment to the time "in the beginning, before the desire of having more than man needed, had altered the intrinsic value of things" (37); and this nostalgic voice returns to the natural use-economy of his Indian scene: "But ... this I dare boldly affirm, that the same rule of property, viz. that every man should have as much, as he could make use of, would hold still in the world, without straitening any body; since there is land enough in the world to suffice double the inhabitants, had not the invention of money, and the tacit agreement of men to put a value on it, introduced (by consent) larger possessions, and a right to them" (36). The assertion of "tacit agreement" or "consent" is important. Locke may be of two minds about the introduction of money, but men have consented to it and so have altered their economy in the proper way. Still, the conflicting implications of his discussion of money cannot be overlooked, and recent interpreters of Locke's political and economic philosophy have divided into "bourgeois" or "non-bourgeois" camps according to how they treat this confusion and others like it.

Does Locke want the Greenhill portrait because he needs it, or does his desire exceed his need? Locke claims the former, Stringer the latter. (Recall that Stringer termed the frontispiece story a "Colourable Excuse.") Locke's position seems entirely defensible; except that as he ended up not using it, and probably for the very reasons suggested by Stringer, one might wonder whether more was at work here than use value. With this suggestion we move to the fourth answer: the friend owns the picture. In "Property," Locke praises those desires associated with useful labor and condemns another, transgressive kind of desire: God gave the earth "to the use of the industrious and rational, ...

not to the fancy, or covetousness, of the quarrelsome and contentious" (34). He uses "fancy" as a contrary to reason and a partner (presumably the cause) of covetousness. When desires move outside reason and into fancy, natural economy can turn into contentious chaos. A mild version of such chaos occurs in the portrait dispute, where reason is threatened by the complicated mediations of friendship.

Locke placed great value on friendship. He had the utmost contempt for a thief. He judged it "lawful for a man to kill a thief, who has not in the least hurt him, any farther than . . . to take away his money, or what he pleases from him. . . . I have no reason to suppose, that he, who would take away my liberty, would not, when he had me in his power, take away everything else" (*Second Treatise* 18). Stringer was a problem because he was both a friend and a thief. This problem with Stringer helps point out something missing in Locke's discussion of property: something that happens when two of his presocial individuals become close enough for each to threaten the possessive autonomy of the other, in such a way that friendship and theft become coparts of a single experience. This friend/thief problem comes up in Locke's discussion only subliminally in the *Second Treatise*, when he mentions Cain and Abel and then Jacob and Esau: "Thus, at the beginning, Cain might take as much ground, as he could till, and make it his own land, and yet leave enough for Abel's sheep, to feed on; a few acres would serve for both their possessions. . . . But when there was not room enough, in the same place, for their herds to feed together, they [ancient inhabitants of Biblical lands] . . . separated, and enlarged their pasture, where it best liked them. And for the same reason, Esau went from his father and his brother, and planted in mount Seir" (38). Curiously, Locke uses Cain and Abel, and Jacob and Esau, to illustrate a natural economic harmony. He suppresses all mention of the kin competition everyone associates with these names. We get instead the happy cooperation of Cain and Abel, suspended in time before their desires became momentously entangled; and Jacob and Esau as they agree to separate, well after the dispute over the birthright stolen/purchased by Jacob. Locke's suppression here is at least as thought-provoking as his explicit argument. It shows him excluding but not erasing from his liberal property theory some subversive counterplots of contentious friendship.

Public and Spectral Blake

Blake was much readier to acknowledge "the severe contentions / Of Friendship" (*Milton* 41:32–33), but his battles with friends/thieves were no less troublesome for that. One of the most serious of these battles also had to do with a picture he believed a friend had stolen from him. Even more than with the Locke incident, it is difficult to sort out the facts; but we can at least get a feeling for the possessions and emotions at stake.

At the center of the quarrel were two depictions of Chaucer's Canterbury pilgrims, one by Blake and the other by Thomas Stothard. Blake claimed that the idea for Stothard's painting came from him. When Stothard's painting reached the public first and became quite popular, Blake was furious over what he considered a theft of his artistic property. The Chaucer fight broke out in 1807, but its origins go back to the latter part of 1805 and the negotiations surrounding another work. Robert Cromek, an engraver turned entrepreneur, arranged for Blake to draw and engrave twenty plates for an edition of Blair's *The Grave*. After he saw Blake's first engraving, Cromek decided that his style was too crude and old-fashioned to have a plausible chance of popularity. He decided to use Louis Schiavonetti for the engravings and reduced the number of engraved designs to twelve. This reduction was hard on Blake. At a time in his life when he was earning very little money, he had been counting on the original terms of Cromek's proposal. Furthermore, his engraving skills had been judged unworthy. Blake, of course, was deeply offended, although at the time he seems to have contained his anger well enough. Cromek was irritated at Blake's refusal to adopt a popular, contemporary style of engraving; he believed that Blake was stubbornly determined to ruin his chances in the name of artistic purity, over what amounted to a simple matter of technique.

Against this background, the Chaucer fight took place. Much of what we know comes from Blake's memory of the events. In 1806, according to Blake, Cromek saw at Blake's house a pencil drawing of Chaucer's Canterbury pilgrims. Cromek liked it and wanted Blake to do a finished picture to be engraved and published. Cromek no doubt wanted someone else to do the engraving, because of his objections to Blake's style. It is not clear what sort of arrangement (if any) Cromek made with Blake. Blake claimed that Cromek had commissioned him to paint the pilgrims and to do the engraving. Cromek denied giving any commission whatsoever. He also claimed that the Chaucer subject was his idea in the first place. Beginning with Gilchrist's account of the dispute, the first to blame Cromek decisively, scholarly opinion has tended to line up with Blake on the question of invention. Stothard's son wrote an article in 1863 defending Cromek, but his facts are muddled.[19] More recently, Aileen Ward has argued that Cromek's version of the story makes more sense than Blake's. Ward speculates that Blake generated his own Canterbury pilgrims in 1808 (after Stothard's painting) as a response to "Schiavonetti's facile virtuosity, Stothard's inauthentic medievalism, and Cromek's crass commercialism." When he was telling the story later in life, his memory may have fused the details of the Chaucer episode with the earlier problems surrounding the Blair project.[20]

Ward presents an interesting case against Blake's memory of the facts, but important elements of her argument are (necessarily) speculative. Blake's account remains a plausible alternative to Cromek's. It still seems reasonable that Blake came up with the idea for the design. Cromek was unlikely to have wanted Blake as an engraver, given his experience with *The Grave*. But he admired Blake's inventive genius enough to use him as a creative resource. If he felt he had to be careful with the volatile artist, Cromek might have resorted to some sort of deception in order to clear the way for the project. He might have promised Blake the engraving profits without ever intending to grant them. The more one distrusts Cromek, the more likely Blake's account becomes. But much of Cromek's bad reputation comes from Blake's bitter vilification. If Blake's accusations cannot be trusted entirely—because he angrily misinterpreted Cromek and reshaped his memory of events—Cromek becomes less of a villain. Blake attacked Cromek so passionately in his notebook poems that it is easy to neglect evidence of a different relationship between the two men. Bentley found an 1807 letter from Cromek to a friend in which Cromek not only praises Blake's work but addresses such subjects as the divine poetical imagination in a strikingly Blakean style.[21]

In any event, Cromek suggested the subject to Stothard and commissioned him to do an oil painting. Stothard had been a good friend of Blake's for some twenty-five years. Blake may have seen and praised Stothard's Canterbury picture before it was finished. But when the painting came out and proved a great success, Blake protested that Cromek and Stothard had stolen his idea. He was extremely angry with both of them and with his close friend John Flaxman as well, whom he considered a conspirator. Flaxman was a friend of Cromek's, but no evidence suggests that he participated in any mistreatment of Blake. Scholars also doubt that Stothard knowingly stole from him.

These events obviously unsettled Blake's emotions. Like Locke, he was "naturally choleric." In this case he was angry enough to lose his composure and to alienate at least one or two friends who did not deserve his scorn. However one sorts out the blame, the Chaucer fight did serious damage. It contributed substantially to Blake's professional isolation after 1807.

We can ask the same question for Blake that we did for Locke: who owned the picture of the Canterbury pilgrims? And it might be possible to attempt a parallel answer, in four parts: public, artist, purchaser, friend. But this scheme proves less convenient when applied to Blake. Cromek is a purchaser (perhaps investor is a better word), but we cannot be sure of what he promised and did. Artists and friends abound in the episode, but the two roles cannot be separated cleanly: Stothard and Flaxman act simultaneously as artists and friends. Cromek, in fact, is an artist as well as an investor, and Blake early on even called him a friend. These three answers are relevant but hard to work with. However, the fourth answer—the general public—can point the way to a more helpful approach.

When Blake finished his own version of the pilgrims, he submitted it to the public in his 1809 exhibition. In the prose surrounding this event (the *Descriptive Catalogue* and *Public Address*), he appeals repeatedly to the public as judge and owner of his work. Because "Genius and Inspiration are the great Origin and Bond of Society" (528), the exhibition becomes "a duty which Mr. B. owes to the Public, who have always recognized him, and patronized him, however hidden by artifices" (538). "It has been said of late years the English Public have no Taste for Painting This is a Falshood The English are as Good Judges of Painting as of Poetry" (581). The relative merits of Blake and his artistic adversaries are "now to be Decided by The Public"; and "The Public will know, & Posterity will know" the genius of Blake (571–72). Posterity came through for Blake, but not the public: Stothard's painting was a great success, while Blake's was largely ignored.

In an 1807 letter to Blake, Cromek wonders why the success of Stothard's picture has so upset him: "Why shd you so *furiously rage* at the success of the little picture of 'The Pilgrimage'? 3,000 people have now *seen it and have approved of it*. Believe me, yours is '*the voice of one crying in the wilderness!*'"[22] Cromek's question can easily be construed as an impertinent provocation, and certainly Blake took it as such. If only for the sake of argument, though, we might imagine a defense of Cromek's question. Why should Blake be so upset over property rights to a work of art? The work itself is of paramount importance. Stothard's painting comes from his own imagination and articulates his artistic identity. Even if the subject came from Blake, Blake's idea came from Chaucer, and so on, back through the infinite channels of artistic influence. And even if Stothard's painting is founded on an act of deception, the work of art can still stand by itself. Blake, after all, judged Macpherson's and Chatterton's poems to be of great worth, despite all the evidence of deception and posing ("Annotations to Wordsworth's *Poems*" 665). Their cases are hardly identical to Stothard's, but a similar moral might be drawn: attend to the work of art, not to where it came from.

Cromek's question touched Blake in a vulnerable spot. Blake felt that great art must reach the public. It will probably have to re-create the public in order to gain their appreciation, but in some way the public will recognize it and own it. When Cromek labeled Blake as "the voice of one crying in the wilderness," he placed him in the prophetic isolation to which he was becoming accustomed, but which he found depressing—for philosophical reasons as well as more practical economic ones. Blake defended himself by exalting his alienation. Even in the *Public Address* quoted earlier to demonstrate his respect for the public, he implied a contrary perspective: the genius at odds with and obscure to an ignorant public. "Commerce Cannot endure Individual Merit its insatiable Maw must be fed by what all can do Equally well at least it is so in England as I have found to my Cost these Forty Years" (573). He uses "commerce" instead of "public," but either way he is talking about mass appeal. Blake the public artist expects appreciation from a community whose needs he understands. Blake the private artist defends his obscurity as a credential.

Morris Eaves has analyzed most thoroughly the problem of audience for Blake. Eaves sets out three dangerous relationships between artist and audience, all of which Blake had to avoid. The audience can end up determining the values of the artist; the artist can manipulate the audience with rhetoric; and the artist can withdraw into solitary obscurity.[23] Eaves proposes a romantic solution to Romantic problems of audience. For the Romantics, the judge of art should be attached rather than detached. The ideal audience has "an intimate personal relation tied emotionally to the author." The relationship of artist to audience is more like "lover to beloved" than "entertainer to public, performer to judge, teacher to student." If the audience grants the artist "what Jesus usually calls faith, or what Blake calls love and friendship, he then creates coherence from the center outward until a community forms in his image or imagination, until finally the distinction between the artist at the center and the audience on the circumference becomes irrelevant."[24]

Scholars inclined to be tough on this sort of transcendent conclusion should acknowledge that Eaves has at least conveyed a Romantic ideal. Eaves draws this ideal relationship from Blake's own words about love, friendship, and the public. It would be unwise, however, to let "friendship" stand as a simple, adequate vehicle for conveying this ideal. Blake, like Locke, had trouble with friends who were also thieves, and he addressed the ambiguities of friendship much more directly. The primary conflict might be restated as follows, to align it for comparison with Locke: in Blake, is selfishness part of the problem or part of the solution? As with Locke, both answers must be taken seriously. Locke's selfish possessiveness can be seen both as a passionate transgression of reason (problem) and as an intelligent application of reason (solution). Blake condemns "selfhood" as a primary obstruction to redemption; but it can be difficult to distinguish this obstructive self-centering from its redemptive counterpart, the ferocious pride of a visionary excluding himself from the uninspired. For the sake of this discussion, it will be useful to defer the most common "solution" to this difficulty, whether delivered by Marxist, psychoanalytic, or high Romantic reading: namely, that the opposition between self and other will be exposed as an illusion, when the various specters of false consciousness have been exorcised. The conflict is no less interesting for being spectral.

The place to begin is with selfhood as a problem—because Blake treats the theme so explicitly, especially in the long, later works. (He probably remembered the term from Boehme, who identified "selfhood" as a primary symptom of fallen humanity.)[25] An early treatment of selfishness is found in "The Clod and the Pebble," but the clod's opposition to selfishness is so facile, totalizing, and appropriative that it complements rather than resists the pebble's voice. *Urizen* presents a fall caused by self-enclosure; and in this poem the imagination of a separate self seems unequivocally harmful—even if some elements of Urizen's condition do prefigure the later, obscure Blake: "Here alone I in books formd of metals / Have written the secrets of wisdom" (4:24–25). In *Milton*, the attack on selfhood becomes a principal theme. Milton knows right after "The Bard's Song" that selfhood is his problem. He descends in "self-annihilation" (14:22) to overcome what he calls, at different times, the "fallacious," "deadly," and "warlike selfhood." Milton is confident of his redemptive theme from the moment he descends through his final speech. At times he may seem a little too confident—almost belligerently so—to suit his theme of self-annihilation. Even if self-annihilation means something different from the abolition of self (as Mitchell, for example, has argued),[26] it still calls for such a drastic refiguration that only metaphors of death will convey the process.

In *Jerusalem* self-annihilation remains a prominent theme, but instead of a confident Milton to speak for it we have a troubled Los and his Spectre. An early exchange between Los and the Spectre shows the antiselfhood solution in its latest and most telling configuration. At plate 6 Los will find the Spectre separating from him, and for the rest of the poem (at least until the apocalyptic ending, where the separation is simply declared over by narrative fiat) his identity will be doubled. Even before Los enters, the epic narrator demonstrates a double attitude about friendship and selfhood:

Trembling I sit day and night, my friends are astonish'd at me.
Yet they forgive my wanderings, I rest not from my great task! . . .
O Saviour pour upon me thy Spirit of meekness & love:
Annihilate the Selfhood in me, be thou all my life! (5:16–17, 21–22)

The first two lines show Blake the extravagant visionary making life difficult for his friends. The other two lines suggest an effort to counteract such self-assertion, under the banner of self-annihilation, borrowed from Blake's Milton. "Meekness and love" are supposed to restore friendship. But self-annihilation will be much more difficult for Los than it was for Milton.

Los at the beginning of *Jerusalem* is struggling with anger, the same passion that disturbed Locke's composure. And like Locke, Blake's Los becomes passionate about friends/thieves. The Spectre accuses Los's friends of exploiting his talent and stealing his works. Los wants to resist this message, but he admits that the Spectre "Hast just cause to be irritated" (7:53). The Spectre splits away from Los like a projection of his anger, "bitterly cursing him for his friendship / To Albion" (6:5–6). Los responds angrily to his angry double, but his anger has at least two different causes. Apparently he is angry about the Spectre's anger; but his speeches also suggest that, like the Spectre, Los germinates "murderous thoughts" against friends and society in general. His anger at once disputes and duplicates the Spectre's. Los names pity as the antidote to wrath, although he makes it clear that behavior in this case lags behind theory:

> They have divided themselves by Wrath. they must be united by
> Pity: let us therefore take example & warning O my Spectre,
> O that I could abstain from wrath! O that the Lamb
> Of God would look upon me and pity me in my fury.
> In anguish of regeneration! in terrors of self annihilation:
> Pity must join together those whom wrath has torn in sunder.
> (7:57–62)

Los's solution for wrath has a pious, conservative ring to it—not incongruous within *Jerusalem*, but problematic alongside Blake's earlier poetry. The trouble with this solution, as noted in the preceding chapter, is that wrath may have a stronger claim than pity to be a unifying emotion. Wrath announces that someone has found the passionate, if temporary, integrity of a cause; whereas pity "divides the soul," according to the narrator of *Urizen* (13:53). Los in *Jerusalem* has decided not only to be an agent but a recipient of pity ("O that the Lamb / Of God would look upon me and pity me in my fury"). He declares himself willing to risk self-division for the eventual benefit of community, even if it requires "the terrors of self annihilation." The Spectre resists such terrors, and Los defines him as the antithesis of self-annihilation: "Thou art my Pride & self-righteousness: I have found thee out" (8:30).

It is the Spectre, indeed, who must carry the argument against self-annihilation—the argument, in other words, for selfishness as a solution rather than as a problem. But when the Spectre speaks directly in *Jerusalem*, he can come off too simply as a villain. Despite earning scattered moments of sympathy and praise, the Spectre too often lives up to his graphic depiction as a vampire bat. A good place to look for the effective Spectre is in Blake's letters, especially those surrounding his residence at Felpham, where he made his most strenuous effort to translate Blake the extravagant visionary into Blake the successful public artist. In these letters the term "spectre" appears only a few times, but if we keep in mind Los's definition of the Spectre—"Thou art my Pride & self-righteousness"—then the letters become abundantly spectral. The letters from 1801 through 1804 show Blake trying to fulfill contracts for public work and to maintain friendships with patrons and colleagues, during a time when both of these public elements of his career were becoming increasingly jeopardized. The spectral Blake emerges in the letters as the pride and self-righteousness that he could not or would not finally suppress. By looking at some of these letters we can get a feeling for the satisfactions (as well as the dangers) of Blake's imperial self.

In a famous 1804 letter to Hayley, marking the end of the group under discussion, Blake declared emphatically that he had overcome his spectral problems. "For now! O Glory! and O Delight! I have entirely reduced that Spectrous Fiend to his station, whose annoyance has been the ruin of my labours for the last passed twenty years of my life" (756). The imagery here suggests the Los-Spectre relationship in *Jerusalem*. The letter elsewhere makes clear that the Spectre is Blake's way of accounting for failures in his creative work—both the work of art and of personal relationships. As to the former, the Spectre has caused Blake's "incessantly labouring and incessantly spoiling what I had done well." Blake has suffered especially in his engraving work; but now "I am really drunk with intellectual vision whenever I take a pencil or graver into my hand." By saying pencil or graver, he includes not just his own designing but (for him) the more difficult cooperative work of engraving from someone else's design. As to the spoiling of relationships, Blake calls his Spectre "the enemy of conjugal love," and in both this letter and the similar one that follows it, he cites a renewal of friendships as one of the chief benefits of his enlightenment.

In the letters of 1801–1803, however, the Spectre intermittently appears a solution rather than a problem, therapy rather than neurosis. In a letter to Butts (11 September 1801), he mentions specters for the first time. The letter is interesting because on the surface he uses the word negatively, to apologize to Butts for not having completed promised work; but a careful reading suggests that Blake is bragging at least as much as he is apologizing. He begins by hoping that Butts "will continue to excuse my want of steady perseverance" and then offers a spectral explanation for the delay:

> I labour incessantly & accomplish not one half of what I intend because my Abstract folly hurries me often away while I am at work, carrying me over Mountains & Valleys which are not Real in a Land of Abstraction where Spectres of the Dead wander. This I endeavour to prevent & with my whole might chain my feet to the world of Duty & Reality. but in vain! the faster I bind the better is the Ballast for I so far from being bound down take the world with me in my flights & often it seems lighter than a ball of wool rolled by the wind Bacon & Newton would prescribe ways of making the world heavier to me & Pitt would prescribe distress for a medicinal potion. but as none on Earth can give me Mental Dis-

tress, & I know that all Distress inflicted by Heaven is a Mercy, a Fig for all Corporeal Such Distress is My mock & scorn. Alas wretched happy ineffectual labourer of times moments that I am! who shall deliver me from this Spirit of Abstraction & Improvidence. Such my Dear Sir Is the truth of my state. & I tell it you in palliation of my seeming neglect of your most pleasant orders. (716)

Blake must be speaking of his private work—perhaps *Vala* in particular—as "Abstract folly" in a "Land of Abstraction where Spectres of the Dead wander." Thus his first use of specters in the letters refers not to the customary enemies of Blakean imagination but to the daemonic sublimity that inspires his great work. Although a few passages from *The Four Zoas* and *Jerusalem* provide support for such a connection between specters and visionary inspiration, many interpreters do not want to allow it—and either just ignore the reference or find some way to normalize or dismiss it.[27] These strategies, as sensible as they seem, may be missing something. Spectral themes in Blake always involve some version of separation or abstraction from an original unity or presence, now lost but still imaginable. In the letter above Blake calls spectral his attention to prophetic visions at the expense of more communal and publishable work, which Butts would recognize as more "real." Blake's attitude toward this spectral abstraction is not simple. He says he repents of it and assigns it to the land of the dead. But at the same time he depends on it for self-esteem: herein lies his power to contest Bacon, Newton, and Pitt. And even as he asks for deliverance from it, he nourishes it by establishing a severe dualism between mental and corporeal phenomena. Such dualism will increasingly appear in the letters as a response to problems attending public work and friendships.

In another letter to Butts, about a year later, Blake again writes to stave off Butts's disappointment. Here his apology becomes more aggressively a self-defense. He explains that he has been "very unhappy" due to the frustrations of commercial work; but he rouses himself to end the letter with a declaration of triumph that could be called spectral: "And now let me finish with assuring you that Tho I have been very unhappy I am so no longer I am again Emerged into the light of Day I still & shall to Eternity Embrace Christianity and Adore him who is the Express image of God but I have traveld thro Perils & Darkness not unlike a Champion I have Conquerd and shall still Go on Conquering Nothing can withstand the fury of my Course among the Stars of God & in the Abysses of the Accuser My Enthusiasm is still what it was only Enlarged and confirmd" (720). Blake will periodically announce this triumph for about two years, most prominently in the 1804 letter about the "Spectrous Fiend." Here, though, spectral pride acts as solution rather than problem. He presents himself as a conquering champion, a kind of Christian soldier but of magnified cosmic proportions: he projects himself upward "among the Stars of God." His enthusiasm has become enlarged—perhaps his answer to the miniatures his public likes to order (including Mrs. Butts, whose miniature Blake has just apologized for neglecting). Blake declares a furious, exclusive confidence and entertains no self-accusation. If the Spectre will eventually be seen as Los's pride and self-righteousness, then Blake has certainly relied on the Spectre to fashion this sublime triumph over unhappiness. (It is interesting to note, however, that in a postscript he tempers his fury and guides the letter back down to earth. He offers his friend a little household hint: "A Piece of Sea Weed Serves for a Barometer it gets wet & dry as the weather gets so." As if to apologize or at least compensate for his trip up to the stars of God, he offers a minute particular from the sea of time and space. Butts may now be more content about Blake's ability to cope with the pressures, atmospheric and otherwise, of life in nature.)

As Blake's letters to Butts increasingly express frustration with Hayley, his imperial, spectral self comes forward more frequently. In the letter of 25 April 1803, he says he must leave Felpham so that "I may converse with my friends in Eternity. See Visions, Dream Dreams, & prophecy & speak Parables unobserv'd & at liberty from the Doubts of other Mortals. perhaps Doubts proceeding from Kindness. but Doubts are always pernicious Especially when we Doubt our Friends Christ is very decided on this Point. 'He who is Not With Me is Against Me' There is no Medium or Middle state" (728). Here is Blake at his most exclusive, denying the middle ground that grounds all intersubjectivity, and sublimating friendship to aerial purity ("my friends in Eternity"). Possessed by immortals, he claims unquestionable self-possession. In the next letter he refers to the absolute authority of his "Own Self Will" and wants all friends to leave him entirely to his own judgment. Remembering that he is writing to Butts, he adds, "As you my dear Friend have always left me for which I shall never cease to honour & respect you" (731); thus saving at least one friend, if one whom three years ago Blake had thanked for his "reprehension of follies by me fostered" (711).

Blake's imperial self is often accompanied in these 1803 letters by references to daemonic inspiration. The daemonics serve both to elevate Blake and to excuse his proud exclusiveness. He tells Butts "that I am under the direction of Messengers from Heaven Daily & Nightly but the nature of such things is not as some suppose, without trouble or care." In a later letter the trouble and care drop out as Blake presents an extreme countermyth to the painful work of engraving: "I have written this Poem from immediate Dictation twelve or sometimes twenty or thirty lines at a time without Premeditation & even against my Will. the Time it has taken in writing was thus renderd Non Existent. & an immense Poem Exists which seems to be the Labour of a long Life all producd without Labour or Study" (728–29). By calling this a countermyth I do not mean to act as Blake's father reportedly did and accuse him of lying about his visions; nor do I wish to dispute the phenomenological validity of inspiration as Blake frequently describes it. I simply point to this version of creativity as a conveniently simple reversal of the painstaking, time-consuming process he also describes, sometimes with approval and delight. Visionary dictation means unfallen work with no lapse of time, and, unlike engraving or portrait painting, no other people to get in the way—only the Eternal friends whose minds and hands are at one with his own.

Despite their obvious differences in subject matter and rhetorical conditions, Blake's scene of prelapsarian inspiration might be compared with Locke's scene of original economy set in America. Blake's daemonic possession amounts to supreme self-possession, and Locke's liberal right of self-possession emanates from a privileged, unprovably original possessor. Both are scenes of archaic simplicity, purified of inconveniences for the autonomous subject: before a fall into alienated labor, displacements of value, mediated desire, and friends who are also thieves. Locke and Blake depend on these scenes of the exclusive subject, however much they elsewhere try to surpass them, by one or another theory of self-transcendence and assimilation into a public.

Chapter 7

Printing

In her study of print culture in early modern Europe, Elizabeth Eisenstein emphasizes the close ties between the printing press and the development of Enlightenment patterns of thinking. The expanding power of printing institutions and, less tangibly, the *esprit de systeme* created by modern printed books, "made it possible for Grotius, Descartes, Richard Simon and John Locke to make a permanent impression on the European mind."[1] These deep influences of printing were suggested at least as far back as Bacon: printing, along with gunpowder and the magnet, "changed the whole face and state of things throughout the world ... insomuch that no empire, no sect, no star seems to have exerted greater power and influence in human affairs than these mechanical inventions."[2] More recently, of course, McLuhan had everyone thinking about print societies and what came before and after them. Blake started his work when modern print society was mature and thriving. He wanted to subvert it by "printing in the infernal method," as he says in *The Marriage of Heaven and Hell*. McLuhan paid tribute to Blake's subversion at the end of *The Gutenberg Galaxy*, where he invokes Blake as his presiding muse: "Determined as he was to explain the causes and effects of psychic change, both personal and social, he arrived long ago at the theme of *The Gutenberg Galaxy*: 'The Seven Nations fled before him: they became what they beheld.' Blake makes quite explicit that when sense ratios change, men change. Sense ratios change when any one sense or bodily or mental function is externalized in technological form ... Such was the origin of lineal, fragmented analysis with its remorseless power of homogenization."[3]

For Locke as well as for Blake, printing was more than just a technological medium by which to express and publicize ideas. Print consciousness influenced those ideas in substantive ways. Locke's *Essay* is not only a printed book but is a book about printing, in the figurative sense that shaped Locke's epistemology. In many of Blake's works he resists the implications of Locke's print consciousness, both in explicit thematic arguments and through calculated revisions of ordinary expressive media.

Two scenes from the biographies provide useful background. Locke was a significant champion of freedom of the press (he argued successfully against the Act for the Regulation of Printing),[4] and it was the liberated eighteenth-century press that so effectively spread his ideas. But one of his letters records an interesting moment when he expressed irritation at the mediating vehicle of print. When he was in Amsterdam in 1688 attending to the printing of an epitome of the *Essay*, he complained to Benjamin Furly about the slow process: he was forced "to wait here the leisure of drunken workmen, who have so great a reverence for the holy days that they could not till today quit the cabarets, the places of their devotion, and betake themselves to their profane callings . . . It costs, as I have already told you, not a little pains and patience to be at any rate an author."[5] Postlapsarian authors must suffer the pains of giving birth: there is a gap between intellectual intention and the actual production of ideas, as thoughts become words and words become printed texts. Locke jokes about the "profane calling" of printers, whose Christmas drinking interferes with his full investiture as an author. But the joke may hint just slightly of the religious trouble this author suspects he will raise, once printed and publicized as a profane competitor to the Bible. In a later letter he referred to the *Essay* as his "heterodox testament."[6]

At a similar moment in his career, Blake had more substantial worries about the printing and publication of his work. J. T. Smith gives this account: "Blake, after deeply perplexing himself as to the mode of accomplishing the publication of his illustrated songs, without their being subject to the expenses of letter-press, his brother Robert stood before him in one of his visionary imaginations, and so decidedly directed him in the way in which he ought to proceed, that he immediately followed his advice."[7] The method presented in this vision turned out to be a version of relief etching that allowed the printing of text and designs on plates in a complicated but unified process. Blake learned to write and design with an impervious ink, which would not be affected by a corrosive liquid later applied to the copperplate. The rest of the plate would be eaten away, leaving the raised lettering and designs. As Blake refined this technique, according to Joseph Viscomi, it "enabled him to write and draw directly on the plate as though he were sketching and writing on paper, something that would be impossible in the other graphic media." Because each plate thereby produced "was not a reproduction or imitation of other images, the composition necessarily printed as originally *produced*, free of the visual distortion that characteristically occurs when one set of codes is translated into another."[8] If in the early 1780s Blake thought to disseminate his work by means of traditional print,[9] he abandoned that course and set up his own means of production, now freed from the mediating influences of ordinary press publication.

The story of Robert Blake's visionary instruction loses a little of its impact when we learn that one of his living friends, George Cumberland, had earlier suggested some similar ideas.[10] But the vision should still be treated as a meaningful event. It shows that Blake's solution to fallen production was quite different from Locke's. Locke was vexed but patient with the profane media and entered print culture as one of its exemplary authors. Blake bypassed the profane through visionary instruction, and in so doing he created a body of work that could be appreciated only much later. Even now his work requires the mediation of print for effective publication, despite the misgivings of scholarly purists who worry about translating Blake into the medium he rejected.

Printing and Enthusiasm

I propose the topic of printing as a convenient entry into epistemological conversation between Locke and Blake. The appropriate Locke texts all come from the *Essay*. For Blake, the best place to start would be his personal copy of the *Essay*, full of indignant marginal notes. Evidently there was or is such a book—Blake mentions it in his annotations to *The Works of Sir Joshua Reynolds*—but no one has discovered it. Until it turns up, though, we can make do with the Reynolds marginalia. According to Blake, his Locke notes are similar to those he wrote about Sir Joshua: "I read Burkes Treatise when very Young at the same time I read Locke on Human Understanding & Bacons Advancement of Learning on Every one of these Books I wrote my Opinions & on looking them over find that my Notes on Reynolds in this Book are exactly Similar. I felt the Same Contempt & Abhorrence then; that I do now" (660). His contempt for Reynolds—similar in substance, he tells us, to his contempt for Locke's *Essay*—comes across in two recurrent themes of epistemological criticism. One theme has to do with abstraction and generalization, two habits of mind by which reason preempts the other faculties. The other has to do with the denial of innate ideas and inspiration. These epistemological positions produce two dangerous consequences. The religious consequence is atheism (obvious to Blake despite professions of faith by Locke, Bacon, Reynolds, et al.). The secular consequence is political oppression (obvious to Blake despite the liberal reputation of Locke and those who carried on his work). "This Whole Book was Written to Serve Political Purposes" (641), he writes, as he reacts to some introductory remarks praising Reynolds and lamenting this age of "seditious declamations."

I want to take up first the theme of abstraction and generalization, especially as it relates to print consciousness. Blake reacts against Joshua Reynolds's praise of "the ancient sculptors . . . [who were] indefatigable in the school of nature": "All Forms are Perfect in the Poets Mind. but these are not Abstracted nor Compounded from Nature but are from Imagination" (648). Blake's terminology evokes Lockean epistemology, in which useful ideas are abstracted and compounded from primary sense impressions. One result of all this abstraction is the elevation of general ideas above concrete particulars. Over and over Blake sneers at Reynolds's deference to the general. When Reynolds writes, for example, that "art [must] get above all singular forms, local customs, particularities, and details of every kind," Blake calls this "A Folly: Singular & Particular Detail is the Foundation of the Sublime" (647). Throughout the notes he praises "minute discrimination" and "minute particulars." His most quotable note of this sort comes in response to Edmund Burke's prefatory remarks. According to Burke, "this disposition to abstractions, to generalizing and classification, is the great glory of the human mind." Blake replies, "To Generalize is to be an Idiot" (641). He blames Lockean epistemology for the rout of inspiration in the name of reason. He bristles whenever Reynolds celebrates reason at the expense of enthusiasm: "What has Reasoning to do with the Art of Painting?" (647).

For our present focus, we might reformulate his question: what has reasoning to do with the technology of printing? According to McLuhan and more recent scholars, the printing press has a profound connection with reason and the cluster of subfaculties and virtues associated with reason. McLuhan lists five characteristics of print logic: abstraction, uniformity, repeatability, visuality, and quantification. The keystone in this list would have to be abstraction, the process by which some element of a specific perception, idea, text, or event is removed so as to be usefully transferable. Machines that use movable type stimulate and stand for an increasingly systematic and abstractive style of thinking. Eisenstein points to such features as regularly numbered pages, punctuation marks, section breaks, running heads, and indices as visual patterns shaping the new orderliness and uniformity of print consciousness.[11] Walter J. Ong describes all this with more angst than appreciation: "Typographic control typically impresses more by its tidiness and inevitability: the lines perfectly regular, all justified on the right side, everything coming out even visually . . . This is an insistent world of cold, non-human facts." Print reduced sensory experience to a visual surface and "encouraged human beings to think of their own interior conscious and unconscious resources as more and more thing-like, impersonal and religiously neutral. Print encouraged the mind to sense that its possessions were held in some sort of inert mental space."[12] McLuhan earlier pointed to "the uniform processing of minds by the habit of reading the printed work," a "technology of homogeneous citizens" fostered by print consciousness.[13] A more recent study by Michael Warner discusses how "print ideology" created "a neutral and rational ground of public representation" and "valorized the general above the personal."[14] Blake's reaction against abstraction, generalization, and cold reason, it seems clear enough, can stand at least partially as a reaction against print consciousness. (Appropriately, he recorded his indignation by writing in the margins of Reynolds, working against the authoritative tidiness of the printed book.) The significance of this layer of meaning should not be underestimated. Alvin Kernan observes that the nature of truth was at stake: England of the 1790s was a highly developed print society, characterized by "the absolute mark of print culture, a generally accepted view that what is printed is true, or at least truer than any other type of record."[15]

One way of approaching Locke's immersion in print consciousness and Blake's reaction against it is to look at some aesthetic differences between the *Essay Concerning Human Understanding* and Blake's illuminated printing. There has never been much discussion of the artistry of the *Essay*, and this is not surprising: his long-winded style is tolerated more than admired, and Locke himself treated his prose as a mundane, unexceptional product that he was perfectly willing to see condensed and abstracted. Blake at the beginning of *Jerusalem* tells us that "Every word and every letter is studied and put into its fit place." He encourages his audience to pay the utmost attention to detail. In Blake's aesthetics, no text of real value can be abstracted or abridged.

Locke was perfectly willing to let the *Essay* be published in an abridged version. In fact, he went to some trouble in 1687 and 1688 to see that Jean le Clerc's French abridgment was published, reprinted, and circulated. (He got up from a sickbed to see it through the press.)[16] Even after the full *Essay* had been published in two editions, he strongly encouraged the publication of another abridgment, this time in English by an Oxford don, John Wynne. Locke told Wynne that much of the explicatory material might be omitted without damage to the work.[17] He welcomed abridgment because he had no aesthetic pretensions about his prose. In his "Epistle to the Reader" at the beginning of the *Essay*, he speaks almost disparagingly of his writing: it has been a "diversion" for his "idle hours"; it was "begun by chance" and written in "incoherent parcels"; it should probably be "reduced" or "contracted," but he is "now too lazie, or too busie to make it shorter"; it is not written "for Men of large Thoughts and quick Apprehensions" but is "fitted to Men of my own size" (6–8).

With this last comment, Locke's tropes of modesty begin to modulate toward self-congratulation. What look like literary faults turn out to be philosophical virtues. The great advantage of the *Essay* is its accessibility to a public endowed with nothing more than common sense. Ordinary readers will now be able to grasp "some Truths, which established Prejudice, or the Abstractness of the *Ideas* themselves, might render difficult" (8). No longer will prejudice and arcana block understanding by posing as innate ideas. Locke promises an equal opportunity for philosophical knowledge, a clean slate for common instruction. Locke does not abandon his modest reluctance to appear in print ("I have so little Affection to be in Print" [9]), but more and more this modesty looks like a convention of good manners, borrowed from an older system of courtly letters.[18] Biographical records suggest that there was nothing more important to him than appearing in print—where he was determined to make, as he says in his "Epistle," "a clear and lasting Impression." "My appearing therefore in Print, being on purpose to be as useful as I may, I think it necessary to make what I have to say, as easie and intelligible to all sorts of Readers as I can" (9).

For Blake, the *Essay*'s printed truth made it all too easy for Locke to shape a common mind. Recall Blake's early pun on the title: "An Easy of Huming Understanding" (*An Island in the Moon*, 456). Blake's aesthetics call for something more difficult. Various scholars have noticed that Blake's theory and practice of art constitute a radical form of Romantic expressive aesthetics.[19] He asks his audience to discard simple distinctions between production and product and to view each work as an ongoing embodiment of imagination, which he celebrates as the foremost human activity. To abstract or abridge a work, or to reproduce it by soulless mechanical means, threatens the integrity of imaginative presence on which its significance depends. As we have seen, Blake went to much trouble to devise a means by which he could bypass the ordinary machinery of printing and publishing. Copies of his illuminated books differ one from another in coloring and other finishing details and sometimes quite obviously in altered sequences of plates. Although many differences in finishing detail must be consequences of tools and format (as Essick and Viscomi have persuasively argued),[20] other differences from one copy to another are more significant; and Blake's ideas about art privilege the unique moment of inspired expression. The Santa Cruz Blake Study Group (Thomas Vogler, Nelson Hilton, and Paul Mann) has drawn the most radical implications from this line of inquiry. They criticize Erdman's edition for altering and diminishing Blake's work.[21] The charge may seem strange, given Erdman's efforts to produce an unnormalized, minutely faithful text; indeed, one might expect the opposite sort of complaint, about the difficulties of eccentric spelling, spacing, and punctuation. But the Santa Cruz Group argues that Erdman's edition erases differences as it tries for a unitary "best" text and reduces Blake's imaginative abundance to suit the mass-reproducing print medium he rejected.

Paul Mann has elsewhere admitted that this radically purist approach is itself problematic. Blake's works cannot be reproduced and interpreted "without ceasing to be Blake's, without becoming an object precluded by [Blake's] production-aesthetic"; and there is an inherent tension in Blake's aesthetics between "the autotelic and the instrumental . . . between insemination and dissemination, between production and distribution." Nevertheless, Mann emphasizes Blake's resistance to the ordinary mediations of literary production. "Since the primary function of Blake's book is to (re)present or rather to *embody* imaginative activity, the 'Poetic Genius' in all its dimensions and operations," it follows that "the 'meaning' of any Blake book is thus, first and foremost, that Blake made it, and made it *this way*, not just textually, not even only as a composite art, but fully, materially, as 'Itself & Not Intermeasurable with or by any Thing Else.'"[22] Although many scholars do not worry about reproduction as much as the Santa Cruz group does, everyone recognizes Blake's attack on "the fatal Slumber into which Booksellers & Trading Dealers have thrown [Englishmen]" ("Public Address"). Literary work turned out by machines for a publisher lends itself much more readily to abstraction and generalization than a work that insists on the minute particulars of its unique imaginative moment. Blake's anger at the generalizing tendencies of Reynolds, Burke, and Locke can be seen in part as a reaction against the medium of their publication.

Before settling too comfortably into these conclusions, however, we need to address a few complications in the matter of generalization versus minute particulars. Locke is in one sense a philosopher of particulars, and Blake sometimes sounds like an artist of the general. When Locke talks about substance and essence, he conveys a double message about generalization. He says that generalization is necessary for any advanced mental activity: "to talk of specifick Differences in Nature, without reference to general *Ideas* and Names, is to talk unintelligibly" (3.6.5). This is the sort of passage that must have disgusted Blake as he read the *Essay*. But the whole chapter, even as it praises the utility of abstract generalization, actually focuses on the particularities that are lost in general ideas, which are "designedly imperfect: And 'tis visible at first sight, that several of those Qualities, that are to be found in the Things themselves, are purposely left out of *generical Ideas*" (3.6.32). Locke wants to debunk the common notion of "essence": he argues that what we know is a collection of particulars, no one of which can be considered essential or accidental. When we form ideas of essence, we are dealing with "nominal essence"—that is, we are giving a name which records an overlap of observable qualities; we are not identifying the "real essence," which is "that particular constitution, which every Thing has within it self" (3.6.6). Only God and angels can know real essence. Locke's argument acknowledges the primacy of particulars against the nominal generalizations of reason. According to Yolton, "it is in the account of particulars that [Locke] breaks most markedly with tradition" in metaphysics.[23]

In some sense, then, Locke is Blake's ally against Reynolds. When Reynolds de-emphasizes "the minute accidental discriminations of particular objects," Blake protests: "Minute Discrimination is Not Accidental All Sublimity is founded on Minute Discrimination" (643). Locke's disruption of the essence-accident distinction would similarly complicate Reynolds. Blake might acknowledge this, however, and still complain. He might tell Locke in a marginal note that humans, like God and angels, can know real particulars perfectly well, if only they can shake off the slumber of abstract philosophy and revive their poetic genius. But Blake's genius does not always reside in minute particulars. In fact, when Blake is writing in his most Platonic voice, he assumes a sharp distinction between accident and essential substance. Here is an example from the *Descriptive Catalogue,* as he instructs people how to view his picture of the Canterbury pilgrims: "The characters of Chaucer's Pilgrims are the characters which compose all ages and nations . . . for we see the same characters repeated again and again, in animals, vegetables, minerals, and in men; nothing new occurs in identical existence; Accident ever varies, Substance can never suffer change nor decay" (532). Another example would be the following lines from *Milton*—more like a prayer than a lecture but philosophically similar to the first passage:

> Whatever can be Created can be Annihilated Forms cannot
> The Oak is cut down by the Ax, the Lamb falls by the Knife
> But their Forms Eternal Exist, For-ever. Amen Hallelujah. (32:36–38)

"To Generalize is to be an Idiot," but Blake cultivates the general—and risks the idiotic, from an empirical philosopher's point of view—when his imagination takes a Platonic turn.

Blake's approval of Platonism was not consistent or comprehensive, but he did ordinarily disdain reason and memory as visionary resources. They depend heavily on abstraction and generalization. They deny epistemological priority to inspiration and grant it to sensory imprintings, which are then shepherded by the various faculties of a posteriori mind. Blake grouped Locke with Bacon and Newton in a trinity of materialist thinkers dangerously affiliated with the atheistic atomism of Epicurus and Lucretius.[24] Classical atomism had definite attractions for Enlightenment thinkers trying to overthrow Aristotle. They came to see Epicurean physics as a respectable theoretical model, even though many of its conjectures and elaborations were clearly outdated. The theories of Democritus, Epicurus, and Lucretius account for sensation by a process of atomic shedding and the reception of likenesses by organs of sense. Locke, who was significantly influenced by the French Epicurean Gassendi, gives an account of sensation which shares basic features with the atomistic model. Locke mentions atomism infrequently and usually to condemn randomness or the exclusion of the immaterial. It is nevertheless clear that he felt its pull.

Locke repeatedly had to fend off the atheistic implications of some of its more attractive arguments. In journals he frequently noted new arguments against atheism, especially the kind founded on some sort of material organizing principle for the universe. In one such entry, for example, he quickly dismisses the atomistic "blind jumble" then scorns the more dangerously respectable concept of "anima mundi" (a shaping force diffused throughout the material universe): "Thus because we cannot comprehend how a blinde jumble of Atoms can frame the curious bodys of animals, nor yet thinking it fit to engage the immediate hand of God, we invent anima mundi," but this amounts to no more than "a new name" in which to cloak our ignorance.[25] Still, a cleaned up version of atomic concourse might become a serious temptation. Locke suggests as much in a late note from a commonplace book. He confesses that in his adulthood he had often been "assaulted" by religious doubts, and had it not been for "the Special help of God . . . I had certainly apostasized to infidelity."[26]

Despite Locke's victorious piety, religious critics of the eighteenth century were inclined to blame him for the spread of atheistic materialism. Appreciative French philosophers like Voltaire gave him credit for renovating modern thinking.[27] Intellectual historians of Blake's era often traced Lockean thinking back to atomism: "The Epicurism of Gassendi was embraced by the most eminent modern philosophers, and at last appears to have obtained an eternal triumph from its application, by Newton and Huygens to the department of natural philosophy, and by Locke and Condillac, to that of metaphysics."[28] Scottish philosopher Thomas Reid wanted to bring into the open an embarrassingly heavy debt to Epicureanism. He says that Locke "borrowed more from [Gassendi] than from any other author," and he considered atomism part of the classical tradition leading directly to Locke's epistemology.[29] Reid, it should be noted, was arguing from an adversarial position, and he profited from emphasizing similarities between Locke and ancient atheists. But Reid's arguments, whatever their intrinsic worth, may be a good clue to Blake's similarly adversarial outlook.

Locke, of course, did not consider himself an atheist (as Henry Crabb Robinson reminded Blake). But both his antagonists and his supporters saw similarities between Lucretius' theory of perception and Locke's theory of imprinted ideas. Like many important Enlightenment philosophers with whose work he was familiar, he tried to accommodate atomism to Christian belief. Gassendi embraced Epicurean theories as a way of explaining experimental evidence, but he revised atomism by maintaining a distinction between matter and spirit. Galileo was also attempting a risky mixture of Christianity and atomism. As Pietro Redondi has recently argued, Galileo's dangerous heresy was not Copernican cosmology, but atomism—which threatened the doctrine of transubstantiation.[30] The Cambridge Platonists argued explicitly that

Democritan atomism was not incompatible with Christianity. Ralph Cudworth devoted many early sections of *The True Intellectual System of the Universe* to this problem. He argued that atomistic theories can properly be used to support, not to refute, Christian theism (although he felt a need to bolster this reasoning with an odd theory that Moses invented Democritan atomism.)[31] Newton's thinking mixed "a truly active process of integration" with atomistic tendencies.[32] Locke was in good company, then, in his guarded attraction to corpuscular atomism as a means of explaining such things as thermodynamics, neurophysiology, and (most fundamentally) epistemology.

By various means, then—by metaphor and by rationalist theology, by metaphysics and by physics—atomism and Christianity became compatible. This was most unsettling to Blake: "Every Body Knows that this is Epi[c]urus and Lucretius & Yet Every Body Says that it is Christian Philosophy how is this Possible" (620). Locke was not troubled in any obvious way by spiritual deficiencies of his epistemology. In fact, he was more concerned with an opposite problem, the excessive spiritual confidence known as enthusiasm.

When Blake read the *Essay*, he must have reacted quite strongly against the chapter "Of Enthusiasm," where Locke explains the dangers of pseudoinspiration. His notes to Reynolds include several indignant defenses of enthusiasm. When Reynolds says that "mere enthusiasm will carry you but a little way," Blake responds, "Meer Enthusiasm is the All in All!—Bacons Philosophy has Ruind England Bacon is only Epicurus over again" (645). Similarly, to Reynolds's warning that "enthusiastick admiration seldom promotes knowledge," he writes, "Enthusiastic Admiration is the first Principle of Knowledge & its last." It was this sort of thinking that Locke wanted to debunk. The topic of enthusiasm was obviously an important one for him. "Of Enthusiasm" was one of two chapters he added to a late edition. He must have been alarmed at the growing number of dissenting English sects founded by self-proclaimed prophets. Their passionate revisions of the Christianity with which he was comfortable, often accompanied by expressions of political discontent, threatened a social order he considered well founded on rational principles. Perhaps he was also thinking about the strong criticism of the *Essay* coming from some religious authorities. As Locke defines it, enthusiasm is a false faith "which laying by Reason would set up Revelation without it. Whereby in effect it takes away both Reason and Revelation, and substitutes in the room of it, the ungrounded Fancies of a Man's own Brain, and assumes them for a Foundation both of Opinion and Conduct" (4.19.3). Reason and revelation are the two legitimate sources of truth, and they work together.

> Reason is natural *Revelation*, whereby the eternal Father of Light, and Fountain of all Knowledge communicates to Mankind that portion of

Truth, which he has laid within the reach of their natural Faculties; *Revelation* is natural *Reason* enlarged by a new set of Discoveries communicated by GOD immediately, which *Reason* vouches the Truth of, by the Testimony and Proofs it gives, that they come from GOD. So that he that takes away *Reason*, to make the way for *Revelation*, puts out the Light of both, and does much what the same, as if he would perswade a Man to put out his Eyes the better to receive the remote Light of an invisible Star by a Telescope. (4.19.4)

Blake thought this was all upside down. Locke allows for the sort of "immediate" revelation that Blake called imagination or enthusiasm, but he puts it to the test of rational proof and thereby takes away its authoritative priority. Blake condemned this sort of natural religion as a mockery of true inspiration. He might have interpreted the last sentence as an affront to Milton, whose blindness clarified things invisible to mortal sight. Locke, for his part, thought that defenses of enthusiasm were foolishly circular. "This is the way of talking of these Men: they are sure, because they are sure: and their Perswasions are right, only because they are strong in them . . . [A]nd this Light, they are so dazled with, is nothing, but an *ignis fatuus* that leads them continually round in this Circle. *It is a Revelation, because they firmly believe it, and they believe it, because it is a Revelation*" (4.19.9,10). Blake responded with counterarguments using similar phrasing and imagery. In *The Marriage of Heaven and Hell* he is speaking with Isaiah: "Then I asked: does a firm perswasion that a thing is so, make it so? He replied, All poets believe that it does, & in ages of imagination this firm perswasion removed mountains; but many are not capable of a firm perswasion of any thing" (38–39). In the early "There Is No Natural Religion," he uses Locke's circular image against him: "Conclusion. If it were not for the Poetic or Prophetic character, the Philosophic & Experimental would soon be at the ratio of all things & stand still, unable to do other than repeat the same dull round over again" (3). This passage calls up a mill wheel more than an *ignis fatuus,* but the purpose is identical. When the topic is first sources of knowledge, it is always easy to detect circularity in someone else's thinking.

Locke must have been interested in the causes of enthusiasm, but his chapter leaves only hints and gives mixed signals. Sometimes enthusiasm seems to be the result of neurophysiological defects. There have always been "Men, in whom melancholy has mixed with Devotion" (4.19.5); and enthusiasm rises "from the Conceits of a warmed or over-weening Brain" (4.19.7). Locke was up to date in theories of nervous disorder, one of which described an overheating of the brain by fermenting or otherwise disturbed animal spirits. (Blake was also familiar with this sort of diagnosis: Albion calls the narrator of *Jerusa-*

lem a "Phantom of the over heated brain!" [4:24].) But Locke's sentence about the warmed brain also refers to an "over-weening brain" and thus hints at a different kind of cause, more moral than physiological. A little further on he describes the moral defect of enthusiasts more emphatically:

> The Love of something extraordinary, the Ease and Glory it is to be inspired and be above the common and natural ways of Knowledge so flatters many Men's Laziness, Ignorance, and Vanity, that when once they are got into this way of immediate Revelation . . . 'tis a hard matter to get them out of it. Reason is lost upon them, they are above it: they see the Light infused into their Understandings, and cannot be mistaken; 'tis clear and visible there; like the Light of bright Sunshine, shews it self, and needs no other Proof, but its own Evidence: they feel the Hand of GOD moving them within, and the impulses of the Spirit, and cannot be mistaken in what they feel. (4.19.8)

Enthusiastic pseudoinspiration is the moral opposite of Locke's print-based democracy: a near blasphemous conceit against the modesty of a man who speaks for the common mind. (In the introduction to *Jerusalem*, Blake knows he must defend "the Enthusiasm of the following Poem" from charges of "presumptuousness or arrogance.")[33]

Locke charges Blake with blasphemous vanity; Blake charges Locke with atheism. Blake's charge did not hold up very well to the common sense of someone like H. C. Robinson, who was satisfied by Locke's rational defenses of Christian faith. By looking carefully at certain passages of the *Essay*, however, we can see hints of complication for the obvious piety of the argument. As Locke sets out his epistemology in book 2, there are traces of a counterplot, having to do with a fear of deficient spirituality.

THE CRYSTAL CABINET

Locke relies on a metaphor of printing to explain how ideas and minds are formed. Over and over he uses the same figure of speech: objects imprint or impress themselves on minds. "Let us then suppose the Mind to be, as we say, white Paper, void of all Characters, without any *Ideas*" (2.1.2). Here he is careful to mark the metaphor as a metaphor—"Let us suppose," "as we say"—but his use of this printing metaphor is so pervasive that it becomes installed as something more than an occasional figure of speech. It becomes a rational model. Various earlier philosophers had suggested imagery of floating skins (shed by objects), wax, and sealing stamps, but Locke's imagery draws on more modern technology. The printing metaphor appealed to Locke for its implications of order and permanence, two features associated by McLuhan with print's display of truth. In a passage near the beginning of book 2, Locke distinguishes his own epistemological values from his atomistic precursors: he emphasizes the importance of permanent, purposeful impressions in contrast with the temporary, fortuitous ones of a purely Epicurean model: "They, who make the Soul a thinking Thing at this rate, will not make it a much more noble Being, than those do, whom they condemn, for allowing it to be nothing but the subtilest parts of Matter. Characters drawn on Dust, that the first breath of wind effaces; or Impressions made on a heap of Atoms, or animal Spirits, are altogether as useful, and render the Subject as noble, as the Thoughts of a Soul that perish in thinking; that once out of sight are gone for ever, and leave no memory of themselves behind them" (2.1.15).

He is summoning the readability of printed texts to defend his new epistemology against anticipated charges of atheistic randomness. Imprinted ideas may be read, abstracted and generalized, and remembered. Under the controlling metaphor of printed texts, the *Essay* tends to merge perception and retention into a single process (or at least the distinctions between them are minimized). Blake was irritated by this suggestion. "Reynoldss Opinion was that Genius May be Taught & that all Pretence to Inspiration is a Lie & a Deceit to say the least of it For if it is a Deceit the Whole Bible is Madness This Opinion originates in the Greeks Caling the Muses Daughters of Memory." Again he is challenging the piety of Lockeans, and in one of his Reynolds notes he brings in Milton as a witness: "A Work of Genius is a Work 'Not to be obtaind by the Invocation of Memory & her Syren Daughters. but by Devout prayer to that Eternal Spirit. who can enrich with all utterance & knowledge & sends out his Seraphim with the hallowed fire of his Altar to touch & purify the lips of whom he pleases.' Milton" (646).

Locke, as we have seen, expected this kind of response from old-fashioned enthusiasts. He was not troubled in any obvious way by such accusations. His main arguments remain thoughtfully consistent with Christian assumptions. But within his chapters on "Perception" and "Retention," supplementary meanings leak out—mainly from his illustrations and figurative language—to the effect that this epistemological printing process might be feared as well as desired. The *Essay* leaves faint hints of the imprinted images as idols, somehow deficient in spiritual content. Locke's new mind, printed in bodily characters, cannot entirely rid itself of a nostalgic demand for inspiration.

The first hint comes in passages such as the following, concerning "The Original of our Ideas." As he spells out the theory of simple sensory imprinting, the consequences are generally positive. Ideas are available to everyone, in a kind of epistemological democracy—a freedom of the impression. But there is another side to this primary imprinting:

> In this Part, the *Understanding* is meerly *passive;* and whether or no, it will have these Beginnings, and as it were materials of Knowledge, is not

> in its own Power. For the Objects of our Sense, do, many of them, obtrude their particular *Ideas* upon our minds, whether we will or no . . . These *simple Ideas*, when offered to the mind, *the Understanding can no more refuse to have, nor alter, when they are imprinted, nor blot them out, and make new ones in it self*, than a mirror can refuse, alter, or obliterate the Images or *Ideas*, which, the Objects set before it, do therein produce. As the Bodies that surround us, do diversely affect our Organs, the mind is forced to receive the Impressions. (2.1.25)

Here the epistemological freedom of the press turns around and becomes coercion, an oppression visited freely upon all. The mind is "meerly passive," stripped of a power it apparently never had but can still imagine. Objects force themselves on minds that might want to refuse or remake them. Locke briefly shifts his metaphor from printed text to mirror—a mirror is a perfect sort of printing, carried out with light instead of dark—but mirrors still yield images, *eidola*, as Socrates makes plain in book 10 of *The Republic*.

Blake thought this process yielded only idols or specters. He also saw that Lockean epistemology, with its admitted passiveness, might serve to protect any political status quo. Whoever controls the ideas sent out to blank minds has a huge advantage. "This Whole Book was Written to Serve Political Purposes," Blake wrote in Reynolds's margin, and later he elaborates: "The Enquiry in England is not whether a Man has Talents. & Genius? But whether he is Passive & Polite & a Virtuous Ass: & obedient to Noblemens Opinions in Art & Science. If he is; he is a Good Man: If Not he must be starved" (642). As Michael Ferber has pointed out, despite the fact that "Locke's attack on innateness . . . acted as a corrosive that ate away [the] props of hierarchical society" and despite the generally liberal affiliations of his work,

> Locke's empiricist principle . . . encountered in the mid-eighteenth century a critique from the left by some of the same Dissenters who revamped his doctrine of natural rights and who had doubts about unbridled commercialism . . . In a set of vivid expressions akin to those Blake used later, Price wrote that the passive faculty of sense 'lies prostrate under its object' and 'must therefore remain a stranger to the objects.' Price spoke of an 'innate light' or an 'eye of the mind,' not unlike the Inner Light of the Quakers, that can directly intuit moral truths . . . Thus man had a measure of independence from his environment . . . And among the conditions he was able to free himself from were the laws and customs of an oppressive, hierarchical England. Locke was unable to discriminate, according to Price, between an act that is right because it is God's will (as our intuition tells us) and an act that is right because it conforms to *'the decrees of the magistrate, or the fashion of the country.'*[34]

Locke was intelligent enough to anticipate this sort of complaint. He knew the risk of positing blank minds as part of an epistemological printing process that could be seen as entirely arbitrary or politically contingent. He made some gestures to counteract these implications. In the chapter "Of the Association of Ideas" (another late addition), he admits that many of our ideas are connected "wholly owing to Chance or Custom"; however, "Some of our *Ideas* have a natural Correspondence and Connexion one with another: It is the Office and Excellency of our Reason to trace these, and hold them together in that Union and Correspondence which is founded in their peculiar Beings" (2.33.5). He was uncomfortable with an epistemology founded on random or politically contingent influx; hence he set up standards of nature and reason to govern the formation of ideas. Although he has been called the father of associationist psychology, his concept of the association of ideas enters the *Essay* as a way of explaining tenacious unreasonableness. He does not see the passiveness of the mind as an insurmountable problem—just a common one: men are very often misled "by Education, Custom, and the constant din of their Party" (2.33.18).

Back in the chapter on "Perception," the following passage also reduces uneasiness about bullying externals and victimized minds, although this time the effect is subtler:

> As there are some *Ideas,* which we may reasonably suppose may be introduced into the Minds of Children in the Womb, subservient to the necessities of their Life, and Being there: So after they are born, *those Ideas* are the *earliest imprinted, which happen to be the sensible Qualities, which first occur* to them; amongst which, Light is not the least considerable, nor of the weakest efficacy. And how covetous the Mind is, to be furnished with all such *Ideas,* as have no pain accompanying them, may be a little guess'd, by what is observable in Children new-born, who always turn their Eyes to that part, from whence the Light comes, lay them how you please. (2.9.7)

Now the mind is "covetous . . . to be furnished with Ideas," no longer uneasy about its inability to choose or remake them. For support he summons a heliotropic baby. This is Locke's version of Wordsworth's Seer Blest, who comes to this world trailing clouds of glory. Locke's baby may have a half-sketched naturalistic explanation for her light instincts, but she seems like a Neoplatonic baby in disguise. The baby ameliorates the passive blankness of the earlier passage.[35]

In the next chapter of the *Essay,* "Retention," Locke again elevates the printing process as a key to mental privilege. The more comprehensive and secure the imprintings, the greater the mind. The most retentive minds below God belong to angels, then to a few exceptional humans like Pascal, and then to other humans, to a greater or lesser degree depending on particularities of bodily constitution. He continues this discussion with a series of figurative explanations of memory, and within these figures some complications begin to show. In cases of weak memory due to "the temper of the Body, or some other default," "*Ideas* in the Mind quickly fade, and often vanish quite out of the Understanding, leaving no more footsteps or remaining Characters of themselves, than Shadows do flying over Fields of Corn" (2.10.4). The characters turn into shadows (even worse for Plato than mirror images), and the unretentive minds become fields of corn, thriving on their ability to shed the little voids passing over. Locke then shifts to two new comparisons, in a passage more charged with pathos than one might expect in this context: "Thus the *Ideas*, as well as Children, of our Youth, often die before us: And our Minds represent to us those Tombs, to which we are approaching; where though the Brass and Marble remain, yet the Inscriptions are effaced by time, and the Imagery moulders away" (2.10.5). When he compares ideas to children who die young, he uses pathos in the service of a straightforward empiricism: mental greatness depends on the accumulation and retention of imprinted ideas. But then the figuration changes. Now minds are compared to tombs and thus become associated once again with the shadow of death. The passage has an interestingly irrelevant moment of mortal anxiety ("those Tombs, to which we are approaching"). The Lockean mind becomes a site of death, even as it retains as much as it can of its imprintings.

Two final pieces of rhetoric extend this shadowy subplot. Both have biblical subtexts. As he finishes a discussion of the sensory origins of ideas, his figure of speech suggests the Tower of Babel: "All those sublime Thoughts, which towre above the Clouds, and reach as high as Heaven it self, take their Rise and Footing here: In all that great Extent wherein the mind wanders, in those remote Speculations, it may seem to be elevated with, it stirs not one jot beyond those *Ideas*, which *Sense* or *Reflection*, have offered for its Contemplation" (2.1.24). He belittles, almost chastises the mind's accomplishments, scattering the intellectual towers back to their humble originals. In a second passage, Locke is drawing on his work as a physician: "we oftentimes find a Disease quite strip the Mind of all its *Ideas*, and the flames of a Fever, in a few days, calcine all those Images to dust and confusion, which seem'd to be as lasting as if graved in Marble" (2.10.5). There is a curiously biblical ring to this sentence, with its flames, dust, and destruction of graven images. The fever does the work of an avenging God, disappointed with the imaginative weakness of his creatures. Locke's printed ideas occasionally fall into association with shadows, *eidola*, idols and may call up just the faintest shudder of spiritual death. In a short essay on idolatry from his 1676 journal, Locke attributes the Bible's particular emphasis on this sin to God's knowing "how apt we are all to rest our thoughts upon sensible objects."[36]

Blake had no doubts about the spiritual depravity of Locke's imprinted specters. He repeatedly recommended his own printing to readers who wanted to stay in touch with divine truth:

> Reader! [lover] of books! [lover] of heaven,
> And of that God from whom [all books are given,]
> Who in mysterious Sinais awful cave
> To Man the wond'rous art of writing gave,
> Again he speaks in thunder and in fire!
> Thunder of Thought, & flames of fierce desire:
> Even from the depths of Hell his voice I hear,
> Within the unfathomd caverns of my Ear.
> Therefore I print; nor vain my types shall be:
> Heaven, Earth & Hell, henceforth shall live in harmony. (*Jerusalem* 3 ["To the Public"])

If Locke's subtexts (Babel, graven images) imply divine correction of ambitious intellect, Blake makes Yahweh on Sinai into a Promethean God, urging human intellect toward greater expressive capacity. Here and several other places he combines images of fire—privileged biblical image of divinity—with those of printing, as he announces his apocalyptic rewriting of the Enlightenment's spectral printing. But there is a counterplot to be detected within Blake's work, too. Locke's *Essay* contains subtle hints of deficient spirituality against a background of pious natural religion. Blake's work, with its prevailing confidence of enthusiasm, sometimes suggests a need to limit or restrain this voice of private inspiration. There can be a danger of excessive spirituality, in other words—of an inner light overwhelming public knowledge and hindering the imagination. Two texts will serve to illustrate: the manuscript poem "The Crystal Cabinet" and the "doors of perception" plate from *The Marriage of Heaven and Hell*.

"The Crystal Cabinet" is one of the suggestive but elusive lyrics from the Pickering Manuscript:

> The Maiden caught me in the Wild
> Where I was dancing merrily
> She put me into her Cabinet
> And Lockd me up with a golden Key
>
> This Cabinet is formd of Gold
> And Pearl & Crystal shining bright

> And within it opens into a World
> And a little lovely Moony Night
>
> Another England there I saw
> Another London with its Tower
> Another Thames & other Hills
> And another pleasant Surrey Bower
>
> Another Maiden like herself
> Translucent lovely shining clear
> Threefold each in the other closd
> O what a pleasant trembling fear
>
> O what a smile a threefold Smile
> Filld me that like a flame I burnd
> I bent to Kiss the lovely Maid
> And found a Threefold Kiss returnd
>
> I strove to sieze the inmost Form
> With ardor fierce & hands of flame
> But burst the Crystal Cabinet
> And like a Weeping Babe became
>
> A weeping Babe upon the wild
> And Weeping Woman pale reclind
> And in the outward air again
> I filld with woes the passing Wind (488–89)

There can be several valid approaches to interpreting this poem. The most obvious would focus on ironies of sexual desire and possessiveness. A few clues suggest that this poem might also be read in the context of Locke's epistemology. First is a possible pun in the fourth line—"And Lockd me up with a golden Key." The pun might seem an interpretive reach except for reinforcing imagery in the poem and the presence of the same pun (obviously marked as such) in *An Island in the Moon*. Another clue is the image of the cabinet. The *Essay* uses cabinet as one of its metaphors for the mind. The following passage provides an interesting example, because here Locke is belittling the pretensions of human intellect: "He that will not set himself proudly at the top of all things; but will consider the Immensity of this Fabrick, and the great variety, that is to be found in this little and inconsiderable part of it, which he has to do with, may be apt to think, that in other Mansions of it, there may be other, and different intelligent Beings, of whose Faculties, he has as little Knowledge or

Apprehension, as a Worm shut up in one drawer of a Cabinet, hath of the Senses or Understanding of a Man" (2.3.3). Blake considered this sort of thinking a dangerous deception. He blamed the "Loom of Locke" for weaving an immense "Fabrick" that turns men into cabinet worms.

The strongest exterior evidence for this poem as a response to Lockean epistemology comes in a passage from *Jerusalem* that echoes the threefold kiss of "The Crystal Cabinet":

> Imputing Sin & Righteousness to Individuals; Rahab
> Sat deep within him hid: his Feminine Power unreveal'd
> Brooding Abstract Philosophy. to destroy Imagination, the Divine
> Humanity A Three-fold Wonder: feminine: most beautiful: Threefold
> Each within other. On her white marble & even Neck, her Heart
> Inorb'd and bonified: with locks of shadowing modesty, shining
> Over her beautiful Female features, soft flourishing in beauty
> Beams mild, all love and all perfection, that when the lips
> Recieve a kiss from Gods or Men, a threefold kiss returns
> From the pressd loveliness: so her whole immortal form three-fold
> Three-fold embrace returns: consuming lives of Gods & Men
> In fires of beauty melting them as gold & silver in the furnace. (70:17–28)

Here the threefold female from "The Crystal Cabinet" is explicitly identified with "Abstract Philosophy." Just before the quoted passage, the association with Locke is made even more explicit. A sinister threefold male holds "all Wisdom / To consist. in the agreements & disagree[me]nts of Ideas" (70:7–8), quoting Locke's definition of truth from the *Essay*. Then the sons of Albion "combine into Three Forms, named Bacon & Newton & Locke" (70:15) who go about the destruction of imagination.

In this *Jerusalem* passage, in "The Crystal Cabinet," and elsewhere, Blake gives epistemology an erotic dimension. Lockean empiricists become seductive female figures. Especially in his later work, Blake used female imagery to represent intellectual styles and psychological strategies that hindered imaginative life. Such use of gender imagery is of course a troublesome and interesting topic which scholars have recently taken more seriously than in the past. Fewer readers are willing to dismiss his gendered imagery as irrelevant to the higher argument. For the specific purposes of this discussion, it is enough to observe that he classifies Lockean epistemology as feminine (in his own use of that word) and to suggest why he does so. Blake defines a "Female Space" as the illusion of an infinite, incomprehensible other that intimidates and diminishes a fallen subject. Whether in its sexual, religious, or intellectual contexts, the feminine for Blake means a claim to infinite value or truth combined with a denial of access to that value or truth. He must have called Locke's epistemology feminine because of its denial that humans can know the "real essence" or the "true, internal constitution" of anything. Humans construct nominal essences, but only God and possibly angels know the full truth. If we were granted access to the real essence of the species "man," he says, "our idea of any individual man would be as far different from what it now is, as is his who knows all the springs and wheels and other contrivances within of the famous clock at Strasbourg, from that which a gazing countryman has of it, who barely sees the motion of the hand, and hears the clock strike, and observes only some of the outward appearances" (3.6.3). Philosophers of the holistic schools went astray "by having their minds set upon fruitless inquiries after substantial forms, wholly unintelligible" (3.6.10).

In "The Crystal Cabinet," the speaker finds himself in a feminine substitute for the world in which he starts. It seems plausible to read this substitute world as the sensorium taken captive by Lockean epistemology. (This reading does not necessarily displace other plausible interpretive ideas, such as Damon's suggestion of an illicit love affair or Erdman's association with a Urizenic, militarized London—both of which are compatible with the epistemological focus.)[37] The speaker is struck by the completeness and realism of this world, and he is attracted to its promise of bodily fulfillment. But he violates the spirit of Locke when he attempts to "sieze the inmost Form / With ardor fierce & hands of flame." Epistemology becomes sexual because sex seems to offer what nothing else in this world can, a privileged access to essence.

The end of the poem suggests that there may be limits to the imaginative effectiveness of this kind of spiritual quest. The speaker only succeeds in bursting the cabinet and activating the depressing cycle of desire best described in "The Mental Traveller." "The Crystal Cabinet" does not imply that resistance to Lockean epistemology is futile, but it does suggest that enthusiasm can lead to the frustrated isolation of an imagination become impotent: "I filld with woes the passing Wind."

Plate 14 of *The Marriage of Heaven and Hell* offers a different, more optimistic scene of anti-Lockean enthusiasm. The passage is well known and eminently quotable, if not quite as simple as it first appears.

> The ancient tradition that the world will be consumed in fire at the end of six thousand years is true. as I have heard from Hell.
> For the cherub with his flaming sword is hereby commanded to leave his guard at the tree of life, and when he does, the whole creation will be consumed, and appear infinite. and holy whereas it now appears finite & corrupt.

>   This will come to pass by an improvement of sensual enjoyment.
>
>   But first the notion that man has a body distinct from his soul, is to be expunged; this I shall do, by printing in the infernal method, by corrosives, which in Hell are salutary and medicinal, melting apparent surfaces away, and displaying the infinite which was hid.
>
>   If the doors of perception were cleansed every thing would appear to man as it is: infinite.
>
>   For man has closed himself up, till he sees all things thro' narrow chinks of his cavern. (39)

He begins with apocalypse by fire, announced confidently, almost blandly. It might be helpful here to recall the passage from Locke's *Essay* about the "flames of a Fever" that "calcine all those Images to dust and confusion." Locke's disaster is Blake's salvation. In the next sentence, he alters this apocalypse in two ways. First, he brings it into the present and puts it under more personal imaginative control: the angel "is hereby commanded to leave his guard." Second, he tempers the destruction by balancing "consume" with "appear." The third sentence continues this adjustment by describing the apocalypse as a matter of sensual enjoyment, as if to preempt any Gnostic or Platonic misreadings. He then finds it necessary to prevent misreadings of an opposite kind: an apocalypse of sensual enjoyment does not imply a materialist, Epicurean world. On the contrary, the Lockean world must by expunged and reprinted with Blakean fire, so that surface appearances yield to infinite truths.

In the final two sentences, however, it becomes clear that the sensory mind created by Locke's epistemology is not a Platonic prison to escape from or a mere shell to be destroyed by divine fire. It is something to be "cleansed." These last sentences bring to mind images from high canonical sources. The cavern suggests Plato's cave, and the cleansing of the doors of perception recalls St. Paul: "For now we see through a glass, darkly; but then face to face: now I know in part; but then shall I know even as also I am known" (1 Corinthians 13:12). Just as important are the allusions to Locke. The following passage from the *Essay* serves as a useful subtext:

>   I . . . confess here again, That external and internal Sensation, are the only passages that I can find, of Knowledge, to the Understanding. These alone, as far as I can discover, are the Windows by which light is let into this *dark Room*. For, methinks, the *Understanding* is not much unlike a Closet wholly shut from light, with only some little openings left, to let in external visible Resemblances, or *Ideas* of things without; would the Pictures coming into such a dark Room but stay there, and lie so orderly as to be found upon occasion, it would very much resemble the Understanding of a Man, in reference to all Objects of sight, and the *Ideas* of them. (2.11.17)

Locke begins with another modesty trope, in deference to the influential epistemologies he is revising. Plato's cave becomes a more prosaic dark room. Blake, in effect, has superimposed Locke on Plato: he takes Locke's "little openings" and adapts them to the Platonic cave as "narrow chinks." He also turns Locke's windows into doors—simply to subvert a cliché, or perhaps to imply that our senses have become opaque; or even to suggest his own copperplates (sometimes depicted as doors in his designs). In any event, the sense of the apocalypse has shifted from the simple consuming fire at the beginning of plate 14. The apocalyptic autonomy with which he began has found a more mediated voice, attentive to the Daughters of Memory as well as Inspiration. The renovation or reprinting must work from the site of the Lockean cavern, instead of just burning it up with the flames of enthusiasm.

This sense of accommodation is reinforced by an interesting allusion to the *Essay* in the next plate. Plate 15 offers a Memorable Fancy about "a Printing house in Hell," showing "the method in which knowledge is transmitted from generation to generation": "In the first chamber was a Dragon-Man, clearing away the rubbish from a caves mouth; within, a number of Dragons were hollowing the cave" (40). It sounds as if Blake is remembering the passage from Locke's "Epistle to the Reader" in which he minimizes his own work alongside such giants as Boyle, Sydenham, and Newton: Locke is "an Under-Labourer" employed in "clearing Ground a little, and removing some of the Rubbish, that lies in the way to Knowledge" (10). Blake admits Dragon-Man Locke and his colleagues to the company of knowledge printers, albeit in a preliminary, evacuative stage of the work. To some extent, then, Blake is actually repeating Locke's own opinion of his work. Locke made good use of the Enlightenment press, but he seemed a little uneasy about the authority it gave him. He liked to frame the *Essay* as only a preliminary step toward truth, in deference to minds of greater reach.

Chapter 8

Epitaphs

Locke composed his own epitaph. It was inscribed on a marble tablet for his grave in the churchyard of High Laver. Blake thought epitaphs were foolish, and he composed them only in mockery, as in this notebook entry: "Come knock your heads against this stone / For sorrow that poor John Thompsons gone." Stone markers were for Druids. Probably due more to poverty than preference, Blake's grave at Bunhill Fields went unmarked. However, about a year before he died, he did compose something that had the ring of an epitaph, when he signed his name in William Upcott's autograph album.

Here is Locke's Latin epitaph (along with Cranston's translation), followed by Blake's autograph:

> Hic juxta situs est JOHANNES LOCKE. Si qualis fuerit rogas, mediocritate sua contentum se vixisse respondet. Literis innutritus eo usque tantum profecit, ut veritati unice litaret. Hoc ex scriptis illius disce; quae quod de eo reliquum est majori fide tibe exhibebunt, quam epitaphii suspecta elogia. Virtutes si quas habuit, minores sane quam sibi laudi duceret tibi in exemplum proponeret; vitia una sepeliantur. Morum exemplum si squaeras in Evangelio habes: vitiorum utinam nusquam: mortalitatis certe (quod prosit) hic et ubique.

> Natum Anno Dom. 1632 Aug. 29

> Mortuum Anno Dom. 1704 Oct. 28

> Memorat haec tabula brevi et ipse interitura.

> [Near this place lies John Locke. If you wonder what kind of man he was, the answer is that he was one contented with his modest lot. A scholar by training, he devoted his studies wholly to the pursuit of truth. Such you may learn from his writings, which will also tell you whatever else

there is to be said about him more faithfully than the dubious eulogies of an epitaph. His virtues, if he had any, were too slight to serve either to his own credit or as an example to you. Let his vices be interred with him. An example of virtue, you have already in the Gospels; an example of vice is something one could wish did not exist; an example of mortality (and you may learn from it) you have assuredly here and everywhere. That he was born on August 29, 1632, and died on October 28, 1704, this tablet, which itself will quickly perish, is a record.]

William Blake one who is very much delighted with being in good Company

Born 28 Nov 1757 in London & has died several times since. [In the midst of these words Blake drew a naked male figure floating comfortably and supporting a kind of curving frame around them.]

The above was written & the drawing annexed by the desire of Mr Leigh how far it is an Autograph is a Question I do not think an Artist can write an Autograph especially one who has Studied in the Florentine & Roman Schools as such an one will Consider what he is doing but an Autograph as I understand it, is Writ helter skelter like a hog upon a rope or a Man who walks without Considering whether he shall run against a Post or a House or a Horse or a Man & I am apt to believe that what is done without meaning is very different from that which a Man Does with his Thought & Mind & ought not to be Calld by the Same Name.

I consider the Autograph of Mr Cruikshank which very justly stands first in the Book & that Beautiful Specimen of Writing by Mr Comfield & my own; as standing [in] the same Predicament they are in some measure Works of Art & not of Nature or Chance

Heaven born the Soul a Heavenward Course must hold

For what delights the Sense is False & Weak

Beyond the Visible World she soars to Seek

Ideal Form, The Universal Mold

Michael Angelo. Sonnet as Translated by Mr Wordsworth.

Locke's self-image is characteristically different from Blake's. Locke presents his scholarly career with an emphasis on upbringing or nourishment rather than endowment ("literis innutritus"), whereas Blake is an artist inspired by "Ideal Form." Locke is "content with his modest lot"; Blake is "delighted" but never simply content: he has "died" repeatedly in a series of sacrifices and transformations.

Interestingly, one common theme does appear. Both of them worry about the brutal meaninglessness of merely natural life. Locke concludes his epitaph with a reminder of mortality more shivering than one might have expected. He gives the last word to the inanimate "tabula," which will become a blank slate soon enough when nature reclaims it. The account of his virtues and vices is listless enough to sound almost indifferent. On the night before he died, he told Lady Masham that "this life is nothing but vanity."[1] Blake's autograph has a more cheerful tone but delivers a kindred complaint about natural chaos. Artists try to create meaningful structures against the reign of "Nature" and "Chance," full of hogs and humans, signifying nothing. As "delighted" as he might be with good company, he simultaneously rejects "what delights the sense" as "False & Weak."

Blake died on a Sunday night "in a most glorious manner," according to his friend George Richmond. "Just before he died His Countenance became fair— His eyes brighten'd and He burst out in singing of the things he saw in Heaven."[2] Locke died less gloriously. "Lady Masham . . . sat at his side, talking or reading from the Psalms. At three o'clock in the afternoon he became restless. He moved to another seat. Then he lifted his hands to his face, closed his eyes, and died."[3] The two death scenes nicely convey how different the two men were. Blake's face lit up and he began singing, because he could see the glories of heaven. Locke covered his face and died quietly. He had always been skeptical of people who claimed to see heaven. He once read a book called *Joyfull News from Heaven* by Ludowick Muggleton (perhaps a significant influence on Blake, if E. P. Thompson is right);[4] he dismissed it as "extravagant," but he also wrote down details of crystal brilliance, music, and fiery bodies.[5] Perhaps he was a little disappointed that he could not see the sort of things that made people sing as they faced eternity. But he did what he could. He died listening to the Psalms, read by an Enthusiast who loved him.

Notes

Chapter 1: From Caricature to Conversation

1. A recent extended discussion of these matters can be found in Perkins, *Is Literary History Possible?*, which addresses the poststructuralist rejection of a "traditional, romantic model of literary change as continuous development" in favor of "the discontinuity and contingency of history" (11).
2. The standard Locke biography is Cranston's, which replaced Fox Bourne's. Cranston was the first biographer to have full access to the Lovelace papers in the Bodleian Library, the largest collection of primary materials. The extensive correspondence has been edited by E. S. DeBeer. Aspects of Locke's political life were illuminated in Laslett's edition of *Two Treatises of Government*; the fullest such analysis can be found in Richard Ashcraft's *Revolutionary Politics*, although some scholars are skeptical of his boldest conclusions about Locke's activism. Dewhurst's *John Locke: Physician and Philosopher* provides very helpful details of his medical interests.

    By far the most useful single resource for Blake biography is Bentley's *Blake Records* (updated in *Blake Records Supplement*), a volume which collects "as many as possible of the references to Blake made by his contemporaries "(xxiii). Gilchrist's *Life* (1863) was the first extensive biography and remains valuable despite inaccuracies and doubtful stories; Gilchrist did not know Blake but heard accounts from several people who did. Mona Wilson's leaner biography from 1927 (updated in 1971 by Keynes) pays more respectful attention to the longer works, although the interpretive work is of less value now.
3. Jameson, "On *Habits of the Heart*," 550. He is referring to Robert Bellah's assumption that Enlightenment philosophy significantly influenced modern notions of an unencumbered self.
4. Rorty, *Philosophy and the Mirror of Nature*, 389–90, 157.
5. The most interesting record of Newton's uneasiness with the *Essay* comes in a letter of apology to Locke. Evidently Newton had written him a strongly accusatory letter during one of his bouts of nervous agitation. Later he felt better and repented:

    > Sir, Being of opinion that you endeavoured to embroil me with women and by other means I was so much affected with it as that when one told me you were sickly and would not live I answered twere better if you were dead. I

desire you to forgive me this uncharitableness . . . I beg your pardon for my having hard thoughts of you for it and for representing that you struck at the root of morality in a principle you laid down in your book of Ideas and designed to pursue in another book and that I took you for a Hobbist.

Locke politely asked which parts of the *Essay* "struck at the root of morality," but Newton answered that he could not recall his train of thought at the time. Newton may have been thinking either of Locke's emphasis on pleasure and pain as a foundation of ethical analysis or more generally of the repudiation of innate ideas.

6. See Cranston, "John Locke and John Aubrey." Locke played "in a meadow near that village [Stanton Drew] among the famous stones which have stood there since prehistoric times"(553). Aubrey, who also played there, later wrote a book called *Templa Druidum;* he once had a conversation about Druids with Locke and Lord Pembroke. Locke recommended to him a book on "Druids and Delphi."
7. Hilton, *Literal Imagination*, 107.
8. BL MS.Locke c.30:87, 111.
9. BL MS.Locke c.30:111.
10. BL MS.Locke b.5:14.
11. Robinson, *Diary, Reminiscences, and Correspondence* 2:29.
12. I take these figures from John Yolton, *Locke Dictionary*, 26.
13. BL MS.Locke c.27:258–62. Locke concludes that the "conflagration of the earth" will come exactly 7,000 years after the creation of Adam.
14. For a useful discussion of similarities between Paine's ideas about the Bible and Blake's, see Mee, *Dangerous Enthusiasm*, 168–74.
15. Wittgenstein, "A Lecture on Ethics," 10–11.
16. DeBeer 2:591.
17. "Resurrectio et Quae Sequuntur," in King, *Life and Letters of John Locke*, 318.

Chapter 2: Mothers, the Matrix, and Marriage

1. See Storch, *Sons and Adversaries*, xiii.
2. Cranston, *John Locke*, 13.
3. BL MS.Locke e.4. The title page has "Farrago" above "John Locke" and "Agnis Locke."
4. BM Add.MS.15642. The note is dated 14 February 1679.
5. BL MS.Locke c.42B:36.
6. See the discussion by Stone in *Family, Sex and Marriage*, 426–32. In the second half of the seventeenth century arguments against the use of wet nurses began to appear, but for at least another century most upper-class families used them.
7. Lorenne M. G. Clark makes this point in "Women and John Locke." See also Pateman and Brennan, "'Mere Auxiliaries to the Commonwealth,'" and Pringle, *Nature Virtue and Gratitude*, 226–39.
8. DeBeer 2:707.
9. See Apperson, *English Proverbs*, 714.

10. DeBeer 2:686.
11. Cranston, *John Locke*, 25. Cranston speculates that Mary Lower was the sister of a fellow student, Richard Lower.
12. Quoted in Cranston, *John Locke*, 35. Locke obscured the name of the woman to whom this letter was addressed, but Cranston believes it is either his hostess at Hampton Court or a younger woman in the household.
13. Cranston, *John Locke*, 35.
14. Quoted in *Educational Writings of John Locke*, ed. Axtell, 33. The report comes at two removes, from Coste through Joseph Spence. Von Leyden has listed some of the romances Locke read, including *Le Grand Cyrus* by de Scudéry: see *Essays on the Law of Nature*, 19. Locke and Damaris Cudworth discussed the work of de Scudery when they first met.
15. La Calprenede, *Hymen's Praeludia*, 2, 11.
16. DeBeer 1:100.
17. DeBeer 1:131.
18. DeBeer 1:101.
19. Quoted in Cranston, *John Locke*, 54. Cranston notes that Atkins came to a "Falstaffian" bad end, although he cites no evidence.
20. Edwards, *A Brief Vindication*. The relevant passage is quoted in *Educational Writings*, ed. Axtell, 253n.
21. BL MS.Locke c.32:14.
22. DeBeer 1:297. DeBeer cautions that our knowledge of Locke and Elinor Parry is uncertain and incomplete: "Almost all our knowledge of Locke's relations with Elinor Parry is derived from the surviving letters between them, letters whose authorship or direction is sometimes questionable, and whose dates are frequently problematical. In any case the letters would not tell the whole story as the couple were frequently resident in the same town" (298n.).
23. DeBeer 1:307.
24. DeBeer 1:311.
25. DeBeer 1:319.
26. For Locke's letter comparing marriage and death, see DeBeer 2:113. Locke's earlier teasing about wife selling (DeBeer 2:32) comes as he facetiously tempts Toinard to visit by selecting an English wife for him: "N'aiez pas peur . . . si elle ne vous agre pas apres que vous l'avez experimentee quelques tems vous le venderez et je crois a plus grande prix qu'un homme retira pour sa femme a Londres la semaine passee ou il la venda pour quatre sous la livre, je crois que la vostre vous rendra 5 ou 6s par livre parcequ'elle est belle jeune et bien tendre."
27. BL MS.Locke c.28:1. The quotation comes from the "Preface to the Reader" of a proposed treatise on toleration.
28. Cranston, *John Locke*, 54, 111.
29. DeBeer 1:491.
30. BL MS.Locke f.2:38–39 (from his 1677 journal).
31. DeBeer 2:472.
32. DeBeer 2:484–85.
33. DeBeer 2:488.

34. DeBeer 2:490.
35. DeBeer 2:494.
36. DeBeer 2:539.
37. DeBeer 2:503.
38. DeBeer 3:431. Cudworth had read the abridgement that was published shortly before the first edition of the *Essay*. In general she was quite complimentary. No doubt anticipating clerical objections to the book, she emphasized the soundness of its religious foundation.
39. Quoted in Passmore, *Ralph Cudworth*, 52–53. Passmore is quoting from unpublished manuscripts that were inherited by Damaris Cudworth (then Lady Masham). In 1762 Lord Masham sold them, along with a part of Locke's library, to bookseller Robert Davies. In a curious irony, Davies assumed that Locke was the author and tried to market them as such.
40. See Passmore, *Ralph Cudworth*, 56, 75.
41. DeBeer 2:557–58.
42. DeBeer 2:562.
43. For Cudworth's letter, see DeBeer 2:571–73; Locke's reply follows (2:573–75).
44. DeBeer 2:630.
45. DeBeer 2:638.
46. DeBeer 2:678.
47. BL MS.Locke f.8:114–21.
48. Quoted in Saxby, *Quest for the New Jerusalem*, 231.
49. Cranston, *John Locke*, 344. Cranston draws some of this rather quaintly from physiognomic analysis of a portrait of Masham. Apparently Masham was not important enough to have his life recorded in any detail.
50. DeBeer 2:702.
51. DeBeer 2:726.
52. DeBeer 2:734.
53. Cranston, *John Locke*, 343.
54. See BL MS.Locke c.25:71 for the complete list of legacies.
55. Quoted in Bentley, *Blake Records*, 508–9.
56. Quoted in Bentley, *Blake Records*, 508.
57. Quoted in Bentley, *Blake Records*, 526.
58. Blake's various attitudes toward women and sexuality cannot be reduced to a chronological scheme of periods and shifts, even though a few loose trends might be observed. Ostriker ("Desire Gratified and Ungratified") isolates four different Blakean positions on sexuality: "the Blake who celebrates sexuality and attacks repression"; the Jungian Blake attentive to emanation and anima; the Blake "who sees sexuality as a tender trap"; and "the Blake to whom it was necessary . . . to see the female principle as subordinate to the male" (156).
59. Quoted in Bentley, *Blake Records*, 346. These words come from a summary by John Linnell Jr. of his father's letters.
60. Quoted in Bentley, *Blake Records*, 518.
61. Quoted in Bentley, *Blake Records*, 97, 106.
62. Quoted in Bentley, *Blake Records*, 374, 410.

63. Quoted in Bentley, *Blake Records*, 517.
64. Quoted in Bentley, *Blake Records*, 21.
65. Quoted in Bentley, *Blake Records*, 237.
66. Bentley, *Blake Records*, 237n.
67. Wilson, *Life*, 72. With this and many other remarks, Blake seems to have enjoyed unsettling Robinson's common sense. It should probably be interpreted more in this ludic sense than as a careful, resolute conclusion.
68. Bentley raises a doubt about the X as prima facie evidence of illiteracy: "Signing with an X . . . was by no means uncommon at the time, particularly among women, and did not necessarily denote illiteracy. Of the thirty four people married in the church in 1782, fourteen signed only with a mark. For some of these fourteen, writing was perhaps a difficult and precarious skill which it was thought best not to attempt in moments of emotional stress" (*Blake Records*, 24).
69. Gilchrist, quoted in Bentley, *Blake Records*, 237.
70. Gilchrist, quoted in Bentley, *Blake Records*, 30.
71. Boehme, *Mysterium Magnum*, 83–88. This and all subsequent citations refer to the London edition of 1654, translated by John Sparrow. (The German original was published in 1623.) Boehme's works were available in eighteenth-century republications of the early translations.
72. Boehme, *Mysterium Magnum*, 78.
73. Boehme, *Mysterium Magnum*, 77.
74. Boehme, *The Way to Christ*, 85.
75. Norman O. Brown, *Life against Death*, 310.
76. Boehme, *Mysterium Magnum*, 88.
77. Robinson, *Diary, Reminiscences, and Correspondence* 2:29.
78. Milton, *Doctrine and Discipline of Divorce*, 707.
79. Swedenborg, *Wisdom Concerning Conjugial Love*, 183, 178. Swedenborg's use of "conjugial" instead of "conjugal" is explained by his translators as a matter of etymological connotation: "conjugal" derives from the verb for yoking together, which is not "in harmony with the author's doctrine concerning marriage," because it implies "domination and servitude" (*Heaven and Hell*, 247n.). Swedenborg's idea of "equality" in marriage coexists rather uncomfortably with his gender essentialism and division of labor.
80. Robinson, *Diary, Reminiscences, and Correspondence* 2:28. Because of this remark about a dangerous sexual system, Damon assumes that Blake was familiar with Swedenborg's *Conjugial Love* (*Blake Dictionary*, 392). This seems like a good guess, but it is possible that Blake gleaned key ideas about marriage from *Heaven and Hell*, one of three books by Swedenborg that he owned and annotated. *Heaven and Hell* contains a chapter on "Marriages in Heaven" that sketches some basic ideas of *Conjugial Love*, including gender distinctions in mental faculties and the necessity of monogamy.
81. Swedenborg, *Heaven and Hell*, 253.
82. Swedenborg, *Conjugial Love*, 292.
83. See Swedenborg, *Conjugial Love*, 137–46 and 167–70.
84. Bentley, *Blake Records*, 37. The repetition might indicate that married love was a subject of some dispute in the society, perhaps having to do with the legitimacy of

pious or radical alternatives to marriage. In any case the resolutions were approved unanimously at the end of the meeting.
85. Stevenson, *Poems of William Blake*, 793.
86. Damrosch points to this passage as a sure sign that Blake is drawing on aspects of Catherine's behavior in Felpham (*Symbol and Truth in Blake's Myth*, 210). This observation is helpful but needs to be qualified: Blake is presenting his construction of Catherine's behavior. The Felpham problems were so vexing and complicated for him that he had already written an extended mythic account, in "The Bard's Song" from *Milton;* by the time of *Jerusalem*, the "real" events were accessible only through several mediating layers of memory and prophetic narrative. For another discussion of these biographical references, see Sutherland, "Crisis of Love and Jealousy."
87. For a condensed interpretive summary of the figures in plate 25 and possible sources of design elements, see Paley's notes to the facsimile edition of *Jerusalem*, 169. The three females can be plausibly identified as Rahab, Vala, and Tirzah, all of them associated with maternal and natural power. Paley cites Schuchard's "Blake's Healing Trio" in support of the mesmerism thesis.
88. From Bloom's commentary in Erdman's edition, 944.
89. Vogler, "'In vain the Eloquent Tongue,'" in *Critical Paths,* ed. Miller, Bracher, and Ault. "Oothoon seems to acknowledge . . . that her goal is to 'reflect / The image of Theotormon on my pure transparent breast.' As a representation of speaking woman, she serves conveniently as a ventriloquating mirror for acts of narcissistic self-completion on the part of those male readers who like to have their truths of feminine desire come out of the mouths of 'women'" (300). In the same collection of essays, Webster's "Blake, Women, and Sexuality" offers a psychoanalytical explanation of Blake's gestures toward free love, based on primal desire for the mother and consequent jealousy and hostility.
90. This identification of Satan with Hayley and Palamabron with Blake follows the generally accepted allegorical code for interpreting "The Bard's Song" from *Milton*. Of course no Blakean character should ever be reduced to its biographical referent; reading the poem biographically invites oversimplification and encourages the invention of biographical details to fill in representational connections. But these identifications fit well enough with what we know from other records about the relationship of Blake and Hayley, and *Milton* is, after all, a poem with obvious biographical references, including a design labelled "Blake's Cottage at Felpham."
91. Damon, *Blake Dictionary*, 178. Damon supports his reading with a quick biographical sketch of Hayley: he was "deserted by both of his wives, and . . . could never keep a female friend permanently." The argument is slight and accusatory (in an old-fashioned way), but it may help reveal Blake's attitude by reproducing his adversarial perspective.
92. Erdman, *Illuminated Blake,* 263. Erdman also notes that in copy A, Blake's genitals have been obscured by a block of black ink—perhaps the work of a self-appointed Victorian curator, but just as plausibly a censoring afterthought by Blake himself. In the three subsequent copies both Blake's and Los's genitals are covered with unobtrusive underclothing.
93. Mitchell, "Style and Iconography," 66. Mitchell says that he was "unable to locate

any explicit precedent for the oral genitalism suggested by these two plates. It does seem evident, however, that this kind of eroticism is covertly symbolized in the initiation rites of all sorts of brotherhoods" (67). Mitchell then backs away from homoerotics to more familiar, desexualized themes: "We need not believe, with Damon, that Leutha is 'Hayley's repressed homosexuality,' to see that Blake is contrasting two kinds of male love. The first strengthens and enlivens, uniting the individual with all the prophets who have lived before him, using them as vehicles for new explorations of the imagination as Dante uses Vergil, Milton uses Spenser, and Blake uses Milton. The second divides the soul and cripples imaginative exploration" (67).

94. Storch, "The Spectrous Fiend Cast Out," 123.
95. As Erdman notes, in copy A the figures are nude, but in later versions they seem to have underclothing, as was the case with the Los and Blake plate. In copy A Erdman sees on William "a black penis erect against his body" (*Illuminated Blake*, 248).
96. Swedenborg, *Conjugial Love*, 44.
97. More, *Immortality of the Soul*, in *Collection* 2:87.
98. Boehme, *Mysterium Magnum*, 85.

Chapter 3: Two English Physicians

1. DeBeer 4:628–29.
2. Quoted in Dewhurst, *Physician and Philosopher*, 88.
3. BL MS.Locke f.4:105.
4. Dewhurst, *Physician and Philosopher*, 227.
5. Dewhurst, *Physician and Philosopher*, 285.
6. BL MS.Locke d.1:33.
7. Quoted in Dewhurst, *Physician and Philosopher*, 133.
8. DeBeer 4:490.
9. Cranston, *John Locke*, 351.
10. Dewhurst, *Physician and Philosopher*, 285.
11. Paracelsus, *Four Treatises*, 145.
12. Cranston, *John Locke*, 113.
13. Cranston, *John Locke*, 113.
14. Dewhurst, *Physician and Philosopher*, 38.
15. All of these passages are quoted in Dewhurst, *Physician and Philosopher*, 128, 260, 241, 78–79, 163.
16. Dewhurst, *Thomas Willis's Oxford Lectures*, 129.
17. Thomas Willis, *The London Practise of Physick*, 477.
18. For Willis notes, see BL MS.Locke f.19; for Sydenham, BL MS.Locke f.21.
19. The theory of womb ferment retains a place in Locke's thinking, as in this note from his 1678 journal: "Dr. Godefroy imputes hysterical fits to the disorder of the spiritous aire in the hollow of the cranium above the nose when vapours rise from the particular ferment of the womb" (BL MS.Locke f.3:197).
20. Quoted in Dewhurst, *Thomas Willis's Oxford Lectures*, 88.
21. Sydenham, *Whole Works*, 308.
22. 10 July 1670, DeBeer 1:340.

23. 12 December 1677, DeBeer 1:538.
24. Quoted in Dewhurst, *Physician and Philosopher*, 162.
25. Quoted in Temkin, *The Falling Sickness*, 241.
26. Rousseau, "Nerves, Spirits, and Fibres," 152.
27. Sydenham, *Whole Works*, 306.
28. BL MS.Locke f.3:26–27.
29. Quoted in Dewhurst, *Thomas Willis's Oxford Lectures*, 81.
30. Sydenham, *Whole Works*, 306.
31. DeBeer 5:701.
32. Quoted in Temkin, *Falling Sickness*, 183.
33. Dewhurst, *Thomas Willis's Oxford Lectures*, 127.
34. DeBeer 1:416.
35. DeBeer 4:90.
36. Frosch, *The Awakening of Albion*, 29.
37. For a valuable discussion of Blake's use of "fibre" and similar words (and the connections between fibres and nerves in eighteenth-century thinking), see Hilton, *Literal Imagination*, 79–101.
38. BL MS.Locke f.9:14–15 (notes dated June 1686). Locke had some trouble seeing all the details that Van Leeuwenhoek pointed out, both in the sample of blood and the "spermatique animals" (from a dog's womb) he also looked at.
39. The most thorough accounts of Blake's Platonism can be found in Harper's *Neoplatonism of William Blake* and Raine's *Blake and Tradition*.
40. Quoted in Bentley, *Blake Records*, 105–6.
41. Quoted in Bentley, *Blake Records*, 164.
42. Quoted in Bentley, *Blake Records*, 398.
43. Quoted in Bentley, *Blake Records*, 317–18.

Chapter 4: Slavery

1. Farr also finds three versions of accounting for Locke's involvement in slavery in "'So Vile and Miserable an Estate.'" Farr's three versions are similar to mine, although his third group is defined more narrowly and includes only the argument about racism. I would classify Farr's own argument as a combination of my third or integral approach (like David Brion Davis, he finds that Locke's theory of natural rights permits a justification of slavery) and my first or deviation approach (there can be no grounds for justifying African-American chattel slavery).
2. The figure of six hundred pounds I take from Cranston, *John Locke*, 115.
3. See Haley, *Shaftesbury*, 233. Only the duke of York and Sir Robert Viner made larger investments. Haley assumes that Shaftesbury advised Locke to put money in the company. This seems reasonable, although Locke would never have risked money without careful consideration or under any sort of coercion.
4. Haley, *Shaftesbury*, 230. Haley notes cautiously that the *Rose* was said to be in the "Guinea Trade," which "might refer to the trade in gums, wood, ivory . . . but it is more likely to refer to the usual triangular trade."
5. Both documents (the Charter of the Royal African Company and the report of the first year) can be found in Donnan, *Documents* 1:177–93.

6. For this overview of the company's performance, I am relying primarily on Craton, *Sinews of Empire*, 58–66.
7. Fox Bourne, *Life of John Locke* 1:291–92.
8. Craton, *History of the Bahamas*, 69–70.
9. This document (from the Colonial State Papers, West Indies) is cited by both Fox Bourne and Craton, *History of the Bahamas*. Fox Bourne prints an extract (1:290).
10. DeBeer 1:380.
11. Fox Bourne, *Life* 1:292; Craton, *History of the Bahamas*, 69.
12. See Haley, *Shaftesbury*, 245: "Some of Locke's friends later maintained that Locke had told them that this clause providing for the establishment of the Church of England as the state church was inserted contrary to his wishes by 'some of the chief of the proprietors.'"
13. Fox Bourne, *Life* 1:287.
14. Cranston, *John Locke*, 406.
15. Laslett, "John Locke: The Great Recoinage."
16. Squadrito, "Locke's View of Essence," 53n.
17. Grant, *John Locke's Liberalism*, 68n. Grant questions what I am calling the tortured approach of Seliger and Laslett. She charges that Laslett "misuses" his two sources (the *Fundamental Constitutions* and a letter to Governor Nicholson of Virginia), but she does not explain further. The most likely objections would focus on questions of authorship.
18. A useful discussion of these models can be found in Davis, *The Problem of Slavery*, 65–92.
19. Seliger's discussion can be found in *Liberal Politics of John Locke*, 114–24. For a more condensed version of the same argument, see Seliger's "Locke, Liberalism, and Nationalism," 27–29.
20. Craton, *Sinews of Empire*, 72.
21. Laslett, *Two Treatises of Government*, 303n.
22. Seliger mentions the similarity between Locke's argument and the passage from More (*Liberal Politics*, 114), but he makes no definite claim of influence. We know that Locke owned a copy of *Utopia*; but he does not discuss it anywhere in his writings, except for an occasional reference to something "Utopian." Of course, Locke was influenced by many books to which he never acknowledged a debt. Most notoriously he denied the influence of Hobbes, against both internal and external evidence to the contrary.
23. More, *Utopia*, tr. Surtz, 76.
24. BL MS.Locke f.2:44.
25. Squadrito, *John Locke*, 128.
26. Haley, *Shaftesbury*, 250.
27. Bacon, "Of Plantations," 106–8.
28. Fox Bourne, *Life*, 1:245.
29. The minister was John Bulkley, who made his argument in an introduction to Roger Wolcott's *Poetical Meditations* (1725). For excerpts and a brief analysis, see Dunn, "Politics of Locke in England and America," 72–73.
30. Macpherson, *Possessive Individualism*, 269.

31. Strauss, *Natural Right and History*, 246.
32. Tully, *Discourse on Property;* Ashcraft, *Revolutionary Politics.* Another discussion of the concept of the bourgeois Locke and its challengers can be found in Wood, *John Locke and Agrarian Capitalism.*
33. Poliakov, *The Aryan Myth,* 145–50.
34. Bracken, "Essence, Accident, and Race," 93. Another presentation of the argument can be found in Popkin, "Philosophical Bases of Modern Racism."
35. Miller, "Political Language," 178n.
36. Squadrito, "A Reply," 54n.
37. Wood, *Politics of Locke's Philosophy,* 81–82.
38. *Draft A of Locke's "Essay,"* ed. Nidditch, 33.
39. Poliakov, *Aryan Myth,* 145.
40. Davis, *Problem of Slavery,* 119–20.
41. Lebovics observes that Locke's "ethnographic reading proved a great aid" to his theory here, as it taught him "that Wampompeke was used in ceremonial situations not primarily as a means of commercial exchange ('common Money') in the sense that coins of precious metals were in Europe." See "The Uses of America," 578.
42. This passage from Combe's novel is cited by Sypher, *Guinea's Captive Kings,* 286.
43. Keynes, "William Blake and John Gabriel Stedman."
44. Van Lier, *Narrative,* xiv.
45. Erdman was the first Blake scholar to study the flaws of Stedman's *Narrative* as an abolitionist text. In so doing he has already suggested some of the arguments I present below. See "Blake's Vision of Slavery," 244–45. Erdman incorporates much of this essay into *Prophet against Empire,* 230–41.
46. All citations from Stedman's *Narrative* refer to Van Lier's edition. Page numbers are given in parentheses.
47. Goslee suggests that by refusing to go with Stedman, Joanna "rewrote the romantic narrative" with a different motive: she was "reluctant to leave the multi-racial society where she had, though a slave, much communal respect, for a Europe where she feared she would be stigmatized by race and class, though not by law." See "Slavery and Sexual Character," 110.
48. Craton, *Sinews of Empire,* 252.
49. Keynes, "William Blake and John Gabriel Stedman," 100; Essick, *William Blake, Printmaker,* 53.
50. Erdman, *Prophet against Empire,* 231.
51. Gugelberger, "Blake, Neruda, Ngugi wa Thiong'o," 470–71.
52. Ekechi, "History of Ideas in Africa," 67.
53. Chinweizu and Madubuike, *Decolonization of African Literature,* 5.
54. Pratt, "Scratches on the Face of the Country," 121.
55. Erdman, *Prophet against Empire,* 239.
56. A useful general guide to these conventions can be found in Curtin, *The Image of Africa.* Sypher's *Guinea's Captive Kings* gives a more detailed account of the specifically literary conventions of pseudo-Africa.
57. Curtin, *Image of Africa,* 9.

58. Sypher, *Guinea's Captive Kings*, 160.
59. Thomson, "Summer," lines 875–90, *The Seasons*, ed. Sambrook, 101.
60. Swedenborg, "Continuation of the Spiritual World," *Miscellaneous Theological Works*, tr. Whitehead, 611–12.
61. Curtin, *Image of Africa*, 50.
62. Lavater, *Essays on Physiognomy*, tr. Holcroft, 271.
63. Samuel Smith, *Essay on the Causes of the Variety*, 76–77.
64. Goslee argues that *Visions of the Daughters of Albion* merges questions of slavery and gender in a way that diminishes both emphases. See "Slavery and Sexual Character," 101–28.
65. Hinkel, "From Pivotal Idea to Poetic Ideal," 45. Because this first approach to the poem has been the dominant one for some time, it can be found in a number of places. The following discussions, along with Hinkel's, explore the possibilities most helpfully: Adler, "Symbol and Meaning,"; Adams, *Shorter Poems*, 263–66; Bloom, *Blake's Apocalypse*, 48–51; and Manlove, "Engineered Innocence."
66. For a brief record of these variations, see Erdman, *Illuminated Blake*, 51.
67. Glazer, "Blake's Little Black Boys."
68. Glazer's interpretive assumptions about the two copies have been challenged by Essick and Viscomi, who point out that some of the changes in color and design she attributes to artistic vision are actually technical effects of printing conditions. For the most recent examination of these matters, see Viscomi, *Blake and the Idea of the Book*, 164 and *passim*. Glazer's analysis remains relevant here as a critical example even if some of its details may not have the substantive significance she assumed.
69. This remark appears in Keynes's commentary to "The Little Black Boy" in the Trianon edition of *Songs*.
70. Adams, *Shorter Poems*, 264.
71. 12 February 1818, *Collected Letters*, ed. Griggs, 4:837.
72. Erdman, *Prophet against Empire*, 132.

Chapter 5: Seditious Plots

1. See Ashcraft, *Revolutionary Politics*, 465. He quotes the Skelton reply from a manuscript in the British Library (Additional MS. 41812, fol. 100). Ashcraft notes further that some prominent radicals were also omitted from the first government list.
2. For the complete text of the act (13 Car. II, St. I, c. 1), see Costin and Watson, eds., *Law and Working of the Constitution* 1:5–9.
3. From the essay "Of Magistracy," quoted in Howell, *A Complete Collection of State Trials* 11:1344.
4. All details of Johnson's trial are taken from Howell, *A Complete Collection of State Trials* 11:1339–51.
5. Macauley, *History of England* 1:490.
6. Quoted in Cranston, *John Locke*, 221.
7. Cranston, *John Locke*, 252.
8. In his 1681 journal Locke made notes citing Hooker's types of law, more numerous

and more explicitly defined than his own. Along with "law of reason" (tantamount to law of nature), "humane law" (Locke's positive law, but with more consistently favorable connotations), and "nature's law" (determining the actions of lower creatures), Hooker names three types of supernatural law: "law celestial" (for angels), "law eternal" (God's purpose for man), and "divine law" ("that which bindeth [men] and is not known but by special revelation"). See BL MS.Locke f.5:74–76.

9. See *Essays on the Law of Nature*, ed. von Leyden.
10. Locke recorded a few passages from his reading in which laws were said to be better for being minimal or tacit. "Les Mengrelliens n'ont point de loix ecrites, et la justice ne laisse pas d'y estre mieux administree. Le sens commun est la loy de ces peuples" (BL MS.Locke f.8:283); "The Sithonians in 700 years never made a new law which made their commonwealth last longer than any one in all Greece" (BL MS.Locke c.33:11).
11. See Ashcraft, *Revolutionary Politics*, 410.
12. DeBeer 2:708. See discussion in Ashcraft, *Revolutionary Politics*, 463.
13. Ashcraft, *Revolutionary Politics*, 463.
14. Ashcraft, *Revolutionary Politics*, 385.
15. DeBeer 2:582–83.
16. Ashcraft, *Revolutionary Politics*, 386–87.
17. Cranston, *John Locke*, 305.
18. DeBeer, 2:661–66.
19. The case for Locke's collaboration on *A Letter from a Person of Quality* is stronger than the case for *No Protestant Plot*, but both are reasonably persuasive. In Shaftesbury's letter, there are strong similarities with notes on toleration from Locke's journals. The case for Locke's collaboration with Ferguson is plausible, if more conjectural and circumstantial: see Ashcraft, *Revolutionary Politics*, 349.
20. For the purpose of clarity I will be normalizing the spelling of the surname of Blake's accuser (using "Scolfield," from a court document, which Bentley speculates is correct). Blake in *Jerusalem* spells it five different ways, none of which agrees with the "correct" version: Scofield, Schofield, Scofeld, Skofield, and Skofeld. Even though Blake was not a particularly regular speller, it seems plausible to take these misspellings—especially the aggressive ones with *k*s—as expressions of hostility.
21. Erdman, *Prophet against Empire*, 393.
22. Costin and Watson, *Law and Working of the Constitution* 2:11.
23. Bentley, *Blake Records*, 126.
24. Bentley, *Blake Records*, 124–25.
25. Erdman, *Prophet against Empire*, 406.
26. Quoted in Bentley, *Blake Records*, 42.
27. Erdman, *Prophet against Empire*, 494.
28. Bentley, *Blake Records*, 236.
29. Bentley, *Blake Records*, 126.
30. Bentley, *Blake Records*, 132.
31. Bentley, *Blake Records*, 145. The recollection appears in Gilchrist.
32. Bentley, *Blake Records*, 142–43.

33. See "Trial of William Blake," *Nineteenth Century*, 858–59.
34. For discussions of Christian antinomianism in Blake's thinking, see Ferber's *Social Vision of William Blake*, 116–30, and Thompson's *Witness against the Beast*.
35. For a good example of such a reading, see Erdman, *Prophet against Empire*, 193.
36. Erdman, *Complete Poetry and Prose*, 796.
37. For a full discussion of the problem of repentance in *Milton*, see Glausser, "*Milton* and the Pangs of Repentance."
38. Damon, *Blake Dictionary*, 57.
39. Stevenson, *The Poems of William Blake*, 527.

Chapter 6: Possessions

1. Reeve, *Property*, 56.
2. As Nidditch points out, Greenhill evidently painted two portraits of Locke. One was an oval, and the other—the one taken by the Stringers—was larger and rectangular. The oval now belongs to the National Portrait Gallery and has been reproduced for several books about Locke; the larger painting has been lost. See *Essay*, xxiiin.
3. Quoted in Cranston, *John Locke*, 187.
4. DeBeer 3:411.
5. DeBeer 3:429.
6. DeBeer 3:449.
7. DeBeer 3:456.
8. Although Locke was indignant that Stringer presumed to instruct him about portraits and engravings, evidence would suggest that Stringer's advice was sound. Stringer said that such plates work out better if the engraver uses a black and white drawing from life (DeBeer 3:411). This is precisely what Locke ended up using for the frontispiece.
9. Cranston, *John Locke*, 438.
10. For this context I prefer "stinginess" to more formal synonyms then current, like "illiberality." I have come across one use of the word "stinginesse" in Locke's writing. In a secretive letter to Edward Clarke he tells his friend what to keep and what to send along to Holland: "I take not those things out of his hand out of any stinginesse or unkindnesse to him but quite the contrary" (DeBeer 2:709).
11. Cranston, *John Locke*, 70.
12. Cranston, *John Locke*, 398.
13. DeBeer 2:767.
14. DeBeer 2:726.
15. Cranston, *John Locke*, 377.
16. Lebovics has argued that the archaic American setting does not prevent Locke from acknowledging modern contexts of property as capital: see "The Uses of America," 570. But Locke wants his American scene to work not just as a reflection of modern economy but as an authentic version of an original condition. Only to the extent that it does both will it serve his purposes.
17. There has been considerable scholarly debate over the economics and sociology of

land distribution in preindustrial England, but no one would deny the contrast between Locke's American scene and contemporary conditions in England. Lebovics provides a useful bibliography of the debate and reaches this conclusion: "In the sense in which he understood the word not many people possessed 'property,' i. e., land in freehold, in Locke's day" (575).

18. Although the connection between labor and property may seem a commonplace, Wood observes that "Locke was the first classic political theorist to place such great emphasis on labor" (*John Locke and Agrarian Capitalism*, 53).
19. R. T. Stothard's defense of his father is cited and summarized in Bentley, *Blake Records*, 180. Bentley points out some telling deficiencies of the account.
20. Ward, "Canterbury Revisited: The Blake-Cromek Controversy," 85.
21. Bentley, "Blake and Cromek." Bentley concludes from the new letter that "there was a surprising breadth of aesthetic and intellectual sympathy between Blake and Cromek, at least for a time" (366). The new evidence does nothing to change Bentley's denunciation of Cromek's manipulative cunning in business matters. Bentley's notes in *Blake Records* expose some of Cromek's subtler tricks.
22. Quoted in Bentley, *Blake Records*, 186.
23. Eaves, *William Blake's Theory of Art*, 193.
24. Eaves, *William Blake's Theory of Art*, 185–6; 195.
25. See, for example, Boehme, *Signatura Rerum* 15.3–22.
26. Selfhood is not an "unambiguous source of evil" but a "necessary part of the structure of consciousness." "Self-annihilation does not mean the permanent abolition of selfhood; it is the prelude to the creation of a *new* selfhood which will serve the imagination" (Mitchell, *Blake's Composite Art*, 91n.). Like others who have tried to express a similar thought, Mitchell cannot transcend the limitations of terminology. "Selfhood" remains an indispensable but onerous word, so that "new" and "imagination" must come to its rescue.
27. Keynes, for example, notes that Blake uses "spectres of the dead" in more than one sense and chooses an interpretive gloss from Sloss and Wallis which makes these spectres consistent with their anti-imaginative kin: they represent "the abstract idea for which the artist cannot, save by inspiration, find the living form, the eternally right expression" (*Letters of William Blake*, 51; quoting Sloss and Wallis, *William Blake's Prophetic Writings* 2:227). Damrosch is not inclined to sever these specters' ties with inspiration so conveniently—he grants their affiliation with the "visionary forms" of imagination, but he dismisses the letter as the product of a diminished Blake: "Here speaks the Spectre of Urthona" (*Symbol and Truth*, 314).

Chapter 7: Printing

1. Eisenstein, *Printing Press*, 420.
2. Bacon, *Novum Organum*, ed. Devey, 105.
3. McLuhan, *The Gutenberg Galaxy*, 265.
4. It should be noted that Locke's public arguments against the renewal of the act tended to emphasize economic objections above considerations of civil liberty. Cranston summarizes as follows: "But the principle of liberty was not the only nor

even the primary reason Locke gave for advocating the repeal of the Act. His first considerations were of expediency. He argued that the monopoly vested in the Company of Stationers was uneconomic and contrary to the public interest" (*John Locke,* 387).

5. DeBeer 3:331.
6. DeBeer 5:174. Locke is surprised at the success of the *Essay* and by the absence of criticism so far: "nec adhuc invenit dissertatio illa utcunque heterodoxa oppugnatorem."
7. Quoted in Bentley, *Blake Records,* 460. What may be Blake's first relief etching, *The Approach of Doom,* is based on a drawing done by Robert.
8. Viscomi, *Blake and the Idea of the Book,* 31.
9. Essick suggests this as the probable shape of Blake's early career, although the evidence is not definitive. See *William Blake, Printmaker,* 255.
10. As Bentley observes, "In the 1780s there was much interest in stereotype printing in France and Britian, with inventions in 1784 and 1785 by Franz Ignaz Joseph Hoffmann, Alexander Tilloch, and George Cumberland. Blake probably learned something of these experiments from his friend Cumberland" (*Blake Records,* 32).
11. Eisenstein, *Printing Press,* 88–107.
12. Ong, *Orality and Literacy,* 122, 132.
13. McLuhan, *Gutenberg Galaxy,* 209.
14. Warner, "Franklin and the Letters of the Republic," 112.
15. Kernan, *Printing Technology,* 48–49.
16. For an account of these biographical details, see Cranston, *John Locke,* 287–91.
17. See DeBeer 5:266–67, and Cranston's account, *John Locke,* 384–85.
18. Kernan writes of an "aristocratic disdain for print" that was fairly common during the eighteenth century (*Printing Technology,* 65). Locke worked on the border between the "older system of polite or courtly letters—primarily oral, aristocratic, amateur, authoritarian, court-centered" and the "new print-based, market-centered, democratic literary system" (4). Despite his modesty tropes, however, and his aristocratic patronage, his affiliations with the new system are much stronger than with the older system.
19. The most important study of Blake's Romantic aesthetics can be found in Eaves, *William Blake's Theory of Art.* Eaves's influential earlier essay, "Blake and the Artistic Machine," is particulary helpful for the present discussion of Blake and printing.
20. Essick's *William Blake, Printmaker* and Viscomi's *Blake and the Idea of the Book* have revised scholarly opinion about Blake's technique and examined various editorial and interpretive consequences of their discoveries. Viscomi undertook to replicate Blake's workshop and made prints using his methods of relief etching. He has concluded, among other things, that Blake wrote backward on his plates (not forward, with a process of transfer), produced his illuminated books in editions (not one by one for intermittent customers), and could not have expected to sell them to a broad market (they were too expensive). In general, Essick and Viscomi have made editors and interpreters more sensitive to the effects of Blake's medium and thereby subverted simple assumptions about authorial intention. Their work

leaves intact, however, the idea of Blake as an artist whose medium of production reflects his aesthetic, epistemological, and moral objections to mainstream print culture.
21. Santa Cruz Blake Study Group, review of Erdman, ed., *Complete Poetry and Prose of William Blake*. Viscomi criticizes the Santa Cruz group for approaching "the meaning of spatial form from a purely ahistorical, poststructuralist perspective" but acknowledges that he shares their emphasis on "the importance of the reading experience, and the effect of the book's form on reading" (402n.).
22. Mann, "Apocalypse and Recuperation," 27, 5, 2.
23. John Yolton, *Locke: An Introduction*, 105.
24. For a full discussion of Blake and the atomistic tradition, see Glausser, "Atomistic Simulacra."
25. BL MS.Locke c.33:28.
26. BL MS.Locke d.1:iii.
27. For a full discussion of the French reception of Locke's work as a foundation for "materialism, irreligion, and free thinking," see John Yolton, *Locke and French Materialism*, 38–59. Yolton studies the process by which Locke's work was read selectively and oversimplified to generate this reputation.
28. Good, "Preface" to *De Rerum Natura*, cxxx.
29. Reid, *Essays on the Intellectual Powers of Man*, 19.
30. See Redondi, *Galileo: Heretic*, tr. Rosenthal.
31. Cudworth, *True Intellectual System of the Universe*. Cudworth cites Posidonius, who claimed that "Moschus, a Phoenician" invented atomism. Cudworth speculates that the mysterious Moschus is actually Moses.
32. Ault, *Visionary Physics*, 11.
33. Blake actually deleted the second half of this sentence. After "The Enthusiasm of the following Poem, the Author hopes," he engraved but then took out the rest of the sentence: "no Reader will think presumptuousness or arrogance when he is reminded that the Ancients acknowledge their love to the Deities, to the full as Enthusiastically as I have who Acknowledge mine for my Saviour and Lord, for they were wholly absorb'd in their Gods" (145). Perhaps he felt that this sentence placed too much emphasis on ancient deities at a time in his career when he was preoccupied with Christian enthusiasm. (The next sentence, which he keeps, invokes "Jesus our Lord . . . whom the Ancients look'd and saw his day afar off, with trembling & amazement" [145].)
34. Ferber, *Social Vision of William Blake*, 17–18.
35. Caruth, whose reading of Locke's *Essay* resembles mine in its attention to rhetorical plots beyond explicit arguments, observes that figures of children provide one of the means by which the apparent foundations of empiricism can be deconstructed. These figures stand at the putative origin of empirical narrative, but they disrupt the assumptions of immediate perception and self-transparency that empiricism claims. "The obsession with causes and origins in empirical narratives can be read, now, not as mere reductiveness, an ignoring of the rich activity of mental life, but as a telling of the conditions of empirical language. The stories of influence, of the dangers of the origin—of the sensory origin in the external world, or the reflective

origin in childhood—tell, also, of the excesses of the language which made possible the claims of the empirical argument" (*Empirical Truths*, 41).
36. Translated in Von Leyden, *Law of Nature*, 322.
37. For Damon's reading, see *Blake Dictionary*, 95: "It may be the record of some casual affair in Surrey, which ended unhappily." For Erdman's, see *Prophet against Empire*, 394–95.

Chapter 8: Epitaphs

1. Cranston, *John Locke*, 480.
2. Quoted in Bentley, *Blake Records*, 347. Richmond was writing to Samuel Palmer, who was out of town when Blake died.
3. Cranston, *John Locke*, 480.
4. See *Witness against the Beast*, 65–105. Thompson speculates (on the basis of plausible but by no means certain evidence) that Blake's mother had family connections to the Muggletonians, whose antinomianism may have significantly influenced young Blake.
5. BL MS.Locke f.8:12.

Bibliography

Adams, Hazard. *William Blake: A Reading of the Shorter Poems*. Seattle: University of Washington Press, 1963.
Adler, Jacob H. "Symbol and Meaning in 'The Little Black Boy.'" *Modern Language Notes* 72 (1957): 412–15.
Apperson, G. L. *English Proverbs and Proverbial Phrases*. London: J. M. Dent, 1929.
Ashcraft, Richard. *Revolutionary Politics and Locke's "Two Treatises of Government."* Princeton: Princeton University Press, 1986.
Ault, Donald. *Visionary Physics: Blake's Response to Newton*. Chicago: University of Chicago Press, 1974.
Axtell, James L., ed. *The Educational Writings of John Locke*. Cambridge: Cambridge University Press, 1968.
Bacon, Francis. *Novum Organum*. Edited by Joseph Devey. New York: Macmillan, 1902.
———. "Of Plantations." In *The Essays or Counsels, Civill and Morall*, edited by Michael Kiernan, 106–8. Oxford: Oxford University Press, 1985.
Bentley, G. E. Jr. "Blake and Cromek: The Wheat and the Tares." *Modern Philology* 71 (1974): 366–79.
———. *Blake Records*. Oxford: Oxford University Press, 1969.
———. *Blake Records Supplement*. Oxford: Oxford University Press, 1989.
Blake, William. *Jerusalem: The Emanation of the Giant Albion*. Edited by Morton D. Paley. Princeton: Princeton University Press, 1991.
———. *Songs of Innocence and of Experience*. Edited by Geoffrey Keynes. New York: Orion, 1967.
Bloom, Harold. *Blake's Apocalypse: A Study in Poetic Argument*. Garden City, N.Y.: Doubleday, 1963.
Boehme, Jacob. *Mysterium Magnum*. London, 1654. Microfilm.
———. *Signature Rerum, or, The Signature of All Things*. London, 1651. Microfilm.
———. *The Way to Christ*. Translated by John Joseph Stoudt. New York: Harper Brothers, 1947.
Bracken, H. M. "Essence, Accident, and Race." *Hermathena* 116 (1973): 88–103.
Brown, Norman O. *Life against Death*. Middletown, Conn.: Wesleyan University Press, 1959.
Caruth, Cathy. *Empirical Truths and Critical Fictions: Locke, Wordsworth, Kant, Freud*. Baltimore: Johns Hopkins University Press, 1991.
Chinweizu, Onwuchekwa Jemie, and Ihechukwu Madubuike. *Toward the Decolonization of African Literature*. Washington, D.C.: Howard University Press, 1983.

Clark, Lorenne M. G. "Women and John Locke; or, Who Owns the Apples in the Garden of Eden?" *Canadian Journal of Philosophy* 7 (1977): 699–724.
Costin, W. C., and J. Steven Watson. *The Law and Working of the Constitution: Documents 1660–1914*. 2 vols. London: Adam and Charles Black, 1952.
Cranston, Maurice. *John Locke: A Biography*. Oxford: Oxford University Press, 1957.
———. "John Locke and John Aubrey." *Notes and Queries* 195 (1950): 552–54.
Craton, Michael. *A History of the Bahamas*. London: Collins, 1962.
———. *Sinews of Empire: A Short History of British Slavery*. London: Temple Smith, 1974.
Cudworth, Ralph. *The True Intellectual System of the Universe*. 3 vols. London, 1678.
Curtin, Philip D. *The Image of Africa: British Ideas and Action, 1780–1850*. Madison: University of Wisconsin Press, 1964.
Damon, S. Foster. *A Blake Dictionary*. New York: Dutton, 1971.
Damrosch, Leopold. *Symbol and Truth in Blake's Myth*. Princeton: Princeton University Press, 1980.
Davis, David Brion. *The Problem of Slavery in Western Culture*. Ithaca, N.Y.: Cornell University Press, 1966.
DeBeer, E. S., ed. *The Correspondence of John Locke*. 8 vols. Oxford: Oxford University Press, 1976–83.
Dewhurst, Kenneth. *John Locke: Physician and Philosopher*. London: Wellcome Historical Medical Library, 1963.
———. *Thomas Willis's Oxford Lectures*. Oxford: Sandford Publications, 1980.
Donnan, Elizabeth. *Documents Illustrative of the History of the Slave Trade to America*. 2 vols. New York: Octagon Books, 1965.
Dunn, John. "The Politics of Locke in England and America." In *John Locke: Problems and Perspectives*, edited by John W. Yolton, 58–84. Cambridge: Cambridge University Press, 1969.
Eaves, Morris. "Blake and the Artistic Machine: An Essay in Decorum and Technology." *PMLA* 92 (1977): 903–27.
———. *William Blake's Theory of Art*. Princeton: Princeton University Press, 1982.
Eisenstein, Elizabeth. *The Printing Press as an Agent of Change*. Cambridge: Cambridge University Press, 1979.
Ekechi, Felix. "The Future of the History of Ideas in Africa." *African Studies Review* 30 (1988): 63–80.
Erdman, David. "Blake's Vision of Slavery." *Journal of the Warburg and Courtauld Institutes* 15 (1952): 237–60.
———. *The Illuminated Blake*. New York: Doubleday, 1973.
———. *William Blake: Prophet against Empire*. 3rd ed. Princeton: Princeton University Press, 1977.
Essick, Robert N. *William Blake, Printmaker*. Princeton: Princeton University Press, 1980.
Farr, James. "'So Vile and Miserable an Estate': The Problem of Slavery in Locke's Political Thought." *Political Theory* 14 (1986): 263–89.

Ferber, Michael. *The Social Vision of William Blake.* Princeton: Princeton University Press, 1985.

Fox Bourne, H. R. *The Life of John Locke.* 2 vols. London, 1876.

Frosch, Thomas R. *The Awakening of Albion: The Renovation of the Body in the Poetry of William Blake.* Ithaca, N.Y.: Cornell University Press, 1974.

Frye, Northrop. *Fearful Symmetry: A Study of William Blake.* Princeton: Princeton University Press, 1947.

Gilchrist, Alexander. *Life of William Blake.* London, 1863.

Glausser, Wayne. "Atomistic Simulacra in the Enlightenment and in Blake's Post-Enlightenment." *Eighteenth Century: Theory and Interpretation* 32 (1993): 73–88.

———. "*Milton* and the Pangs of Repentance." *Blake: An Illustrated Quarterly* 13 (1980): 192–99.

Glazer, Myra. "Blake's Little Black Boys: On the Dynamics of Blake's Composite Art." *Colby Library Quarterly* 16 (1980): 220–36.

Goslee, Nancy Moore. "Slavery and Sexual Character: Questioning the Master Trope in Blake's *Visions of the Daughters of Albion.*" *ELH* 57 (1990): 98–117.

Grant, Ruth. *John Locke's Liberalism.* Chicago: University of Chicago Press, 1987.

Griggs, Earl L. *The Collected Letters of Samuel Taylor Coleridge.* Oxford: Oxford University Press, 1959.

Gugelberger, Georg M. "Blake, Neruda, Ngugi wa Thiong'o: Issues in Third World Literature." *Comparative Literature Studies* 21 (1984): 465–89.

Haley, K. H. D. *The First Earl of Shaftesbury.* Oxford: Oxford University Press, 1968.

Harper, George Mills. *The Neoplatonism of William Blake.* Chapel Hill: University of North Carolina Press, 1961.

Hilton, Nelson. *Literal Imagination: Blake's Vision of Words.* Berkeley and Los Angeles: University of California Press, 1983.

Hinkel, Howard. "From Pivotal Idea to Poetic Ideal: Blake's Theory of Contraries and 'The Little Black Boy.'" *Papers on Language and Literature* 11 (1975): 38–57.

Howell, T. B. *A Complete Collection of State Trials and Proceedings for High Treason and Other Crimes and Misdemeanors.* London, 1817.

Jameson, Fredric. "On Habits of the Heart." *South Atlantic Quarterly* 86 (1987): 545–65.

Kernan, Alvin. *Printing Technology, Letters, and Samuel Johnson.* Princeton: Princeton University Press, 1987.

Keynes, Geoffrey. *The Letters of William Blake.* Cambridge, Mass.: Harvard University Press, 1980.

———. "William Blake and John Gabriel Stedman." In *Blake Studies: Essays on His Life and Work.* 2nd ed., 98–104. Oxford: Oxford University Press, 1971.

King, Peter. *The Life and Letters of John Locke.* London: Henry Bohn, 1858.

La Calprenede, Gaultier de Coste. *Hymen's Praeludia, or Love's Master-piece, Being a Translation of Cleopatre.* Ann Arbor: University Microfilms, 1977.

Laslett, Peter. "John Locke: The Great Recoinage and the Board of Trade, 1695–1698." *William and Mary Quarterly* 14 (1957): 370–402.

Lavater, Johann Caspar. *Essays on Physiognomy.* Translated by Thomas Holcroft. London, 1804.

Lebovics, Herman. "The Uses of America in Locke's *Second Treatise of Government.*" *Journal of the History of Ideas* 47 (1986): 566–87.

Locke, John. *Two Treatises of Government.* Edited by Peter Laslett. Cambridge: Cambridge University Press, 1960.

Lucretius. *De Rerum Natura.* Edited by J. M. Good. London, 1805.

Macaulay, Thomas Babington. *The History of England from the Accession of James II.* 5 vols. New York: Thomas Nelson and Sons, n.d.

McLuhan, Marshall. *The Gutenberg Galaxy: The Making of Typographic Man.* Toronto: University of Toronto Press, 1962.

Macpherson, C. B. *The Political Theory of Possessive Individualism.* Oxford: Oxford University Press, 1962.

Manlove, C. N. "Engineered Innocence: Blake's 'The Little Black Boy' and 'The Fly.'" *Essays in Criticism* 27 (1977): 112–21.

Mann, Paul. "Apocalypse and Recuperation: Blake and the Maw of Commerce." *ELH* 52 (1985): 1–29.

Mee, Jon. *Dangerous Enthusiasm: William Blake and the Culture of Radicalism in the 1790's.* Oxford: Clarendon, 1992.

Miller, Eugene. "Locke on the Meaning of Political Language." *Political Science Reviewer* 9 (1979): 167–89.

Milton, John. *The Doctrine and Discipline of Divorce.* In *Complete Poems and Major Prose,* edited by Merritt Y. Hughes. New York: Odyssey Press, 1957.

———. *Paradise Lost.* In *Complete Poems and Major Prose,* edited by Merritt Y. Hughes. New York: Odyssey Press, 1957.

Mitchell, W. J. T. *Blake's Composite Art.* Princeton: Princeton University Press, 1978.

———. "Style and Iconography in the Illustrations of Blake's *Milton.*" *Blake Studies* 6 (1973): 54–79.

More, Henry. *The Immortality of the Soul.* In *A Collection of Several Philosophical Writings of Henry More.* 2 vols. New York: Garland Press, 1978.

More, Thomas. *Utopia.* Translated by Edward Surtz, S.J. New Haven, Conn.: Yale University Press, 1964.

Nidditch, Peter H., ed. *Draft A of Locke's "Essay Concerning Human Understanding": The Earliest Extant Autograph Edition.* Sheffield: University of Sheffield Printing Unit, 1980.

Ong, Walter J. *Orality and Literacy: The Technologizing of the Word.* London and New York: Methuen, 1982.

Ostriker, Alicia. "Desire Gratified and Ungratified: William Blake and Sexuality." *Blake: An Illustrated Quarterly* 16 (1983): 156–65.

Paracelsus. *Four Treatises of Theophrastus von Hohenheim called Paracelsus.* Edited by Henry E. Sigerist. Baltimore: Johns Hopkins University Press, 1941.

Passmore, J. A. *Ralph Cudworth: An Interpretation.* Cambridge: Cambridge University Press, 1951.

Pateman, Carole, and Teresa Brennan, "'Mere Auxiliaries to the Commonwealth': Women and the Origins of Liberalism." *Political Studies* 27 (1979): 183–200.

Perkins, David. *Is Literary History Possible?* Baltimore: Johns Hopkins University Press, 1992.

Poliakov, Leon. *The Aryan Myth: A History of Racist and Nationalist Ideas in Europe.* Translated by Edmund Howard. New York: New American Library, 1977.

Popkin, Richard H. "The Philosophical Bases of Modern Racism." In *Philosophy and the Civilizing Arts,* edited by Craig Walton and John P. Anton, 126–65. Athens: Ohio University Press, 1974.

Pratt, Mary Louise. "Scratches on the Face of the Country; or, What Mr. Barrow Saw in the Land of the Bushmen." *Critical Inquiry* 12 (1985): 119–43.

Pringle, Helen Mary. *Nature Virtue and Gratitude: Locke's Representation of Power.* Ann Arbor: University Microfilms, 1992.

Raine, Kathleen. *Blake and Tradition.* 2 vols. Princeton: Princeton University Press, 1968.

Redondi, Pietro. *Galileo: Heretic.* Translated by Raymond Rosenthal. Princeton: Princeton University Press, 1987.

Reeve, Andrew. *Property.* Atlantic Highlands, N.J.: Humanities Press International, 1986.

Reid, Thomas. *Essays on the Intellectual Powers of Man.* Cambridge, Mass.: Harvard University Press, 1969.

Robinson, Henry Crabb. *Diary, Reminiscences, and Correspondence.* 2 vols. Boston: Houghton Mifflin, 1877.

Rorty, Richard. *Philosophy and the Mirror of Nature.* Princeton: Princeton University Press, 1979.

Rousseau, G. S. "Nerves, Spirits, and Fibres: Towards Defining the Origins of Sensibility." In *Studies in the Eighteenth Century,* edited by R. F. Brissenden and J. C. Eads, 140–57. Toronto: University of Toronto Press, 1976.

Santa Cruz Blake Study Group. Review of *The Complete Poetry and Prose of William Blake,* edited by David V. Erdman. *Blake: An Illustrated Quarterly* 18 (1984): 43–51.

Saxby, T. J. *The Quest for the New Jerusalem: Jean de Labadie and the Labadists, 1610–1744.* Dordrecht: Martinus Nijhoff, 1987.

Schuchard, M. K. "Blake's Healing Trio: Magnetism, Medicine, and Mania." *Blake: An Illustrated Quarterly* 23 (1989): 20–31.

Seliger, Martin. *The Liberal Politics of John Locke.* New York: Frederick A. Praeger, 1969.

———. "Locke, Liberalism, and Nationalism." In *John Locke: Problems and Perspectives,* edited by John W. Yolton, 17–38. Cambridge: Cambridge University Press, 1969.

Sloss, D. J., and J. P. R. Wallis. *William Blake's Prophetic Writings.* 2 vols. Oxford: Oxford University Press, 1926.

Smith, Samuel Stanhope. *An Essay on the Causes of the Variety of Complexion and Figure in the Human Species.* 1787. Rpt., edited by Winthrop D. Jordan. Cambridge, Mass.: Harvard University Press, 1965.

Squadrito, Kathleen. *John Locke.* Boston: Twayne, 1979.

———. "Locke's View of Essence and Its Relation to Racism: A Reply to Professor Bracken." *Locke Newsletter* 6 (1975): 50–57.

Stedman, John Gabriel. *Narrative of an Expedition against the Revolted Negroes of*

      Surinam. Edited by R. A. J. van Lier. Amherst: University of Massachusetts Press, 1972.

Stevenson, W. H., ed. *The Poems of William Blake*. London: Longman, 1971.

Stone, Lawrence. *The Family, Sex, and Marriage in England, 1500–1800*. New York: Harper and Row, 1977.

Storch, Margaret. *Sons and Adversaries: Women in William Blake and D. H. Lawrence*. Knoxville: University of Tennessee Press, 1990.

———. "The Spectrous Fiend Cast Out: Blake's Crisis at Felpham." *Modern Language Quarterly* 44 (1983): 112–31.

Strauss, Leo. *Natural Right and History*. Chicago: University of Chicago Press, 1953.

Sutherland, John. "Blake: A Crisis of Love and Jealousy." *PMLA* 87 (1972): 424–31.

Swedenborg, Emanuel. "Continuation of the Spiritual World." In *Miscellaneous Theological Works*. Translated by John Whitehead, 606–38. New York: Swedenborg Foundation, 1976.

———. *Delights of Wisdom Concerning Conjugial Love*. Boston: Otis Clapp, 1852.

———. *Heaven and Hell*. Philadelphia: J. B. Lippincott, 1874.

Sydenham, Thomas. *Whole Works*. Translated by John Pechey. London, 1740.

Sypher, Wylie. *Guinea's Captive Kings: British Anti-Slavery Literature of the Eighteenth Century*. 1942. Rpt., New York: Octagon Books, 1969.

Temkin, Owsei. *The Falling Sickness: A History of Epilepsy from the Greeks to the Beginnings of Modern Neurology*. 2d ed. Baltimore: Johns Hopkins University Press, 1971.

Thompson, E. P. *Witness against the Beast: William Blake and the Moral Law*. New York: New Press, 1993.

Thomson, James. *The Seasons*. Edited by James Sambrook. Oxford: Oxford University Press, 1981.

"Trial of William Blake for High Treason." *Nineteenth Century* 67 (1910): 853–61.

Tully, James. *A Discourse on Property: John Locke and His Adversaries*. Cambridge: Cambridge University Press, 1980.

Viscomi, Joseph. *Blake and the Idea of the Book*. Princeton: Princeton University Press, 1993.

Vogler, Thomas A. "'In vain the Eloquent Tongue': An Un-Reading of *Visions of the Daughters of Albion*." In *Critical Paths: Blake and the Argument of Method*, edited by Dan Miller, Mark Bracher, and Donald Ault, 271–309. Durham, N.C.: Duke University Press, 1987.

Von Leyden, Wolfgang. *John Locke: Essays on the Law of Nature*. Oxford: Oxford University Press, 1954.

Ward, Aileen. "Canterbury Revisited: The Blake-Cromek Controversy." *Blake: An Illustrated Quarterly* 22 (1989): 80–92.

Warner, Michael. "Franklin and the Letters of the Republic." *Representations* 16 (1986): 107–30.

Webster, Brenda. "Blake, Women, and Sexuality." In *Critical Paths: Blake and the Argument of Method*, edited by Dan Miller, Mark Bracher, and Donald Ault, 204–24. Durham, N.C.: Duke University Press, 1987.

Willis, Thomas. *The London Practise of Physick*. 1685. Rpt., Boston: Longwood Press, 1977.

Wilson, Mona. *The Life of William Blake*. 1927. Rpt., edited by Geoffrey Keynes. Oxford: Oxford University Press, 1971.

Wittgenstein, Ludwig. "A Lecture on Ethics." *Philosophical Review* 74 (1965): 3–19.

Wood, Neal. *John Locke and Agrarian Capitalism*. Berkeley and Los Angeles: University of California Press, 1984.

———. *The Politics of Locke's Philosophy*. Berkeley and Los Angeles: University of California Press, 1983.

Yolton, John W. *Locke: An Introduction*. Oxford: Blackwell, 1985.

———. *Locke and French Materialism*. Oxford: Oxford University Press, 1991.

———. *A Locke Dictionary*. Oxford: Blackwell, 1993.

Index

Act for the Regulation of Printing, 142
Act to Preserve the Person and Government of the King (1661), 93–94
Adam (biblical): and creation of woman, 29–37, 55; and sexuality, 40–41
Adams, Hazard, 89–90
Africa: and national character, 78; poetic conventions about, 84–85; and spirituality, 85; stereotypes of, 83, 85–86. *See also* natives; slavery
aggressors: effects of, 105–6; natives as, 69–70, 74–75. *See also* crime/criminals
alchemy, 44–45
anger: of Locke, 123–26; and selfhood, 135–36
anticlericalism, 7–8
apocalypse, Blake on, 160–62
Aristotle, 72, 148
art: details in, 144–48; and property, 132–40
Ashcraft, Richard: on Locke as bourgeois, 71–72; on Locke's politics, 166n.2; on Locke's sedition, 92–93, 95–96, 103–4
Ashley (Lord). *See* Cooper, Anthony Ashley (Lord Ashley)
astrology, 44–45
atheism, and Locke's doctrine, 1, 5–6, 143, 149–50, 152, 153
Atkins, Frank, 16–17
atomism, 44, 148–50
Aubrey, John, 167n.6
audience. *See* public

Bacon, Francis, 70, 108, 141, 143, 150
Bahaman Islands, development of, 63–65
Barbados, investments in, 63
Bartolozzi, Francesco, 79–80
Beddoes, Thomas, 50
belief. *See* faith
Bellah, Robert, 166n.3
Bentley, G. E., Jr.: Blake collection by, 166n.2; on Blake's art, 132, 179n.19; on Blake's marriage, 28; on illiteracy, 170n.68; on printing, 180n.10
Bible: Blake's interest in, 30, 151; and forgiveness, 117–18; and God's law, 100; idolatry in, 156–57; interpretations of, 29–37, 54–55; Locke's interest in, 6–8, 65–66, 100; miracles in, 8–11; and property theories, 130; willful king in, 113–14. *See also* faith; God; religion
Bicknell, Alexander (poet), 85
biomechanics, 86
black (color), Blake's use of, 83–86, 89–91
Blair, Robert, *The Grave,* 131–32
Blake, Catherine (William's mother), 27
Blake, Catherine (William's wife): and Blake's sedition, 109–10; designs colored by, 36, 41; illness of, 60; marriage of, 27–29, 42; and Swedenborg's resolutions, 34; visions of, 29
Blake, John, 26–27
Blake, Robert, 29, 39–40, 142–43

Blake, William: approach to, 1–3, 87; background of, 5–7, 13, 26–27; characterization of, 27, 55, 111–12; epitaph by, 163–65; illness of, 53, 58–61; influences on, 26, 34, 40, 86, 165; inspiration for, 138–40; isolation of, 132, 133–34; and law/innocence, 106–7, 112–20; on liberation, 86–87; on Locke, 1–2, 4–6, 146–47, 157, 158–59, 161–62; and love, 26–42; marriage of, 27–29, 34, 42; and medical interests, 43, 53–61; painting stolen from, 121, 130–40; and printing, 141–48, 150–53; reenchantment of body by, 53–61; sedition of, 92, 96, 107–20; and slave trade, 57, 62, 75–91; spectral themes of, 135–39; techniques of, 142–43, 146–47; works: *America*, 81–84, 110, 115; *The Book of Urizen*, 30, 34, 41, 54–55, 135–36; "The Crystal Cabinet," 157–60; *A Descriptive Catalogue*, 148; *The Four Zoas*, 30, 34, 40, 138; *The French Revolution*, 115; *An Island in the Moon*, 4, 158; "The Little Black Boy," 84–85, 87–91; "My Spectre round me night and day," 34; *The Song of Los*, 83; *Songs of Innocence*, 88–89, 106–7; *Songs of Innocence and Experience*, 88–89, 115, 117; *Visions of the Daughters of Albion*, 27, 37–38, 57, 82–83, 87. See also *Jerusalem* (Blake); *The Marriage of Heaven and Hell* (Blake); *Milton* (Blake)

Bloom, Harold, 37
Board of Trade, 65, 66
body: Blake's version of, 53–61; Locke's version of, 46–52, 54; as site of oppression, 57–58; vs. soul, 60–61, 88, 90, 161. See also sexuality
Boehme, Jacob: on creation of woman, 30–36; influence by, 26, 30; on magical sexuality, 41; on selfhood, 135
bourgeois ideology, 71–72, 129. See also social class
Boyle, Robert, 45

Bracken, H. M., 72
Brown, Norman O., 30–31
Brownover, Sylvanus, 123
Bulkley, John, 174n.29
Burke, Edmund, 143, 144, 147
Butts, Thomas, 60, 137–39

Canterbury Tales (Chaucer), art for, 131–33, 148
canting, in correspondence, 103–4
capitalism, Locke as advocate of, 46, 71–72, 74
Caruth, Cathy, 181–82n.35
Charles II (King of England), 47, 93, 95
Chatterton, Thomas, 133
Chaucer, Geoffrey, *Canterbury Tales*, 131–33, 148
children, nurture of, 13–15, 155–56. See also education
Christianity: and anticlericalism, 7–8; and atomism, 149–50; and forgiveness, 117–18; and marriage, 18; and pseudoprophets, 150–51; and slavery, 65–67, 81–82; zealot sects in, 23–25. See also faith; Protestant visionaries
Church of England, established in Carolina, 65
Clarke, Edward, 103–4, 122–23, 178n.10
class. See social class
Clora (character in pastoral poetry), 21–23. See also Cudworth, Damaris
Coleridge, Samuel Taylor, 90
Colleton, Peter, 64–65
Combe, William, *Devil Upon Two Sticks in England*, 76
common, Locke's use of, 74–75
Company of Royal Adventurers into Africa, 63
Condillac, Étienne Bonnot de, 149
conjugal love: vs. free love, 37–39; vs. homoerotic desire, 39–40; vs. polymorphous imagination, 40–41; Protestant visionaries on, 27–29
conversation, description of, 3–4, 17
Cooke, Mary, 125

Cooper, Anthony Ashley (Lord Ashley): and Carolina constitution, 65–66; landpurchases by, 70; and Locke's portrait, 121–22; medical treatment for, 44, 47–48; and sedition, 105; slave-trade investments by, 63–65
correspondence, encryption of, 95, 103–4
Coste, Pierre, 16, 123–24
Council of Trade and Plantations, 65, 66
Cowper, William, 27–28, 54, 59, 77
Cranston, Maurice: biography by, 166n.2; on Cudworth's marriage, 25; on Locke and Board of Trade, 66; on Locke and printing, 179–80n.4; on Locke's medical work, 45, 47; on Locke's mother, 13; on Locke's romantic ways, 16; on Locke's sedition, 95–96, 103; on Locke's temperament, 18, 123, 125
Craton, Michael, 64–65, 67, 68, 79
crime/criminals, Locke on, 48, 74–75, 99, 102, 105, 130. *See also* aggressors
Cromek, Robert, 131–33
Cudworth, Damaris (later Lady Masham): background of, 15; on Locke's anger, 123–24; and Locke's death, 165; Locke's relationship with, 19–25, 41–42; marriage of, 23, 25; pastoral poems by, 21–23
Cudworth, Ralph, 19, 21, 150
Cumberland, George, 110, 142, 180n.10
Curtin, Philip, 83, 85, 90

Damon, S. Foster, 39, 119, 160, 170n. 80, 171–72n.93
Damon (character in pastoral poetry), 21–23. *See also* Locke, John, and love
Damrosch, Leopold, 171n.86, 179n.27
Dare, Thomas, 125
Davies, Robert, 169n.39
Davis, David Brion, 73–74
Day, Thomas, 85
DeBeer, E. S., 166n.2, 168n.22
Democritus, 148, 150
Dewhurst, Kenneth, 48, 166n.2

diseases: causes of, 53–54, 59–60; diagnosis of, 49–51; as metaphor, 156; mystification of, 44, 49–50; treatments for, 13, 44–45, 47–48, 51–52, 60–61. *See also* medicine; nervous conditions
dualism: Blake's, 60–61, 138; flaws in, 87–88

Eaves, Morris, 134, 180n.19
education, Locke on, 14–15, 17, 19, 123–25
Edwards, John, 17, 25
Eisenstein, Elizabeth, 141, 144
Ekechi, Felix, 81–82
England: colonies administered by, 64–66, 68–70; commercial development by, 77, 84; land distribution in, 128; possible invasion of, 108; print culture in, 145; rebellion in, 93–96, 104; representation of, 53; and slave treatment, 77–78
enthusiasm: in Blake's art, 160–62; for French Revolution, 110, 113; Locke on, 1–2, 150–52; meanings of, 20–21; and printing, 143, 150–52. *See also* imagination; inspiration
envy, Locke on, 124–25
Epicurus, 148–50, 153
epilepsy (sacred disease), 49, 52
epitaphs, of Blake and Locke, 163–65
equality: basis for, 46, 98–99; and Blake's marriage, 29; and competition, 99–100, 102; and property theories, 46, 98
Erdman, David: on Blake's art, 39, 80, 172n.95; on Blake's poetry, 82–83, 90, 160; on Blake's politics, 96; on Blake's sedition, 108, 109; criticism of edition by, 146; on Stedman's *Narrative*, 175n.45
An Essay Concerning Human Understanding (Locke): on enthusiasm, 1–2, 150–52; on formation of mind/ideas, 152–57, 158, 161–62; frontispiece for, 121–22; and human essence, 72–73, 147–48, 160; on marriage, 18;

Essay—Continued
ojections to, 4, 6–7; on passions, 124, 125–26; and printing, 141–43, 145–47; on property, 126; and racism, 98; on revelation vs. reason, 11
Essick, Robert N., 79, 176n.68, 180n.9, 180–81n.20
eternity, Blake's use of, 107, 116
Eve (biblical), creation of, 29–37, 55

faith: certainty of, 9–10; and reason, 10–11, 19–21; regeneration of, 24. *See also* Christianity; God; spirituality
Farr, James, 173n.1
fear, origins of, 14
female space, Blake's use of, 5, 36, 55, 159–60
Ferber, Michael, 154
Ferguson, Robert, *No Protestant Plot*, 105
Filmer, Robert, 67, 70, 103, 127
Flaxman, John, 132
forgiveness, Blake's use of, 117–18
Fox Bourne, H. R., 64–65, 95–96
France: Blake's representation of, 110, 113; Locke's writings in, 145, 149
freedom of the press, 142, 154
free love, Blake's version of, 37–39
French Revolution, Blake's enthusiasm for, 110, 113
friendship: and audience, 134; and Platonism, 20–21; and property theories, 129–30; renewal of, 137; and selfhood, 135–36; sublimation of, 139
Frye, Northrop, 1–2
Fundamental Constitutions of Carolina, 65–66
Furly, Benjamin, 142
Fuseli, Henry, 28

Galen, 43, 45
Galilei, Galileo, 149–50
Gall, Franz Joseph, 86
Gassendi, Pierre, 148–49
gender: and Blake's imagery, 159–60; and medical diagnoses, 49–51; and slavery, 78–80, 176n.64. *See also* body; female space; love; men; sexuality; women
George III (King of England), 115
Gilchrist, Alexander, 28–29, 110, 131, 166n.2
Glazer, Myra, 88–89
God: in Blake's art, 89–90; humanity as property of, 46, 98; knowledge of, 160; law of, 96, 99–103; and private property, 127; as source of revelation and reason, 151, 153, 157. *See also* Bible; faith; religion
Goslee, Nancy Moore, 175n.47, 176n.64
governess, meaning of, 23
Grant, Ruth W., 67
The Grave (Blair), art for, 131–32
Greenhill, John, 121, 128
Gugelberger, Georg M., 80–82

Haley, K. H. D., 70, 173nn.3–4
Hayley, William: Blake's frustration with, 139; and Blake's innocence, 114–15; on Blake's marriage, 27–28; and Blake's nervous condition, 58–61; and Blake's sedition, 108–9, 111; sexuality of, 39, 171–72n.93
health/sanity. *See* diseases; medicine; nervous conditions
Hilton, Nelson, 5, 146
Hinkel, Howard, 88
Hippocrates, 49
Hobbes, Thomas, 106–7, 118, 174n.22
Hoffmann, Franz Ignaz Joseph, 180n.10
homoerotic desire, Blake's version of, 39–40
Hooker, Richard, 176–77n.8
humanity: as beasts, 74–75; community of, 75; constitution of, 72–73; cooperation among, 116; hierarchy among, 98–99, 155–56; natural rights of, 73–75, 173n.1; state of nature of, 97–98
Hume, David, 4, 127
Huygens, Christiaan, 149

hypochondria, 49–50
hysteria, 49–50, 52

iatrochemistry, 43, 45
ideas, formation of, 152–57, 158, 161–62. *See also* education
illiteracy, 29
imagination: limits on, 160; material sublimated through, 116–17; meritocracy of, 113; polymorphous, 40–41; print as embodiment of, 146–47; vs. reason, 51, 53–54, 150–52, 159–60. *See also* enthusiasm; inspiration
Indian religion, miracles in, 10
Indians. *See* natives
individualism. *See* possessive individualism; selfhood
industrialization, 5
infants, nurture of, 13–15, 155–56. *See also* education
innatism: denial of, 143; Locke on, 123–24, 154
innocence: Blake's state of, 106–7; definition of, 105; theory of, 103–7, 114–20. *See also* law
inspiration: defense of, 153; excessive, 157–58; vs. reason, 143–44, 150–52; source of, 138–40. *See also* enthusiasm; imagination
intelligence, and nervous conditions, 51, 52–53, 59

Jamaica, slavery in, 76
James II (King of England), 92, 95
Jameson, Fredric, 3
jealousy: between Blakes, 28, 39; and manipulation, 36–37; Swedenborg on, 33; therapy for, 37–38
Jephthah, as example, 100
Jerusalem (Blake): and conversation, 3–4; influences on, 151–52; on Locke's epistemology, 159; love in, 34–38, 41; and printing, 145; and sedition, 112–18, 177n.20; selfhood in, 135–38; weaving imagery in, 4–5

Job (biblical), as example, 100
Johnson, Joseph, 76, 115
Johnson, Samuel, 93–94
Judeo-Christian religion: miracles in, 8–11, 115; and slavery, 67. *See also* Christianity; God
Justinian Code, 68

Kernan, Alvin, 145, 180n.18
Keynes, Geoffrey, 79, 89, 179n.27
king: and law, 101–3; overthrow of, 93; power of, 67, 94; subversion of confidence in, 92; as tyrant, 108. *See also* tyrant
knowledge: definition of, 9; and enthusiasm, 150; God's power of, 160; as matter of conversation, 3. *See also* mind; reason

Labadie, Jean de, 26
Labadists, Locke-Cudworth correspondence on, 23–25
labor: and equality, 46; private property earned by, 128–29
La Calprenède, Gautier de Costes de, 16
Laslett, Peter: edition of *Two Treatises* by, 166n.2; on Locke and slavery, 66, 69, 174n.17; on Locke's sedition, 103
Lavater, Johann Kaspar, 85, 113
law: characteristics of, 177n.10; convergence of types of, 112; God's, 96, 99–103; hierarchy in types of, 96–97; music associated with, 119; natural, 96–103, 105, 129; for poor, 5; positive, 96–97, 100–102; and reason, 97–99; supernatural, 176–77n.8; and visionary social contract, 116–20; willful, 96, 101–3, 105, 112–14, 116, 119. *See also* innocence
Laws and Liberties of Massachusetts, 68
Lazarus (biblical), and faith, 11
Lebovics, Herman, 175n.41, 178n.16, 178–79n.17
le Clerc, Jean, 104, 145
Leeuwenhoek, Antoni Van, 56

A Letter from a Person of Quality to His Friend in the Country (Shaftesbury), 105
letters, encryption of, 95, 103–4
liberal theory, and slave trade: practice as deviating from, 62–63, 66–69; practice as fulfilling, 63, 71–75; practice as torturing, 62–63, 68–71. *See also* property theories; reason
Linnell, John, 27
literature: and deviation approach, 87–88; vs. philosophy, 2; and poststructuralist approach, 88–89; and race prejudice approach, 89–91; and racism, 76–82. *See also* printing
Little Black Boy, context of, 84–85, 87–91
Lock, Nicholas, 96
Locke, Agnes, 13
Locke, John: anger/stinginess of, 123–26; animal imagery of, 48–49, 74–75, 105–6; approach to, 1–3, 75; background of, 4, 13, 15–16; on body/body politic, 46–52, 54; epitaph by, 163–65; on formation of mind/ideas, 152–57; illness of, 52–53; influences on, 44, 49, 69, 148–49; and law, 96–103, 105, 113, 120; and love, 13–25, 41–42; and medical interests, 43–53, 56, 60–61; pastoral poems by, 21–23; portrait stolen from, 121–30; and printing, 141–43, 145–48, 150–52; and property, 121–30, 140; sedition of, 92–107; and slave trade, 57, 62–75; works: *First Treatise of Government*, 67, 70, 93–94, 103; *The Reasonableness of Christianity*, 7–8, 10; *Some Thoughts Concerning Education*, 14–15, 17, 19, 123, 125. *See also An Essay Concerning Human Understanding* (Locke); *Second Treatise of Government* (Locke)
Lockean Proviso, 128
Lords Proprietors of Carolina, 65
love: and audience, 134; Blake's involvement in, 26–42; free love as, 37–39; homoerotic desire as, 39–40; Locke's involvement in, 13–25, 41–42. *See also* conjugal love; friendship
Lower, Mary, 15
Lower, Richard, 168n.11
Lucretius, 148–50
lycanthropy, 49

Macaulay, Thomas Babington, 95, 112
Macpherson, C. B., 71–72
Macpherson, James, 133
Mann, Paul, 146–47
Mapletoft, John, 64
marginalia, as subversive of printing, 145
marriage: age for, 13; alternative version of, 19–25, 41–42; Blake on, 27–29; components of, 32–33; for Labadists, 24; Locke on, 13–19; meaning of, 30, 31–32; quarrels in, 41; women's relation to, 33–34, 36
The Marriage of Heaven and Hell (Blake): aphorisms in, 113–14; on enthusiasm, 160–62; and printing, 141; on revelation, 151; on soul vs. body, 60–61
Masham, Francis, 25, 169n.39
Masham (Lady). *See* Cudworth, Damaris (later Lady Masham)
Massachusetts, laws in, 68
maternal: and Blake's love, 26–27; as women's role, 14–15, 23. *See also* motherhood
matrix, meanings of, 26–27
McLuhan, Marshall, 141, 144, 152
medicine: and animal imagery, 48–49; competing approaches to, 44–45; Enlightenment context for, 49–51; and microscopes, 56; and reason, 43–44; romanticized, 43–44. *See also* diseases; nervous conditions
melancholy: Blake on, 58–60; Locke on, 21, 49, 151; Willis on, 49
men: diminished power of, 33–34; nervous conditions of, 51. *See also* gender; sexuality

Michelangelo, 164
microcosm: Blake's use of, 56–57; Paracelsus on, 45–46
Middleton, Charles, 92–93
Miller, Eugene, 72
Milton, John: on angelic sex, 40; on creation of woman, 30, 31–32, 33, 35; designs including, 39; on divorce, 32; influence by, 26; on inspiration, 153
Milton (Blake): gender in, 39–40; and law, 116–19; reenchantment of body in, 54–58; selfhood in, 135; spirituality in, 60–61; substance articulated in, 148; willful law in, 113
mind, formation of, 152–57, 158, 161–62. *See also* education
miracles, 8–11, 115
Mitchell, W. J. T., 39, 88, 135
monarchy. *See* king; tyrant
money, function of, 129
Monmouth's Rebellion, 94, 95–96, 104
monogamy, rationale for, 32–33
More, Henry, 20, 40–41
More, Thomas, *Utopia*, 69–71
motherhood, and breastfeeding, 13–14. *See also* maternal
Muggleton, Ludowick, 165
music, law associated with, 119

Napoleon I, 108–10
natives: as aggressors, 69–70, 74–75; Locke's interests in, 70–71; and property theories, 127–29
natural rights: and reason, 74–75; slavery justified in, 73–74, 173n.1
nature: innocence of, 106–7; microscopic view of, 56; stewardship of, 47–48. *See also* law, natural
Nebuchadnezzar (biblical), Blake's drawing of, 113–14
Neoplatonism, 40, 57–58
nervous conditions: of Blake, 53, 58–61; causes of, 51–52, 59–60; diagnosis of, 49; enthusiasm as result of, 151–52; and imagination, 54–61; of Locke, 52–53; mystification of, 49–51; people at risk for, 50–53, 59. *See also* melancholy
nervous fibres, Blake's use of, 55–56
nervous system, literary references to, 55–56
Newton, Isaac, 4, 45, 53, 149–50
Nidditch, Peter H., 178n.2
nominal essence and substance, Locke's theory of, 72–73, 147–48, 160
The Norton Anthology of English Literature, 2

Ong, Walter J., 144
oppression: body as site of, 57–58; cause of, 143; freedom of press as, 154. *See also* tyrant
Ostriker, Alicia, 169n.58
Oxford University, 43–44

Paine, Tom, 6–8, 115
Paley, Morton D., 171n.87
Paracelsus, 45–46
Parry, Elinor, 15–18
Pascal, Blaise, 156
passions: definition of, 124–25; and Locke's anger, 123–26; moderation of, 51–52; and property, 121, 124–26, 129–30; vs. reason, 123–26; and selfhood, 135–36. *See also* jealousy; love
Paul (biblical), 11, 18, 65–66, 161
Pembroke, 104–5
Perkins, David, 166n.1
Persian religion, miracles in, 10
Philander. *See* Locke, John, and love
Philoclea. *See* Cudworth, Damaris, Locke's relationship with
philosophy vs. literature, 2
phrenology, 86
physiognomy, 85–86
pity, Blake's use of, 117
Platonism: and love, 19–21, 25; and printing, 148–50, 161–62
poetry vs. philosophy, 2

Poliakov, Leon, 72–73
polymorphous imagination, 40–41
Posidonius, 181n.31
possession, rejection of, 49
possessive individualism: and Locke's portrait, 121–23; and passions, 123–26; as rational, 126–30
poststructuralism, 2, 88–89
Pratt, Mary Louise, 82
Price, Richard, 154
Prideaux, Humphrey, 95
printing: and abstraction/generalization, 143–48; and enthusiasm, 143, 150–52; illuminated, 145; and images of fire, 157, 160–62; influence by, 141–42; as metaphor for development of mind/ideas, 152–57; reason's association with, 144–45; and social class, 180n.18; stereotype, 180n.10; subversion of, 141; techniques for, 142–43, 146–47, 176n.68
private property: earned by labor, 128–29; principle of, 127–28, 140
propensity, Blake on, 113
property theories: and art works, 132–40; context of, 126–27; and enlightened development, 57, 74–75, 77; and equality, 46, 98; issues in, 127–30, 132–33; and justification for slavery, 73–74; ownership in, 128–29; and passions, 121, 124–26, 129–30; and payment, 123; private property in, 127–29, 140; and reason, 74–75, 127–30; turning point in, 121; and waste land, 69–71, 74
Protestant visionaries: on conjugal love, 27–29; and creation of woman, 29–32; influence by, 26; and nervous conditions, 59
pseudoprophets. *See* enthusiasm, Locke on
public: Blake's appeal to, 133–40, 146, 157; and printing, 144–46
public ministry, credentials for, 47
Pufendorf, Samuel von, 127

racism: basis for, 71–72, 98; Blake's poem on, 87, 89–91; and literature, 76–82; and reason, 71–72. *See also* slavery
reason: abstraction/generalization in, 143–44; and atheism, 1, 5–6, 143; common law of, 74–75; definition of, 48; denunciation of Locke's, 4–6, 24, 56, 99; and faith, 10–11, 19–21; function of, 155; vs. imagination, 51, 53–54, 150–52, 159–60; vs. inspiration, 143–44, 150–52; and law, 97–99; and medicine, 43–44; and miracles, 9–10; and nervous conditions, 51–53; and nominal essence, 72–73, 147–48, 160; vs. passions, 123–26; and possessiveness, 126–30; and printing, 144–45; and property theories, 74–75, 127–30; and racism, 71–72; source of, 151, 153, 157; vs. spiritual motive, 21. *See also* law, natural; knowledge; liberal theory, and slave trade; mind
Redondi, Pierre, 149–50
Reeve, Andrew, 121
regeneration, definition of, 116
Reid, Thomas, 149
religion, of slaves, 65–66. *See also* Bible; Christianity; faith; God; Judeo-Christian religion; Labadists; spirituality; state religion
repentance, Blake's use of, 117
resurrection, 11
revelation: role of, 100, 150–51; source of, 151, 153, 157
revenge, and law, 118
Reynolds, Joshua, Blake on, 143–45, 147–48, 150, 153–54
Richmond, George, 165
Robinson, Henry Crabb: on Blake and sexuality, 28, 31, 32, 39; on Blake's dualism, 61; on Blake's nervous condition, 59; on Locke's religion, 5–6, 149, 152
Romantic ideology, 116, 134, 146

Rorty, Richard, 3
Rose, Samuel, 110–12
Rose (ship), 63
Rousseau, G. S., 50–51
Rousseau, Jean-Jacques, 118
Royal African Company, 63–64, 69
Rye House conspiracy, 94–95, 104

sanguine, definition of, 60
Santa Cruz Blake Study Group, 146–47
Schiavonetti, Louis, 131
Scolfield (soldier), 108–12
Scott, James (duke of Monmouth), 94, 95–96, 104
Scudéry, Georges de, 168n.14
Second Treatise of Government (Locke): on conjugal society, 14; on crime, 48; on development, 77; on equality, 46; on innocence, 103–7; on law, 96–103; on property, 126–27, 130; as seditious, 93–94, 96; on slavery, 62, 67–70, 72, 74
sedition: Blake accused of, 92, 96, 107–20; Blake's trial for, 109–12; charges of, 92–107, 107–20; definition of, 93, 108; evidence of, 95–105; "good," 114; Johnson's trial for, 93–94; justification for, 102–3; Locke accused of, 92–107; mitigation defense against, 111; people accused of, 92–93; punishment for, 94; and willful law, 101; writing changes in response to, 115–16
selfhood, as problem, 135–40. *See also* possessive individualism
Seliger, Martin, 68–71, 74, 174n.17
semiotics, 85–86
sexuality: and apocalypse, 161; Blake on, 54, 169n.58; and creation of woman, 32–35; and essence, 160; and free love, 37–39; and homoerotic desire, 39–40; of Locke, 19, 23; and Locke's epistemology, 158–60; magical, 41; and nervous conditions, 52; and polymorphous imagination, 40–41

Shaftesbury. *See* Cooper, Anthony Ashley (Lord Ashley)
signatures, doctrine of (Parcelsus), 45–46
Sithonians, law of, 177n.10
Skelton, Bevil, 92–93
skin color: and Blake's work, 89–91; and poetic conventions, 84–85; and soul vs. body, 88; and universalism, 79, 83. *See also* black (color)
slavery: abolition of, 86–87; Blake's art on, 76–77, 79–83, 88; Blake's reading on, 76–77; Blake's writing on, 75–76, 82–91; conditions in, 65–66, 77–82; justification for, 68–71, 73–75, 77–78; literature on, 76–82; Locke's participation in, 57, 62–67; Locke's writing on, 62, 67–75; origin of, 73–74; supporters of, 86; vs. universal myth of liberation, 86–87. *See also* liberal theory, and slave trade
slaves, religious freedom of, 65–66
Sloss, D. J., 179n.27
Smith, J. T., 142
Smith, John, *Divine Knowledge*, 20
Smith, Samuel S., 86
social class: and capitalism, 71–72; and medical diagnoses, 50–51; and printing, 180n.18; and universalism, 82. *See also* bourgeois ideology; labor
social contract: Blake's visionary, 116–20; and slavery, 73–74. *See also* property theories; reason
Society for Effecting the Abolition of the Slave Trade, 90
Socrates, 154
soul vs. body, 60–61, 88, 90, 161
Southey, Robert, 59
Spence, Joseph, 168n.14
spirituality: of Africans, 85; danger of excessive, 157–58; effectiveness of, 160; and printing metaphor, 153–54, 156–57; vs. reason, 21
Squadrito, Kathy, 67, 70
state religion, denunciation of, 7

Stedman, John Gabriel: and Blake's art, 62, 79–81, 83; on slavery, 76–79, 83
stereotype printing, 180n.10
Stevenson, W. H., 34, 119
Stillingfleet, Edward, 6–11
stinginess, definition of, 125
Stone, Lawrence, 167n.6
Storch, Margaret, 39–40
Stothard, R. T., 179n.19
Stothard, Thomas, 131–33
Strauss, Leo, 71
Stringer, Thomas, 122–23, 129–30
Strong Man, Blake's mythology of, 110–11
substance and nominal essence, Locke's theory of, 72–73, 147–48, 160
Surinam, slavery in, 76–81
Swedenborg, Emanuel: on Africans' spirituality, 85; on angelic love of sex, 40; on creation of woman, 30, 32–33, 35; influence by, 26; on marriage, 33, 36; on microcosm, 46, 56–57; and society resolutions, 34
Sydenham, Thomas, 43, 49–52
Sypher, Wylie, 84

Tatham, Frederick, 26–28
textile industry, 4–5
Thomas, David, 125
Thomas, William, 125
Thompson, E. P., 165
Thomson, James, 77, 84, 86
Tilloch, Alexander, 180n.10
Toinard, Nicolas, 18
treason, definition of, 93–94. *See also* sedition
Treasonable and Seditious Practices Act (1795), 108
Trenchard, John, 104
True Intellectual System of the Universe (Cudworth), 19, 150
Tully, James, 71, 75
tyrant: definition of, 101; law as, 107; Nebuchadnezzar as, 113–14; and willful law, 102. *See also* king

Tyrrell, James, 125

United States: Locke's involvement with, 63, 65–66, 70; state laws/constitutions in, 65–66, 68. *See also* natives; slavery
universalism, Blake's use of, 79, 81–83, 87, 91
Utopia (More), 69–71

Valentine, Basil, 45
Van Helmont, J. B., 45, 52
Varley, John, 29
vehicles, definition of, 25
vices, 107, 113
Viner, Robert, 173n.3
Virginia, 1622 massacre in, 70
virtues: and abstraction, 118; Blake on, 113; definition of, 124; Locke's separation of, 106–7
Viscomi, Joseph, 142, 176n.68, 180–81n.20, 181n.21
visionary faith, meanings of, 20–21
visions: manifestation of, 29; and printing, 142–43; source of, 138–40, 148
Vogler, Thomas, 38, 146
Voltaire, 149
Von Leyden, Wolfgang, 168n.14

Wallis, J. P. R., 179n.27
war: basis of, 102; captives taken in, 68–70, 73–74, 77; justification for, 68–70, 105–6; reparations after, 70; spiritual vs. natural, 116–17. *See also* slavery
Ward, Aileen, 131–32
Warner, Michael, 144–45
waste land, Locke's theory of, 69–71, 74
Watson, Richard, 6–9, 115
weaving, Blake's imagery of, 4–5
Webster, Brenda, 171n.89
West Indies, as waste land, 69–70
will, Blake on, 113
Willis, Thomas, 48–49, 51–52
Wilson, Mona, 28, 166n.2

Wittgenstein, Ludwig, 9
Wolcott, Roger, 174n.29
Wollstonecraft, Mary, 28
womb vapors, 50
women: Blake's attitudes toward, 13, 27, 36–37, 39; and Blake's imagery, 159–60; creation of, 29–37, 55; and female will, 55; Locke's attitudes toward, 13–18, 23; and male power, 33–34; manipulation by, 36–37; nervous conditions of, 49–52; roles of, 14–15, 23. *See also* female space; maternal; motherhood; sexuality
Wood, Neal, 72–73, 179n.18
Wordsworth, William, 86–87, 155, 164
workers. *See* labor
The Works of Sir Joshua Reynolds. See Reynolds, Joshua
Wynne, John, 145

Yolton, John, 147, 181n.27
Yvon, Pierre, 24

Wayne Glausser is professor of English at DePauw University. He has published articles on Locke and Blake, as well as on various topics in recent American fiction and popular culture. He has won several awards for teaching, and in 1990 was chosen Indiana Professor of the Year by the Council for the Advancement and Support of Education.

OHIO UNIVERSITY LIBRARY

Please return this book as soon as you have finished with it. In order to avoid a fine it must be returned by the latest date stamped below. All books are subject to recall after two weeks or immediately if needed for reserve.

QUARTER LOAN

JUN 1 5 1998

MAY 0 4 1998

JUN 1 6 2003

NOV 3 0 2004

CF